University of London
Institute of Latin American Studies Monographs

4

British Nitrates and Chilean Politics,
1886–1896:
Balmaceda and North

University of London
Institute of Latin American Studies Monographs

1. *The 'Detached Recollections' of General D. F. O'Leary*, edited by R.A. Humphreys. 1969

2. *Accounts of Nineteenth-Century South America: an Annotated Checklist of Works by British and United States Observers*, by Bernard Naylor. 1969.

3. *Commercial Relations between British Overseas Territories and South America, 1806–1914*, by T. W. Keeble. 1970

4. *British Nitrates and Chilean Politics, 1886–1896: Balmaceda and North*, by Harold Blakemore. 1974

British Nitrates and Chilean Politics, 1886–1896: Balmaceda and North

by

HAROLD BLAKEMORE

UNIVERSITY OF LONDON
Published for the
Institute of Latin American Studies
THE ATHLONE PRESS
1974

Published by
THE ATHLONE PRESS
UNIVERSITY OF LONDON
at 4 *Gower Street, London* WC1
Distributed by Tiptree Book Services Ltd
Tiptree, Essex

U.S.A. *and Canada*
Humanities Press Inc
New York

© *University of London* 1974

0 485 17704 8

Printed in Great Britain by
WESTERN PRINTING SERVICES LIMITED
BRISTOL

PREFACE

The origins of this book go back more than twenty years to research on the Chilean revolution of 1891 for a doctoral dissertation of the University of London. The subsequent course of a varied career in university administration interrupted my work, but did not destroy my interest, in modern Chilean history, and when I took up the subject again in a serious fashion I was able to benefit from the wider range of archival resources available and from the sustained interest in this work from many persons who have assisted me in one way or another. Specific acknowledgements will be found in the notes to this book, but, invidious though the exercise may be, I wish to acknowledge specifically here the names of those to whom I am most indebted. My first thanks are due to Professor R. A. Humphreys. It was he who first kindled my interest in Latin American history in general, and in Chile in particular, and I have benefited immeasurably from his knowledge, understanding and friendship for over half my life. Of my many Chilean friends, I am especially grateful to Professor Eugenio Pereira Salas for his great assistance and innumerable kindnesses on my visits to Santiago; to Professor Horacio Aránguiz Donoso for the Balmaceda manuscripts used in this study; to Professor Ramón Rodríguez, formerly head of the Department of International Relations of the University of Chile, for enabling me to spend several weeks in Santiago in 1970 to complete my research in Chile; and, although I disagree profoundly with his own interpretation of the events described in this book, to Professor Hernán Ramírez Necochea, formerly Dean of the Instituto Pedagógico, for a personal friendship and common scholastic interest which override strong differences of opinion. Custodians of archives and libraries also deserve my warmest thanks, particularly Dr A. J. E. Hollaender, Archivist of the Guildhall Library in London, Mr W. R. A. Easthope, formerly Archivist of *The Times*, Don Juan

Eyzaguirre, Director of the Archivo Nacional in Santiago, and Don Mario Medina, Keeper of the Newspaper Collection at the Biblioteca Nacional. I am also indebted to the Committee of Management of the Institute of Latin America Studies for leave of absence in 1970, to Mr J. G. Palmer for occasional research assistance, and to Miss Christine Hill of the Geography Department of University College London, for drawing the map. Last, but very far from least, to my wife, Miriam, and to my children, Christopher and Alison, I owe an unpayable debt for their forbearance and understanding during the period it has taken for this book to come to fruition. Responsibility for any defects is mine, and mine alone.

If this book had a dedication it would be to the land and people of Chile, and it has been written as a contribution to the better understanding of their history by one who will always regard them with sympathy and affection.

London   H.B.

CONTENTS

MAP

I

THE SETTING

Chile in the Nineteenth Century: Political and Economic Development to 1886

Of all the states of Latin America which had once formed part of the Spanish empire, Chile, in the nineteenth century, enjoyed a unique reputation for orderly government and internal peace. The early years of independence were turbulent enough, and Chile did not escape the common experience of the continent—military violence, administrative discontinuity and intestine struggle—in that period of political ferment. But the battle of Lircay in 1830 marked the dawn of a new era in the history of the republic: in that year the armed struggle of Conservatives and Liberals, of Centralists with Federalists, and of *caudillo* with *caudillo*, gave place to a period of Conservative rule under the aegis of Diego Portales, the virtual dictator of Chile.[1]

Portales was chiefly responsible for the establishment in Chile of a constitutional system which remained fundamentally unaltered for over half a century and to which Chile owed its international reputation in later years as 'the model republic of South America'.[2] Yet the political foresight of any one man or group of men would have availed little of itself: geographic and social circumstances helped to solve the problems of political organization.

Chile was an island country, hemmed in on the east by the Andes and on the west by the Pacific ocean, while to the north the Atacama desert provided the most natural, though ill-defined, of frontiers. To the south, the river Bío-Bío marked the limit of settlement, for beyond that river stretched the fjord coastline and, inland, dense forests peopled only by Indians. But between Copiapó on the rim of the northern desert and

[1] The literature on the period of independence is enormous. Simon Collier, *Ideas and Politics of Chilean Independence, 1808–1833* (Cambridge University Press, 1967) provides both an excellent account and a detailed bibliography.

[2] *The Times*, 22 April 1880.

Valdivia and Osorno at the edge of the southern forest area lay
the central valley, some seven hundred miles long but rarely
more than a hundred miles wide, blessed with a Mediterranean
climate and a varied physical character—fertile valleys, wooded
slopes and fresh rivers rising from the snow-capped *cordillera*.
This clearly-defined central region was the real Chile and it has
remained the heart of the nation to the present day.[3]

The society of this area was rural. The *hacendado*, owner of the
great estate, ruled the countryside while the peasantry toiled,
and from the colonial era to the twentieth century Chile could
be described essentially as 'a unique agrarian society character-
ised by an extreme land monopoly and a sharply marked social
stratification'.[4] Only in the late nineteenth century did the rise
of new urban and industrial classes begin seriously to blur the
lines of strict social division between master and man. It was
this rigid distinction which gave its stamp to the nation; the
aristocracy ruled the national life in all its branches while the
illiterate peasantry obeyed. Yet the social and economic unit of
the *fundo*, the great estate, and the social system it produced,
was a great force for stability, and so was the country's racial
structure. The high degree of fusion between white and Indian
that proceeded throughout the colonial period had, by the time
of independence, virtually eliminated the aboriginal races,
leaving a two-tier structure: a dominant minority, predomin-
antly white and numbering, in 1810, about 150,000, and some
350,000 *mestizos*, a fusion of stocks in which the Spanish, not the
Indian, strain predominated.

The years of anarchy following the wars of independence
were ended by Portales in the early 1830s. By crushing militar-
ism, by a severe but necessary policy of repression enforced by
the exercise of extraordinary powers, Portales created conditions of internal order in which the constitution of 1833 could
be promulgated.[5] This constitution was the political mirror of

---

[3] For a more detailed description of Chilean geography in its historical setting,
see my essay in Harold Blakemore and Clifford T. Smith (eds.), *Latin America:
Geographical Perspectives* (London, Methuen, 1971), pp. 475–565.

[4] G. M. McBride, *Chile: Land and Society* (New York, American Geographical
Society, 1936), p. 34.

[5] F. A. Encina, *Historia de Chile* (20 vols., Santiago, 1940–52), x, 443–552, provides a detailed account of the dictatorship of Portales.

the social structure, adjusted perfectly 'to the cultural and economic state and to the actual needs of society'.[6] It restricted the suffrage to literate Chileans who owned property or invested capital valued at a specific figure fixed by law at periodic intervals, and it proclaimed certain fundamental principles which were theoretically applicable to all—equality before the law, equal right to fill public office, the right of petition and liberty of the press.[7]

A bicameral legislature was established, a Congress of Deputies and Senators, the former elected by direct vote from local departments, the latter by indirect vote, with Deputies serving a three-year term and Senators nine, though a third of the Senate was renewable every three years. Congress assisted the executive in the making of laws: its key powers, however, were those of approval of the budget and of granting the executive extraordinary powers in specific cases, in effect a temporary suspension of the constitution.[8]

But the most important powers were conferred on the executive, the President. Elected indirectly like the Senate, the President held office for five years and was re-eligible immediately for a further term. His authority was enormous. He virtually controlled the courts and the administration, both central and local; he was commander-in-chief of the armed forces; he appointed his own ministers and dismissed them at will; he made recommendations to ecclesiastical office. The intendants and governors who carried on local government and provincial administration were his direct representatives, responsible to him alone. The President was assisted by ministers, in effect his secretaries, of whom there were three in 1833 and six by 1890, and he also had a Council of State, whose members were selected by himself from a specified list, to act in an advisory capacity.[9]

The highest judicial power resided in a supreme tribunal whose members were named by the President from lists of three

---

[6] L. Galdames, *La Evolución Constitucional de Chile, 1810–1925* (Santiago, 1926), p. 872.

[7] *Constitución de la República de Chile, jurada y promulgada el 25 de mayo de 1833* (Santiago, 1833), Articles 1–12, pp. 4–8.

[8] Ibid., Articles 13–39, pp. 8–16.

[9] Ibid., Articles 59–107, and 115–21, pp. 21–34; 35–7.

drawn up by the Council of State. Neither President nor congress had judicial functions.[10]

A peculiar feature of the constitution was the Comisión Conservadora. Ordinary sessions of Congress were fixed to run from 1 June to 1 September, after which date the legislature went into recess until called in extraordinary session by the President. To advise him, however, on constitutional matters during the recess, seven senators were elected by the Senate on the last day of the ordinary session; they formed the Comisión Conservadora which was answerable to Congress for its conduct.[11]

The general provisions of the constitution were particularly noteworthy for the articles which declared that general education should receive special attention from the government.[12]

A remarkable document by any standards, the Chilean constitution of 1833 was, in an era of constitution-making, a classic example of political organization which accorded almost perfectly with the prevailing social circumstances:[13]

like the bourgeoisie of France and the fathers of the American Constitution, the creoles . . . were human beings with their interests to protect. . . They owned the land and controlled all the productive institutions of Chile; they had power *de facto* and wanted it *de jure* . . .[14]

The political system thus implanted was a quasi-monarchical one;[15] upheld by an oligarchy of wealth, talent and power, it depended above all on the solidarity of the upper class, and on its capacity—which proved quite remarkable—to absorb other elements which might, in time, have come to oppose it. Yet it would only work well so long as the executive represented, and was seen to represent, the interests of that class. It is significant that, throughout the nineteenth century, despite the existence of antagonistic political groups, of fundamentally divergent ideologies and of conflicts of personality within the aristocracy, an underlying social unity was preserved.[16] Though differences

[10] Ibid., Articles 108–14, pp. 34–5.   [11] Ibid., Articles 57–8, p. 20.
[12] Ibid., Articles 153–4, p. 43.
[13] Ricardo Donoso, *Las Ideas Políticas en Chile* (2nd ed., Santiago, 1967), p. 85.
[14] P. V. Shaw, *The Early Constitutions of Chile, 1810–1833* (New York, 1930), p. 134.
[15] J. Eyzaguirre, *Fisonomía Histórica de Chile* (Santiago, 1948), p. 119.
[16] One interesting indication of this is the fact that, in contrast to other Latin

might produce armed conflict, as in 1851 and, again, in 1859, they did not radically alter the social structure of government. Organizations founded to broaden the basis of representation, such as the *Sociedad de Igualdad* in 1850, modified the spirit but did little to change the structure of the constitutional system. Congress remained 'the council of a governing class where men who, with all their differences of opinion, respect each other, meet and discuss their common interests with dignity and ability'.[17] It was not until much later in Chilean history, with the development of industry and the growth of working-classes having no place in the traditional social structure, that this unity was impaired by the appearance of new lines of political division between men prepared to make the mental adjustments essential for an understanding of a changing society and those who were not. As yet there was no scope for an alignment of parties based on social and economic issues and interests. Political parties were based on religious and constitutional beliefs and on personalities within the governing class.[18]

The years from 1830 to 1861 have been described as the era of the 'autocratic republic' and from 1861 to 1891 as that of the 'liberal republic'.[19] While this is an over-simplification of a complex political development, it denotes the change which took place in the spirit of government in the middle years of the century. Until 1857 two parties held the political stage, the Conservative and the Liberal, and the former's triumph in battle in 1830 gave them power for twenty-five years. But the Liberal opposition underwent a revival in the 1840s and began to press for reforms to weaken executive authority and free the suffrage from governmental interference. This was a basic aim

American states, excepting Brazil, political antagonism was never pursued to the point of physically exterminating enemies. Opponents of the government, even if they took up arms, were usually exiled for a few years, but then allowed to return to full political activity.

[17] P. S. Reinsch, 'Parliamentary Government in Chile', *American Political Science Review*, iii (1908–9), p. 510. The comparison with the squirearchy of eighteenth-century England is noteworthy. Cf., however, the classic essay of A. Edwards Vives, *La fronda aristocrática en Chile* (Santiago, 1928), *passim*.

[18] See A. Edwards Vives and E. Frei Montalva, *Historia de los partidos políticos chilenos* (Santiago, 1949), pp. 11–15.

[19] The phrases are those of L. Galdames, *A History of Chile* (trans. and ed. by I. J. Cox, Univ. of North Carolina Press, 1941).

of all parties in opposition throughout the century. The constitution gave such powers to the President that he was able to regulate the elections and thus ensure adequate congressional support for his policies. The practice also developed of a retiring President virtually choosing his own successor and guaranteeing his election. Every congressional and presidential election which took place in Chile before 1891 was followed by acrimonious dispute between supporters of these practices, that is, supporters of the government, and the opposition.[20]

The 'autocratic republic' ended in 1861. In 1857 the Conservative party split on the question of the relations between Church and State: the more clerical wing retained the name of Conservatives, the more liberal elements, who supported the President, Manuel Montt, in his claims for state supremacy became known eventually as the National Party.[21] On the Liberal side there was a similar, though less clear, fractionalization: moderate Liberals formed one faction, extreme, anticlerical Liberals another, and the latter adopted the name of the Radical party. This fractioning of the two great traditional parties in fact liberalized the regime since the government came to depend more on political alliances and coalitions formed by various combinations of the different groups.

During the presidency of Federico Errázuriz Errázuriz, 1871–76, a number of reforms modified the autocratic character of the constitution. These were significant since they aimed at greater congressional control over the President. In 1871, an amendment was passed to prevent presidents seeking re-election at the end of their first term.[22] This ended the period of ten-year presidencies which had obtained since 1831. In 1874, the Council of State was made less dependent on the President, and the Comisión Conservadora was empowered to request him to call extraordinary sessions of Congress when it saw fit.[23] Moreover, seven deputies were to sit on the Comisión, with the seven senators stipulated in the original constitution.[24] But the

[20] The fullest account is J. M. Yrarrázaval, *El Presidente Balmaceda* (2 vols., Santiago, 1940), i, *passim*.   [21] See Encina, *Historia de Chile*, xii, 187–273.

[22] *Constitución política de la República de Chile de 25 de mayo de 1833 con las reformas efectuadas hasta el 10 de agosto de 1888* (Santiago, 1888), Article 52, p. 29.

[23] Ibid., Article 93, pp. 43–4, and Article 49, pp. 27–8.

[24] Ibid., Article 48, p. 27.

fundamental reform, the elimination of executive interference in elections, still remained the principal point at issue between government and opposition. Parallel to this movement for constitutional reform was a movement for religious reform which came to a head under President Domingo Santa María, 1881–86, when liberty of conscience, secular cemeteries, and civil marriage and registry were established.[25]

The system of orderly government and the comparatively peaceful evolution of Chile from 1830 onwards allowed material progress to be made on the basis of the country's natural resources, agricultural and mineral.[26] The history of the Chilean economy in the nineteenth century may be divided into two periods which are separated by the War of the Pacific, 1879–83. After the war, Chile's economy was geared closely to nitrates; before it, the export trade depended largely on copper. Yet Chile was really an agricultural country, self-sufficient in most foodstuffs, and with a sizeable export trade in wheat throughout the century.[27] But the market in farm products was basically an internal one—wheat alone excepted—and it was from the mine rather than the farm that Chilean export trade derived its strength.

Before the War of the Pacific the principal mineral resources were coal, silver and copper. Coal was mined chiefly in the provinces of Arauco and Concepción, and the industry was developed by native capitalists, but the amount of coal produced was sufficient for Chile's needs only until the 1860s; thereafter, Chile depended on imports of coal from abroad.[28] Silver-mining had been a major industry of colonial Chile and the discovery of fresh lodes in the provinces of Atacama and Coquimbo in the middle years of the nineteenth century began

[25] See Encina, loc. cit., xviii, 147–80.

[26] There is no satisfactory economic history of Chile in the nineteenth century, though Daniel Martner, *Estudio de la política comercial chilena e historia económica nacional* (2 vols., Santiago, 1923), and the same author's *Historia de Chile: Historia Económica* (Santiago, 1929), the first volume of a projected multi-volume history which was not continued, are useful surveys.

[27] For this story, see S. Sepúlveda, 'El trigo chileno en el mercado mundial', *Informaciones Geográficas* (Santiago, Instituto Geográfico de la Universidad de Chile, 1959), año VI (1956), pp. 7–135.

[28] See P. P. Figueroa, *Historia de la fundación de la industria del carbón de piedra en Chile* (Santiago, 1897), *passim*.

a new period of exploitation of the mineral in which many fortunes were made.[29] Further stimulus to this development came in 1870 with the discovery of rich ores at Caracoles, in territory claimed by both Chile and Bolivia, though it was Chilean capital that was employed to mine them.

Copper also had been mined in Atacama and Coquimbo in the days of the Spanish empire, but it was the great expansion of the industry in the 1840s and 1850s which enabled Chile to become, for a time, the world's leading exporter of the metal.[30] In 1860, for example, out of a total export trade valued at 25,451,179 pesos ($),[31] copper exports were worth $14,111,099.[32] By the 1880s, however, owing to the rapid development of mines in the United States and Spain the world standard for the metal ceased to be 'Chile bars' as Chile lost her supremacy in the world market for copper. Yet the exploitation of the mineral had been crucial to Chile's economic progress, stimulating other industrial developments and providing, through export taxes on copper shipments, a sizeable proportion of government revenue for public works. The period from 1830 to 1879 saw the beginning of manufacturing— flour-milling, sugar-refining, glass-blowing, metal foundries and other local industries.[33] It also saw a considerable expansion of communications. Between 1849 and 1852 the first railway in Chile was built, linking Caldera with Copiapó, and by 1863 the capital of the republic, Santiago, was linked by rail to the principal port, Valparaiso.[34] William Wheelwright, an American citizen, constructed the telegraph line from Valparaiso to Santiago in 1851–52, thus initiating a process which extended

[29] See B. Vicuña Mackenna, El libro de la plata (Santiago, 1882), passim, and the excellent modern study, which also embraces copper, of L. R. Pederson, The Mining Industry of the Norte Chico, Chile (Evanston, Ill., Northwestern University Studies in Geography, No. 11, 1966), passim.

[30] B. Vicuña Mackenna, El libro del cobre i del carbón de piedra en Chile (Santiago, 1883), passim; F. M. Aracena, Apuntes de viaje. La industria del cobre en las provincias de Atacama i Coquimbo i los grandes i valiósos depósitos carboníferos de Lota i Coronel (Santiago, 1884), pp. 71 ff., Pederson, loc. cit., passim.

[31] Martner, Estudio de la política comercial, i, 299. The exchange rate was then 41¾d. to the peso.   [32] Martner, loc. cit., ii, 307.

[33] See J. F. Rippy and J. Pfeiffer, 'Notes on the Dawn of Manufacturing in Chile', Hispanic American Historical Review (hereafter HAHR), xxviii (1948), pp. 292–303.

[34] J. F. Rippy, Latin America and the Industrial Age (New York, 1944), pp. 24–5.

to forty-eight towns in Chile by 1876, and put the country into rapid communication with Argentina and Peru by a line across the Andes and a submarine cable under the Pacific ocean.[35] Wheelwright had previously brought the benefits of steam navigation to Chile in 1840, when he founded the Pacific Steam Navigation Company, to establish a line of steamers for regular service between Europe and the Pacific coast republics of South America.[36]

The growth of a railway and telegraphic network, the building of roads, schools and bridges, the rise of banking institutions —another important factor of these years—the appearance of the first Chilean joint-stock companies, and many other features were all trends in the material growth of Chile before the War of the Pacific.[37] And in many of these developments, a considerable role was often played by foreign interests and individual foreign entrepreneurs, attracted to a Latin American country where, as one early observer remarked, the inhabitants showed 'a natural disposition' to 'repose and tranquillity' and a 'conviction of the inestimable advantages to be derived therefrom'.[38] From the period of independence, Chile looked abroad for that expertise which her leaders thought the country lacked, and Chilean policy towards European immigration throughout the nineteenth century was the policy of the open door.[39] As the century passed, the immigrant stream widened and foreign as well as native capitalists began to exploit Chile's natural resources.

[35] See J. J. Johnson, *Pioneer Telegraphy in Chile* (Stanford University Press, 1948), *passim*.

[36] See Claudio Véliz, *Historia de la Marina Mercante de Chile* (Santiago, 1961), pp. 67–74.

[37] On banking, see G. Subercaseaux, *Monetary & Banking Policy of Chile* (Oxford, 1922), pp. 52 ff., and R. E. Santelices, *Los Bancos Chilenos* (Santiago, 1893), *passim*. On the stock exchange, see Luís Escobar Cerda, *El Mercado de Valores* (Santiago, 1959), pp. 44–53.

[38] Consul-General Walpole to Lord Palmerston, Santiago, 21 September 1841. No. 30. Diplomatic. London, Public Record Office, Foreign Office Archives, Chile (cited hereafter as F.O.), 16/44.

[39] Bernardo O'Higgins, the hero of independence, was keen to attract European immigrants to Chile. Collier, *Ideas and Politics*, pp. 249–50. Portales pursued an active policy of recruiting European and American savants, of whom the most distinguished were the Frenchman Claudio Gay, and the Venezuelan Andrés Bello. See Encina, *Historia de Chile*, xi, *passim*. Successive governments continued these policies.

The Anglo-Chilean Connection[40]

Of the foreign elements in Chile by far the most important were the British, and trading ties were not the only ones which bound the two nations in friendship; naval connections were also an important feature. The British had played a prominent part in the manning of the first Chilean navy during the wars of independence, and the commander of that navy, Lord Cochrane, was regarded as 'one of the founders of the Republic'.[41] The Chilean navy was modelled on that of Great Britain and the practice developed whereby Chilean midshipmen served their apprenticeship on British men-of-war, a scheme which helped to cement the traditional friendship which derived from the stormy days of the independence period.[42] And behind this friendship was the realization of Chilean statesmen that sea-power was of crucial importance to their country, whose entire western frontier was the Pacific shoreline.

More important, however, were the commercial relations between the two states. Between 1844 and 1898 the total value of Chilean imports from Great Britain exceeded the total value of imports from France, Germany and the United States combined.[43] The foundations of British commercial supremacy were laid at an early date; by 1820 at least twelve British firms had established branches at Valparaiso.[44] It was also in the first decade of independence that there arrived in Chile those British elements which married into Chilean society and whose names recur throughout the later history of the republic.[45] In

[40] There is ample scope for an interesting study of this relationship. What is presented here is merely a sketch.

[41] A. Montt to Lord Salisbury, London, 14 December 1887. F.O. 16/250. Domestic. Diplomatic. See also R. A. Humphreys, *Liberation in South America, 1806–1827* (London, 1952), pp. 74–6, and D. E. Worcester, *Sea-Power and Chilean Independence* (Gainesville, Fla., 1962), *passim*.

[42] In 1841, the Chilean government requested that this practice be continued, thus indicating that it began some time before. Walpole to Palmerston, Valparaiso, 30 May 1841. F.O. 16/43. Separate.

[43] C. W. Centner, 'Relaciones comerciales de Gran Bretaña con Chile, 1810–1830', *Revista Chilena de historia y geografía* (hereafter *RCHG*), No. 103 (1943), p. 106.

[44] J. A. Gibbs, *The History of Antony and Dorothea Gibbs and the early years of Antony Gibbs and Son* (London, 1922), pp. 393–4. See also R. A. Humphreys, 'British Merchants and South American Independence', *Proceedings of the British Academy*, li (1965), pp. 166–7.

[45] See B. Vicuña Mackenna, *Los primeros ingleses en Valparaíso, 1817–1827* (Valparaiso, 1884), and D. Amunátegui Solar, 'El orígen del comercio inglés en Chile',

1825 some 90 British vessels called at Valparaiso, compared with 70 ships from the United States;[46] fifteen years later this number had increased to 166, compared with 56 from the United States, 48 from France and 17 from Hamburg.[47] Great Britain and her colonies took well over 50 per cent of Chilean exports in 1860 and supplied Chile with 33 per cent of her imports, while by 1875 these proportions had risen to 60 per cent and almost 40 per cent respectively.[48]

As trade increased so did the size of the British community in Chile. An estimate of from 1,000 to 3,000 British subjects at Valparaiso alone, which was made in 1824, was probably somewhat exaggerated,[49] but in 1861 it was reckoned that in the whole of Chile there were some 4,000 British citizens of whom almost 1,900 lived in Valparaiso.[50] The census of 1875 gave the number of Britons in Chile as 4,627.[51] That of citizens of the United States in Chile remained at less than 1,000 throughout the century, though the numbers of other European nationals compared favourably with the number of British there.[52] Many of these were settlers: as the frontier was pushed southwards, the land was colonized, particularly by German and Swiss immigrants.[53] In the ports, however, and particularly in Valparaiso, British influence predominated. Already in 1818, an American

RCHG, No. 103 (1943), pp. 83–95. Such were William Blest, John Walker and David Ross. George Edwards, scion of one of the most important Anglo-Chilean families in Chilean history, arrived in Valparaiso in 1807. V. Figueroa, *Diccionario histórico y biográfico de Chile* (5 vols. in 4, Santiago, 1926–35), iii, 16. Two other useful sources on British subjects in Chile are P. P. Figueroa, *Diccionario biográfico de estranjeros en Chile* (Santiago, 1900) and 'Quien Sabe' (pseud. C. F. Hillman), '*Old Timers*'. *British and Americans in Chile* (Santiago, 1900).

[46] R. A. Humphreys, *British Consular Reports on the Trade and Politics of Latin America, 1824–26* (Royal Historical Society, Camden Third Series, lxiii, London, 1940), p. 94, note 1.

[47] Return of Trade of Valparaiso for 1840 enclosed in Walpole to Palmerston, Valparaiso, 17 May 1841. F.O. 16/43. No. 11. Diplomatic.

[48] Percentages calculated from figures in Martner, *Estudio de la política comercial*, i, 299, and ii, 351–2. For British colonial trade with Chile, see T. W. Keeble, *Commercial Relations between British Overseas Territories and South America, 1806–1914* (London, Institute of Latin American Studies Monographs No. 3, 1970), *passim*.

[49] Humphreys, *Consular Reports*, loc. cit.

[50] Enclosure in Consul Thomson to Lord John Russell, Santiago, 5 June 1861. F.O. 16/117. No. 45. Diplomatic.   [51] *The South American Journal*, 5 May 1882.

[52] See *Sinopsis estadística de la República de Chile, año 1923* (Santiago, 1924), p. 9.

[53] For this story, see M. Jefferson, *Recent Colonisation in Chile* (New York, American Geographical Society, 1921), pp. 19–28; 31–5.

representative had reported that the British in Chile were 'so much more weighty in commercial houses, numbers, wealth, etc., that the American influence and interest' was 'much diminished'.[54] And seventy years later, an American advocate of dynamic, commercial Pan-Americanism directed from Washington complained that Valparaiso, with almost its entire trade conducted in pounds sterling, its English newspaper, and the almost exclusive use of the English language, was 'nothing more than an English colony'.[55]

Yet, despite the early date at which British commercial enterprise was active in Chile, Great Britain did not grant full recognition to the republic until 1841, when her consul-general at Santiago was given the additional rank of chargé d'affaires.[56] Recognition was delayed, apparently, because of Chile's failure in the 1820s to meet payments on the loans she contracted in London in 1822.[57] The situation was regularized further in 1854 by a Treaty of Friendship, Commerce and Navigation between the two countries.[58] And in 1872 the British representative was designated Minister-Resident and Consul-General.[59] Behind these formal indications of developing commercial and political relations between Great Britain and Chile lay the activity of the individual British trader, mechanic and industrialist who played no small part in the country's development.

Of the British trading-houses to establish themselves in Chile, that of Antony Gibbs and Sons, active before the independence of Spanish America in the West Indies trade, in Spain and in Portugal, was to become the most significant.[60] Offices were opened both in Valparaiso and Lima in 1822, and in Santiago

---

[54] Cited in R. A. Humphreys, 'Anglo-American Rivalries and Spanish-American Emancipation', *Transactions of the Royal Historical Society*, 5th series, vol. 16 (1966), p. 146.

[55] W. E. Curtis, *Capitals of Spanish America* (New York, 1888), p. 454.

[56] T. E. Nichols, 'The Establishment of Political Relations between Chile and Great Britain', *HAHR*, xxviii (1948), p. 141.

[57] D. Barros Arana, *Historia jeneral de Chile* (16 vols., Santiago, 1884–1902), xvi, 160.

[58] The text may be found in *British and Foreign State Papers*, xliv (1854), pp. 47–62.

[59] Nichols, loc. cit., p. 143.

[60] W. Maude, *Antony Gibbs & Sons Limited. Merchants and Bankers, 1808–1958* (London, 1958), pp. 17 ff.

in 1826, and, as the century advanced, so did offices and agencies of the firm, not only on the Pacific coast of South America but also elsewhere in the Americas and Australasia. Combining trade, both import and export, with banking, insurance services and contract work, the House of Gibbs was to play a crucial role in the development of the trade in both guano and nitrates, the rich natural fertilizers around which so much of the economic history of Peru and of Chile was to be written. A quarter of a century after Gibbs had established themselves in Chile, three Scotsmen, Alexander Balfour, Stephen Williamson and David Duncan, established at Liverpool the partnership of S. Williamson and Company for shipping goods to the west coast of South America.[61] In 1851–52, the firm was established in Valparaiso and the business expanded during the 1850s, but in 1863 the original partnership was dissolved with the withdrawal of Duncan, the House's name in Valparaiso being changed to Williamson, Balfour and Company. Like Gibbs, the House expanded its business on the west coast of South America and elsewhere in the world, and like them also it was to play a prominent part in the nitrate business. As for Duncan, he helped to found another important British business with extensive interests when in 1863 he joined with H. F. Fox, a partner in the firm of Ravenscroft Brothers, who had been in Valparaiso since 1843, to establish the House of Duncan, Fox and Company.[62]

There were, of course, many other British concerns which were active in mid-nineteenth-century Chile, some of them no less well known and successful than those mentioned above. A few examples must suffice to illustrate the range of British interests. During the period 1840–70, a considerable amount of British capital was invested in Chilean copper, the Copiapó Mining Company being the most important firm.[63] Copper

[61] Wallis Hunt, *Heirs of Great Adventure. The History of Balfour, Williamson and Company Limited* (2 vols., London, 1915), i, 15 ff.

[62] There is no published history of Duncan, Fox & Company, but a typescript *Short History of Duncan, Fox and Co. Ltd., 1843–1956*, the work of E. E. Davies, is located at the Company's headquarters. I am grateful to a former Chairman, Mr J. V. Gallagher, for an opportunity to read this work.

[63] See C. W. Centner, 'Great Britain and Chilean Mining, 1830–1914', *Economic History Review*, xii (1942), pp. 77–8, and also Isaiah Bowman, *Desert Trails of Atacama* (New York, American Geographical Society, 1924), pp. 180–5.

provided other links with Britain since the ores were shipped to Swansea for smelting, and Chile was also the home of a number of Cornish miners who had been recruited to work in the industry.[64] Another important trading connection was the supply of British coal to Chile, amounting by 1883 to nine-tenths of all the coal imported into the country.[65] In 1885 British capital moved directly into coal-mining in Chile for the first time with the foundation in London of the Arauco Company.[66] Agricultural interests were not neglected: when, in 1849–53, Chilean wheat production and exports received a powerful stimulus from the gold rushes in California and Australia, sudden markets which only Chile could supply, among the chief beneficiaries of the boom were British business-houses in Chile which built modern mills in the southern part of the central valley.[67]

British economic interests in Chile were, therefore, already considerable before the War of the Pacific.[68] After the war, however, they increased greatly. In the first place, the accession to Chile of the rich nitrate province of Tarapacá opened up fresh vistas for British capital and enterprise. And, secondly, there appeared on the scene the man whose name became synonymous with nitrate itself, John Thomas North.

The War of the Pacific and the Nitrate Industry[69]

The causes of the War of the Pacific, 1879–83, fought between Chile on the one hand and Peru and Bolivia on the other, were many and involved, but the results were clear and definite. Chile, victorious on land and sea, compelled her adversaries to sue for peace, taking as spoils of war the Peruvian province of

[64] Charles Darwin, *The Voyage of the Beagle* (London, Dent's Everyman edition, 1960), pp. 247–8, records an amusing encounter with one of the Cornish miners.

[65] Consul-General Drummond Hay to the Earl of Granville, Valparaiso, 27 April 1883. F.O. 16/224. No. 2. Commercial.

[66] Centner, loc. cit., p. 77.

[67] Sepúlveda, 'El trigo chileno', pp. 45 ff.

[68] In addition, there were, of course, British holders of bonds who had subscribed to Chilean government loans floated in London. At par, the amount involved by 1875 was £9,820,700. J. F. Rippy, *British Investments in Latin America, 1822–1949* (Hamden, Conn., 1966), p. 29.

[69] There is an extensive literature on both these subjects. Among the more important works on the War of the Pacific are, from the Chilean viewpoint,

Tarapacá and Bolivia's only litoral territory of Antofagasta. These acquisitions increased the size of Chile by more than one-third, pushed her northern frontier from the southern to the northern boundary of the Atacama desert, and brought under Chilean control the rich mineral resources of that otherwise barren region. The war had a profound material effect upon Chile, for it was from the export duties on nitrate extracted from the ceded territories that the government derived a high proportion of its revenue for the next forty years.

Yet the history of the nitrate industry as a Peruvian rather than a Chilean story is also relevant to this narrative, at least in its main outlines. Before the 1860s, nitrate was much less important to Peru than guano—the manure of untold millions of sea-birds, the exploitation of which brought Peru the bulk of her government income between 1830 and 1870 and enabled her leaders to embark on large and expensive programmes of public works.[70] Not only did the Peruvian government have

Gonzalo Bulnes, *Guerra del Pacífico* (3 vols., Santiago, 1911–19) and A. Blanlot Holley, *Historia de la Paz entre Chile i el Perú, 1879–1884* (2nd ed., Santiago, 1910). The enigmatic title refers to the numerous attempts at negotiation while the war, officially, went on. The Peruvian case is argued by M. F. Paz Soldán, *Narración histórica de la Guerra de Chile contra el Perú y Bolivia* (Buenos Aires, 1884) and Andrés A. Cáceres, *La Guerra entre el Perú y Chile, 1879–1883* (Buenos Aires, 1924). Two interesting accounts by contemporary observers, both sympathetic to Peru, are: Sir Clements R. Markham, *The War between Peru and Chile, 1879–1882* (London, 1882) and Tommaso Caivano, *Historia de la guerra de América entre Chile, Perú y Bolivia* (trans. from the Italian by A. de Ballesteros Contín, Iquique, 1904). The best account in English is W. J. Dennis, *Tacna and Arica: an account of the Chile-Peru boundary dispute and the arbitration of the United States* (New Haven, 1931), while the same author's *Documentary History of the Tacna-Arica Dispute* (Iowa City, Univ. of Iowa, 1927) prints many of the relevant documents.

On nitrates, see particularly, E. Semper and E. Michels, *La industria del salitre en Chile* (trans. into Spanish and augmented by O. Gandarillas and G. Salas, Santiago, 1908); Manuel Cruchaga, *Guano y Salitre* (Madrid, 1929); G. Billing-hurst, *Los capitales salitreros de Tarapacá* (Santiago, 1889); Roberto Hernández Cornejo, *El salitre. Resumen histórico desde su decubrimiento y explotación* (Valparaiso, 1930), and, the most detailed account based on extensive documentation, Oscar Bermúdez, *Historia del Salitre desde sus origines hasta la Guerra del Pacífico* (Santiago, 1963). This is vol. 1 of a projected two-volume work. A useful collection of documents is C. Aldunate Solar, *Leyes,Decretos i Documentos relativos a Salitreras* (Santiago, 1907), while M. B. Donald, 'History of the Chile Nitrate Industry', *Annals of Science*, i, No. 1 (January 1936), pp. 29–47, and No. 2 (April 1936), pp. 193–216, provides an excellent short account.

[70] For this story, see A. J. Duffield, *Peru in the Guano Age* (London, 1877); Jonathan V. Levin, *The Export Economies: Their Pattern of Development in Historical Perspective* (Cambridge, Mass., Harvard Univ. Press, 1960), pp. 27–123, and

almost a world monopoly of this rich natural fertilizer; it also possessed, together with the Bolivian government, the world's only resources of natural nitrate, and with the decline of the richest guano deposits on Peru's offshore islands, in the 1860s, Peruvian ministers turned fresh eyes to the country's nitrate wealth. Both the guano and nitrate industries owed their development, to a large extent, to foreign capital, foreign enterprise and foreign labour, but each industry developed on different lines. The guano industry was a Peruvian government monopoly: in return for large loans to finance construction programmes, the government allowed lenders to ship a fixed amount of guano from its deposits and deduct from the proceeds the amount owing to them by the government. On the other hand, the nitrate deposits were exploited by private capital and the producers simply paid an export duty on shipments to the Bolivian or Peruvian governments, both of which remained apparently indifferent so long as this easily-acquired wealth continued to flow into their treasuries. The network of private interests in nitrate, however, both in Peruvian Tarapacá and Bolivian Antofagasta, was primarily Chilean and British. Chilean workmen provided much of the labour force: as early as 1870 it was reported that, of the 16,000 to 18,000 workers in the region of Iquique, the principal port of Tarapacá, almost half came from Chile and Bolivia.[71] This fact proved to be an important subsidiary argument advanced later by Chile for annexing the province.[72] But the amount of Chilean capital invested in the nitrate industry and a long history of frontier disputes with her northern neighbours were more important factors leading to the War of the Pacific.[73]

British interests in Tarapacá were financial and commercial: certain merchant houses, and notably Antony Gibbs, were closely involved with nitrate, as, indeed, they had been earlier

W. M. Mathew, 'Peru and the British Guano Market, 1840–1870', *Economic History Review*, Second Series, xxiii (1970), pp. 112–28.

[71] Acting Vice-Consul Nairn to Minister Jerningham, Iquique, 14 September 1870. Copy encl. in Jerningham to Earl Granville, Lima, 13 October 1870. F.O. 61(Peru)/259. No. 79. Diplomatic.

[72] *Diario Oficial* of Chile, 25 December 1881, encl. in Minister Pakenham to Granville, Santiago, 27 December 1881. F.O. 16/213. No. 91. Diplomatic.

[73] Dennis, *Tacna and Arica, passim*.

in the guano trade.[74] On the outbreak of the War of the Pacific in 1879, it was reported that

the working of the nitrate deposits is mainly in the hands of a powerful Chilian Company of this city [Santiago] and Valparaiso, and . . . the funds thereof are chiefly those of Gibbs, and Edwards and Co., wealthy capitalists of English extraction, and the former connected with the well-known house of A. Gibbs of London.[75]

The amount of British capital involved in Tarapacá was estimated at not less than £1,000,000.[76]

These interests, however, were seriously affected in the 1870s by the policy of the Peruvian government. By 1872, the government had indulged in such prodigal expenditure and had contracted such huge loans abroad that it had recourse to extraordinary means of finding money.[77] In January 1873 a law was passed for the creation of a government sales monopoly in nitrate, the government becoming the sole exporter of the fertilizer.[78] Fierce opposition caused the government to leave the law in abeyance for the time being while it raised the export duty on nitrate and thus achieved the same end as was intended by the monopoly.[79] But in 1875 it was decided to expropriate the foreign capitalist; a law was passed in May which authorized the President to contract a new loan of £7,000,000, of

[74] Gibbs' involvement in guano has been studied in detail by W. M. Mathew, 'Anglo-Peruvian Commercial and Financial Relations, 1820–1865' (unpublished Ph.D. thesis, Univ. of London, 1964), a study based upon the extensive archive of the House. London, Guildhall Library, Archives of Antony Gibbs & Son (cited hereafter as AAG with ms. number). Balfour, Williamson were also interested in guano. See correspondence in the letter-books of Stephen Williamson. London, Roman House, Records of Balfour, Williamson & Company (cited hereafter as Balfour, Williamson Papers, with volume number). I am indebted to Mr Wallis Hunt for the opportunity to see this material.

[75] Pakenham to Lord Salisbury, Santiago, 18 February 1879. F.O. 16/202. No. 6. Diplomatic.

[76] Minister Spencer St John to Salisbury, Lima, 26 November 1879. F.O. 61/319. No. 170. Diplomatic.

[77] A mania for railway building was largely responsible for Peru's indebtedness. See W. S. Stewart, *Henry Meiggs, Yankee Pizarro* (Duke Univ. Press, 1946), *passim*.

[78] Semper and Michels, *La industria del salitre*, p. 122. For a recent, detailed account of the Peruvian government's policy on nitrates in the 1870s, see Robert G. Greenhill and Rory Miller, 'The Peruvian Government and the Nitrate Trade, 1873–1879', *Journal of Latin American Studies*, v, No. 1 (May 1973), pp. 107–131.

[79] Jerningham to Granville, Lima, 13 March 1873. F.O. 61/279. No. 16. Commercial.

which £4,000,000 was to be used to pay for the privately-owned *oficinas*, or nitrate-producing plants.[80] A decree of December 1875 regulated the transfer of the *oficinas* to the government.[81] The producers were to be paid in certificates which were redeemable by the government within two years and which bore an annual interest of 8 per cent. The bonds were made payable to bearer, but they were never cancelled by Peru, since she failed to obtain the loan needed to redeem them.[82]

The effect of these developments on the industry in Tarapacá was serious and by 1878 it was reported that the trade of Iquique was falling owing to the government monopoly.[83] An earthquake in March 1877, which destroyed many of the loading platforms along the coast, further restricted production.[84] And, whereas in 1876 over 7,300,000 *quintals* of nitrate had been exported from Tarapacá, in the following year the figure dropped to 5,000,000 *quintals*.[85] Early in 1879, however, the War of the Pacific broke out. It has been alleged that the real responsibility for that war rests with the dispossessed nitrate producers, the *salitreros*, of Tarapacá who urged upon Chile the advisability of taking over the nitrate areas.[86] There is no doubt that the *salitreros* looked askance at the government monopoly,[87] and it was perfectly true that 'the nitrate districts of Antofagasta and Tarapacá were the real and direct cause of the war'.[88] There is, however, scant evidence that the foreign *salitreros* played a significant part in bringing on the war,

[80] Semper and Michels, loc. cit., p. 123. Aldunate, *Leyes, decretos y documentos*, Part i, pp. 33–4, gives the text of the law.

[81] Ibid., pp. 35–40.

[82] Semper and Michels, loc. cit.

[83] St John to Salisbury, Lima, 23 May 1878. F.O. 61/306. No. 8. Consular.

[84] AAG, MS. 11,138, a miscellaneous bundle of papers, contains interesting eyewitness accounts of the earthquake and its effects.

[85] Semper and Michels, *La industria del salitre*, p. 135. A *quintal* is about 100 lb.

[86] See Dennis, *Tacna and Arica*, pp. 61–83. The leading spokesman for this view was American Secretary of State, James G. Blaine.

[87] Cf. St John to Granville, Lima, 27 December 1881. F.O.61/344. No. 111. Diplomatic: 'Should the result of the war be to secure to Chile the provinces of Atacama [Antofagasta] and Tarapacá, it will certainly be to the advantage of foreign commerce.'

[88] *The Chilean Times*, Valparaiso, 31 December 1881.

though individuals seem to have assisted the Chilean authorities once the war had begun.[89]

The fall of Lima to Chilean troops early in 1881 effectively put an end to military operations, though it was October 1883 before Chile and Peru signed the Treaty of Ancón to end hostilities officially. By the treaty, Chile received the perpetual and unconditional cession of Tarapacá, as well as the cession for ten years of Tacna and Arica; at the end of that time a plebiscite would decide the ownership of these districts, the gainer paying 10,000,000 silver dollars to the loser.[90] A separate peace with Bolivia in 1884 assured to Chile the territory of Antofagasta with its port of the same name and nitrate deposits second only in importance to those of Tarapacá.[91]

While the war was still in progress, the Chilean government began to consider what steps to take with regard to the nitrate industry, and in 1880 a commission was appointed to find some basis for an arrangement by which nitrate could be shipped from the province without prejudicing the rights of producers.[92] As a result, in October 1880, a decree was issued fixing the export duty to be levied on nitrate shipped from Tarapacá.[93] The real significance of the work of the commission, however,

[89] See V. G. Kiernan, 'Foreign Interests in the War of the Pacific', *HAHR*, xxxv (1955), pp. 14–36, for a careful refutation of Blaine's opinion. On the other hand, the role of George Hicks, manager of the Antofagasta Nitrate and Railway Co., in which Gibbs had a large interest, and whose conflict with the Bolivian government was the immediate cause of the war, seems more dubious. This opinion is based upon a typescript collection of copies of letters from the archives of the Anglo-Lautaro Company, made by Arturo Fuenzalida, known as 'Guerra del Pacífico. Cartas'. I am indebted to Señor Samuel B. Mardones of Santiago for this material. Gibbs themselves were blameless, and strongly reproved one of their local staff for being too friendly with the Chileans 'in direct contradiction to all their old principles of not mixing themselves up in any way to compromise their neutrality'. John Hayne to Alfred Bohl at Lima, Valparaiso, 5 March 1879. AAG, MS. 11,120. Private Letters, Valparaiso to Lima, 1873–79.

[90] The text of the treaty is in A. Bascuñan Montes, *Recopilación de Tratados y Convenciones celebrados entre la República de Chile y las potencias estranjeras* (6 vols., Santiago, 1894–1913), ii, 158–66.

[91] Ibid., pp. 167–75.

[92] The fullest account of the complicated situation of the nitrate industry during the war is Oscar Bermúdez, 'El salitre de Tarapacá y Antofagasta durante la ocupación militar Chilena', *Anales de la Universidad del Norte* (Antofagasta), v (1966), pp. 131–82.

[93] Ibid., *passim*. R. Anguita, *Leyes promulgadas en Chile desde 1810 hasta 1912* (4 vols. and index, Santiago, 1912), ii, 494, gives the text of the decree.

lay in the report it made to the Chilean government: this rejected the idea of a government monopoly for nitrate, such as Peru had attempted to create, and expressed a firm belief in a system of free enterprise and private ownership.[94] In view of this report, wide credence was given to the rumour that, having taken Tarapacá, Chile intended not only to annex the province but also to return legally to the *salitreros* the *oficinas* which Peru had theoretically acquired from them in return for unredeemed certificates.

In June 1881, the Chilean government took a decisive step towards the reconstruction of privately-owned nitrate-fields (*salitreras*) in Tarapacá when it promulgated the following decree:

The nitrate establishments of . . . Tarapacá, which were bought by the Peruvian government and in payment for which the government had issued certificates . . . will be provisionally returned, without prejudice to the rights of third parties, to those who will deposit at least three quarters of the certificates issued . . . for each *salitrera* and who will deposit in the treasury a sum of money equal to the price of the remaining quarter, which . . . will be returned . . . when all the certificates issued for the value of the respective *salitrera* are surrendered.[95]

This decree was the outcome of the deliberations of a second commission, appointed early in 1881, which came to the same conclusions as its predecessor.[96] In the following March, two other decrees regulated the return of the nitrate-fields to certificate holders and also provided for the public auction of such properties which were not reclaimed within ninety days.[97]

The decision to return the *salitreras* to private enterprise was the result of a number of factors of which, perhaps, the most important was the widespread belief in principles of laissez-faire. The Peruvian attempt to nationalize the nitrate industry had been a dismal failure, though it must be said that all the attendant circumstances for this move in 1875 were themselves more responsible for the débâcle than the principle itself.[98]

[94] Bermúdez, loc. cit., pp. 145–9.   [95] Aldunate, *Leyes, decretos y documentos*, p. 75.
[96] Bermúdez, loc. cit., pp. 169–76.   [97] Aldunate, loc. cit., pp. 83–90.
[98] See Greenhill and Miller, 'The Peruvian Government and the Nitrate Trade', *passim*. The opinions of the House of Gibbs, which took on the role of consignment

Nevertheless, the Peruvian example of state interference weighed heavily with the Chilean government in its own attitude to the question. The personal opinion of President Domingo Santa María, as well as that of other leading Chileans, was also significant. He believed fundamentally in private ownership and he also thought that recognition of the nitrate certificates by Chile would redound to the country's credit abroad.[99] It has also been alleged that another reason for the government's decision was the influence of the private nitrate interests in financial and political circles in Santiago, and the close links that existed between members of the Chilean aristocracy and foreign entrepreneurs.[100]

Whatever the reasons for the Chilean government's decision, the result was to place in foreign hands a sizeable part of the nitrate industry. During the war, great uncertainty had prevailed among holders of the Peruvian nitrate certificates who did not know what would happen to their holdings in the event of a Chilean victory; as a result, the value of those certificates, which had begun to decline before the outbreak of the war itself, fell steeply as the war progressed. In 1879, nitrate certificates in Lima were selling at 60 per cent of their nominal value, and they continued to fall in price until certificates originally worth £183 were selling at £20 and £30.[101] In these circumstances, a number of speculators bought up large quantities of the depreciated certificates which would, in effect, be the title-deeds to the nitrate-grounds if Chile were to return the industry to private ownership; when the Chilean government took precisely that step, the speculators exchanged the certificates for the appropriate *salitreras* which were worth far more than they had paid for them, and thus realized huge profits on the transaction.[102] The speculators were mainly British and it

agents for Peruvian nitrate under the nationalization, fluctuated considerably in the 1870s. They disagreed with their employer on the operation of the scheme, and their views swung between optimism and pessimism all the time they were operating it.

[99] See Encina, *Historia de Chile*, xviii, 284–307; Bermúdez, 'El salitre de Tarapacá', p. 179.

[100] Hernán Ramírez Necochea, *Balmaceda y la contrarevolución de 1891* (2nd ed,. Santiago, 1969), p. 24. See also below, pp. 125–9.

[101] Billinghurst, *Capitales salitreros de Tarapacá*, p. 49.

[102] Ibid., pp. 49–51. Billinghurst asserted that Mr Read, the manager of Gibbs

was by their operations that the nitrate industry came to be dominated by British interests. In 1878, British capital had controlled 13 per cent of the nitrate industry in Tarapacá; by 1884, the proportion had risen to 34 per cent,[103] and by 1890, after a period of feverish activity on the London Stock Exchange—to be dealt with in detail below—70 per cent of the nitrate industry was in British hands.[104] Many actors played a part in this story, but one in particular assumed the leading role. He was John Thomas North, an English engineer who had lived and worked in Tarapacá for almost twenty years: now, with the War of the Pacific, he saw his chance to tread a larger stage and, as his earlier career had clearly shown, North was not the man to need much prompting.

North's Early Life and Achievements, 1842–1882[105]

In the various accounts of North's beginnings, emphasis is laid on his very humble origins as if to paint in sharper colours his

in Lima, proposed to the London House that they should seize the opportunity to buy up all the certificates, title-deeds to all the *oficinas* except those of the German house of Gildemeister, and he reckoned it would cost them some £600,000. I have found no reference to this in the Gibbs Archive, but there is a good deal of correspondence to show that, in 1879 at least, the House was not optimistic about Chile returning the industry to private hands. Hayne to the Lima House, Valparaiso, 5 October 1879, AAG, MS. 11,120; same to same, 13 October 1879, in ibid.

[103] Semper and Michels, *La industria del salitre*, p. 139.

[104] Ramírez, loc. cit., p. 18.

[105] Information on North and his activities is widely scattered in a large number of sources, but I have found no single corpus of material on which to base a full biography. Short accounts may be found in P. P. Figueroa, *Diccionario Biográfico de Estranjeros en Chile*, pp. 159–62; O. Hardy, 'British Nitrates and the Balmaceda Revolution', *Pacific Historical Review*, xvii (1948), pp. 171–80; Enrique Bunster, *Bombardeo de Valparaiso y otros relatos* (Santiago, 1948), pp. 151–76; Ramírez, *Balmaceda*, pp. 41 ff., and in many of the books on nitrate cited in note 69. Almost all writers on North used the interview he gave to the French reporter Gaston Calmette which was published as 'Le Roi des Nitrates', *Le Figaro*, Paris, 23 April 1896. In addition to these sources, I have used the British press and notably extensive obituary notices on North in *The Leeds Mercury*, 6 May 1896, and in *The Sidcup and District Times*, 8 May 1896, and two contemporary pamphlets: *Life and Career of the Late Colonel North. How he made his Millions, as told by himself* (Leeds, 1896), in the Public Reference Library of Leeds, and *The Life and Career of Col. North from Apprentice Boy to Millionaire* (Sidcup, Kent, 1896) in the Library of the Borough of Woolwich, London. I have also benefited from conversations at various times with Mr Richard North, Mrs Vera Proctor and Mrs Victoria Fischer, members of the family of North's brother, Gamble, who was also active in nitrates.

dramatic rise to fame and fortune.[106] It was a picture he himself promoted once he had become well known.[107] In fact, however, he had a reasonable start in life. He was born on 30 January 1842, at Holbeck near Leeds in Yorkshire, the son of a prosperous coal-merchant who was also a local churchwarden and clearly a man of some substance. He was educated at a middle-class school in Leeds, and at the age of fifteen was apprenticed to the firm of Shaw, North and Watson of Hunslet, millwrights and shipwrights, one of the partners being a cousin of his father. After eight years learning his trade as a mechanical engineer, North joined the larger firm of Messrs Fowler and Company at Leeds at their well-known Steam Plough Works. In the same year, 1865, he married Jane Woodhead, the daughter of a prominent local Conservative and member of the Leeds Town Council, a match which further emphasizes North's essentially middle-class background.

North's first contact with South America was in 1866 or 1867 when Fowlers sent him to Chile to supervise locomotive construction on the Carrizal railway, and he worked for a time in the locomotive workshops both at Carrizal and at the port of Caldera. He then, apparently, left the service of Fowlers to branch out on his own, and in 1871 he moved to Iquique where he found employment in the nitrate *oficina* of the Peruvian, González Véliz: in this post he got to know both the nitrate region of Tarapacá and the sizeable British colony in the region.

The 1870s was the first great decade of expansion for the nitrate industry. Between 1860 and 1870, some 17,000,000 *quintals* of nitrate had been shipped from the ports of Tarapacá, but in the following decade the figure rose to over 44,000,000 and the ports of Iquique and Pisagua began to assume the appearance of modern towns with civic amenities.[108] As nitrate *oficinas* sprang up in the hinterland, so machine-shops were established to service them, and British foundrymen were much

[106] Ramírez, loc. cit., p. 41, speaks of North as a peasant (*campesino*), transformed by Leeds into a 'cog in the wheel of the capitalist system'.

[107] At a dinner in Coronel in 1889, North referred to working on the Chilean railways for 'four pesos a day', *El Heraldo* of Santiago, 20 March 1889.

[108] See W. F. M. Castle, *Sketch of the City of Iquique, Chile during Fifty Years* (Plymouth, 1887), *passim*.

in evidence in the works of Humphrey, Dickinson and Company, MacAllum, Shaw and Company and, in a branch of North's former employers, Fowler and Bennett.[109] The railway between Iquique and Pisagua, built essentially to link the *oficinas* with the coast, was constructed between 1868 and 1875, and there appeared on the scene many Englishmen associated with the nitrate trade whose names recur throughout the history of the industry—Jameson, Whitelegg, Bush, Inglis, Robertson and many others.[110] Though Antony Gibbs and Sons did not actually establish their branch at Iquique until 1881, they owned nitrate establishments in the interior from the early 1860s, in association with British pioneers in nitrate, George Smith and Melbourne Clark, and it was in the 1870s that the House began its important interest in the trade in iodine, a by-product of nitrate.[111] But it was the port of Iquique which best reflected the growing economy of Tarapacá: its population grew from 2,485 in 1862 to 9,222 in 1876,[112] and three years later the British government appointed its first vice-consul at the port.[113]

It was with the first holder of that post, Maurice Jewell, that North went into partnership, importing machinery, tools and other merchandise for the *oficinas* and the growing population of Iquique itself, and acting as local agents for the steamship lines which now called more frequently at the ports on the fringe of the Atacama desert. Thanks to his initiative and business acumen, North was soon able to acquire nitrate-works of his own, though at this stage of his career he was less interested in owning them than in using them to increase his capital.[114] But other opportunities for advancement soon pre-

---

[109] Hillman, *Old Timers*, p. 202.

[110] Ibid. See also Bermúdez, *Historia del Salitre*, *passim*, the fullest account o British participation in nitrates.

[111] Maude, *Antony Gibbs & Sons, Ltd.*, p. 31; Bermúdez, loc. cit., pp. 166–9; and, on iodine, Robert G. Greenhill, 'Antony Gibbs & Sons and the Organization of the Iodine Trade' (Univ. of Cambridge, Centre of Latin American Studies, Working Papers No. 1, 1972), *passim*.

[112] G. Billinghurst, *Estudio sobre la jeografía de Tarapacá* (Santiago, 1886), p. 93.

[113] Foreign Office to St John, London, 1 December 1879. F.O. 177/160. No. 21. Consular.

[114] Ramírez, *Balmaceda*, pp. 42–3, quoting documents in the Judicial Archives of Iquique.

sented themselves. The chief obstacle to tolerable living conditions in the nitrate regions was lack of water, for scarcely any rain, at least in predictable measure and location, falls on the Atacama desert. Accordingly, in 1878 the *Compañía de Aguas de Tarapacá* was founded at Iquique to bring water to Iquique by tanker from Arica, and build installations to store it. North promptly rented the company's property for two years and operated the service, though he was not new to the business, having in 1875 bought a vessel, the *Marañon*, which he used as a water-tanker at the small port of Huanillos and did a good trade with passing ships.[115] But when the War of the Pacific intervened, the founders of the *Compañía*—all Englishmen—left Iquique, and North was recognized by the Chilean authorities in occupation of Tarapacá as the sole owner of the business. During the war, a good deal of the company's property was destroyed in the fighting by Chilean forces and the *Marañon* was sunk by a Chilean warship, but even this apparent setback North tried to turn to his advantage. After the war, claims commissions were set up between the Chilean government and various foreign states whose nationals in Chile had suffered loss or damage to property as a result of Chilean action.[116] North, not surprisingly, claimed for the loss of the *Marañon* but, while the sinking of the vessel was proved, the commission declared the claim to be outside its jurisdiction and North's claim fell to the ground. He also claimed, entirely in his own name, for the losses suffered by the water company, and in this was partially successful, though the commission reduced his compensation on the grounds that the proofs put in did not establish the fact that the damage done to the claimant's property amounted to the sum claimed.[117] Nevertheless, North did quite well out of

[115] For North and the Compañía, see Ramírez, *Balmaceda*, pp. 45–6, note 44, and for the *Marañon*, Pakenham to Granville, Valparaiso, 2 October 1880, with enclosures, F.O. 16/208. No. 69. Diplomatic.

[116] A. Soto Cárdenas, *Guerra del Pacífico: Los Tribunales Arbitrales, 1882–1888* (Santiago, 1950); pp. 226 and 228 refer specifically to North's claims.

[117] Fraser to Iddesleigh, Santiago, 25 November 1886. F.O. 16/243. No. 102. Diplomatic, and same to same, Santiago, 22 December 1886, in idem., No. 22. Claims. North's original manuscript letter, protesting against a 'most wanton piece of mischief' and demanding an investigation was sent to the Foreign Office in London and forwarded by the office to the British Minister in Lima. Foreign Office to St John, London, 28 October 1879, with enclosures. F.O. 177/160. No. 50. Diplomatic.

the War of the Pacific in this respect, since he owned con-
densing equipment at Iquique which had not been damaged in
the war, and he held the company's tankers: on the basis of
these assets he soon established a monopoly for the supply of
water to the population of Iquique.[118]

The War of the Pacific did much more than this for the rising
entrepreneur in presenting him with a unique opportunity of
securing a dominant position in the nitrate industry itself. For
North was the leading speculator in nitrate certificates at Lima
during the war.[119] And in these operations he utilized long-
standing friendships with two Englishmen who had also gone
to seek their fortune in the nitrate regions, Robert Harvey and
John Dawson.

The career of Robert Harvey had much in common with that
of North, with whom he was to be associated in so many enterprises in Chile and in England.[120] Born at Truro in Cornwall in
1847, the son of the quaymaster of the port, Harvey attended a
local school before joining the Perran Foundry and becoming a
fitter. The foundry then secured a contract to supply machinery
for the Carmelita mine near the Chilean port of Tocopilla and
it was Harvey, at the age of 22, who was sent out to set it up.
He worked at the mine—which was managed by another
Cornishman, as so many Chilean mines were—for four or five
years and then, in 1875, attracted by news of the opportunities
now developing in the nitrate regions, Harvey moved to
Iquique. In Tarapacá he soon found employment in an *oficina*
owned by the Peruvian León Castro, of the *Compañía Salitrera
del Rimac*, and became well known in the region, not least to
the workmen to whom he was 'el gringo colorado' because of
his ruddy complexion. In 1876, however, the Peruvian government having decreed the nationalization of the nitrate industry,
it established a general inspectorate for the nitrate-fields
(*Inspección de Salitreras de Tarapacá*) to determine the extent,
ownership, and capacity of the various *oficinas*, and Harvey
obtained a post with this organization. His friendship with

[118] See below, pp. 56–60 for the continuation of this story.

[119] Evidence that North was in Peru at this time is provided by the fact that his
letter mentioned above in note 117 was posted in Callao on 17 August 1879.

[120] For much of my information on Harvey, I am deeply indebted to his son,
Mr Robert A. Harvey of Truro. See also the various publications cited in note 105.

North was already formed by this time, and he was of some
assistance to the Yorkshireman, through his acquired knowledge of the subject, in North's first entry into the nitrate
business in 1878.[121] Harvey was now well-established in
Tarapacá; he had a house at La Noria in the heart of the
southern nitrate district, on the railway line from Iquique to
Pisagua, and his work for the Peruvian government made him
an important local figure among the large expatriate community of Tarapacá.[122]

As with North, so with Harvey, the War of the Pacific was a
turning-point. Because of his extensive knowledge of the terrain,
the Peruvian government sought his advice and, indeed, made
him an honorary colonel in the army, but the rapid advance of
Chilean troops into Tarapacá and the subsequent rout of the
Peruvian and Bolivian armies saw Harvey a prisoner of the
Chileans, taken to Iquique. There he was seen by the Chilean
military and political commander in Tarapacá, Admiral
Patricio Lynch, to whom, apparently, Harvey justified his pro-
Peruvian conduct on the grounds of natural duty towards the
government which employed him. He was then told that the
Chileans intended to stay in Tarapacá indefinitely and was
asked if he were prepared to put his local knowledge to their
service, an offer he willingly accepted. In February 1880,
probably on the recommendation of Lynch, Harvey was named
Inspector-General of Nitrates by the Chilean government.[123]

As it happened, North had also reason to be grateful to
Lynch. In the same year that Harvey moved from the service
of Peru to that of Chile, North also helped the Chilean war
effort, despite the damage he later claimed to have suffered at
Chilean hands. He loaned one of his steamers to the Chilean
forces for the transport of the wounded, sold them another at a
moderate price, and provided them with eight launches for
landing operations.[124] It was, no doubt, partly in recognition
of this generosity, that Lynch in 1881 sold to North and a

[121] Bermúdez, *Historia del Salitre*, pp. 279–80; Ramírez, *Balmaceda*, pp. 43–5.

[122] Harvey married at Iquique in 1881 the daughter of a French businessman,
married to a Peruvian lady of Lima.

[123] Ramírez, *Balmaceda*, pp. 43–4.

[124] Hardy, 'British Nitrates', p. 172. See also below, p. 101, for North's recollections of this event.

partner of his in yet another enterprise, H. B. Jameson, 40,000 tons of guano at a price which enabled them to realize huge profits on the sale of the fertilizer in Europe.[125] But much bigger possibilities were in the offing for both North and Harvey in consequence of the impact of the War of the Pacific on the Peruvian nitrate industry and in this, their major enterprise, they enlisted the help of their mutual friend, John Dawson.

Much less is known about Dawson than about either North or Harvey, yet his assistance was vital in the acquisition of depreciated nitrate certificates during the War of the Pacific. Dawson was a banker with the London Bank of Mexico and South America, founded in 1863, and he had served as manager at various times at the Bank's branches in Lima and Valparaiso in the 1870s, becoming acquainted with North in the same period.[126] Some time in the late 1870s, Dawson joined the Chilean Bank of Valparaiso, and when Chilean troops occupied Iquique in 1880, he was sent to establish a branch in the nitrate port, beginning the business, in fact, in his bedroom.[127] When North and Harvey began to buy the nitrate certificates, they did so, at least in part, with funds supplied to them by Dawson in his capacity as manager of the Bank of Valparaiso in Iquique.[128]

The Chilean government's decision to return the nitrate industry to private enterprise found North and Harvey in possession of the title-deeds to 'the cream of the Iquique and

---

[125] Hardy, loc. cit.; Bermúdez, 'El Salitre de Tarapacá', p. 159; *Le Figaro*, 23 April 1895. This transaction had widespread repercussions. As the British Minister in Lima pointed out, it was contrary to an agreement made between the Chilean government and the holders of Peruvian bonds in 1880, whereby guano sales from Chilean-occupied territory were to be used to help pay for Peru's pre-war debts. St John to Granville, Lima, 8 June 1881. F.O. 61/344. Bondholders Claims, 1881–2. No. 48. The complicated and protracted history of the Peruvian Bondholders and their relation to the guano and nitrate industries, though related in part to this story, lies outside the central theme of this narrative. A brief outline is given in D. C. M. Platt, *Finance, Trade and Politics in British Foreign Policy, 1815–1914* (Oxford Univ. Press, reprinted, 1971), pp. 336–9. A detailed examination, based on the Foreign Office archives, may be found in my unpublished doctoral dissertation of the University of London, 'The Chilean Revolution of 1891: a Study in the Domestic and International History of Chile', 1955, pp. 74–95 ff.

[126] David Joslin, *A Century of Banking in Latin America. The Bank of London and South America Ltd, 1862–1962* (Oxford Univ. Press, 1963), p. 175.

[127] Castle, *Sketch of the City of Iquique*, p. 16.

[128] Billinghurst, *Los capitales salitreros*, pp. 48 ff.

Pisagua properties'.[129] Among the *oficinas* they acquired in this
way were those of Primitiva, Peruana, Ramírez, Buen Retiro,
Jazpampa and Virginia, all of them worth a good deal more
than they had paid for them.[130] It has been alleged by a number of writers that the enterprising trio of North, Harvey and
Dawson had prior knowledge, through Harvey's official
position, of the Chilean government's intentions long before
they were announced publicly, and that it was this knowledge
which prompted their purchase of the certificates.[131] On the
face of it, this is a plausible assumption, but detailed proof
is lacking. The dates of the purchases, in relation to the Chilean
government's decisions, are not known, and it is, therefore,
impossible to say whether or not North and Harvey were
gambling on a favourable outcome or whether they were
absolutely certain. And, as North's subsequent career was to
show beyond doubt, he was nothing if not a gambler. Certainly
the report of the first government commission of enquiry was
not received uncritically in the Chilean Congress.[132] And while
North himself subsequently claimed that he *knew* not only that
Chile would win the war but that she would also completely
respect the property rights represented by the certificates,[133]
this was the subsequent natural boast of a highly self-confident
man whose success seemed to be based on extraordinary foresight, and whose rise to fame and fortune depended precisely on
his capacity to convince the public of his reliability. At the
time, however, while there was no doubt a good deal of speculation about the Chilean government's ultimate intentions, it
seems hardly likely that there could be certainty.[134]

As for the purchase money for the nitrate certificates coming
from a Chilean bank, a feature of the story which has also

[129] Report of Consul-General Walker, Bogotá, 28 December 1889, in *Monthly
Reports from the Consuls of the United States of America. Miscellaneous Documents of the
House of Representatives for the 1st Session of the 51st Congress*, xxxii (Washington,
1890), pp. 407–8.

[130] Billinghurst, *Los capitales salitreros*, pp. 49–51.

[131] Ibid., p. 48; Semper and Michels, *La Industria del Salitre*, p. 138; Ramírez,
Balmaceda, pp. 43–5.

[132] Bermúdez, 'El Salitre de Tarapacá', pp. 151–5, 169–76.

[133] *Le Figaro*, 23 April 1895.

[134] Cf. Encina, *Historia de Chile*, xviii, pp. 307–15, expressing the same
opinion.

received some attention,[135] there was nothing improper in Dawson advancing funds, presumably at a good rate of interest, to two well-established figures in the nitrate regions. And it is, indeed, quite possible that if, in fact, North and Harvey had prior knowledge of the Chilean government's plans, Dawson did not, but was simply making a perfectly reasonable loan to two good customers who were, in addition, well-known acquaintances of his, if not more. It is, perhaps, relevant to note that Dawson's name does not figure in the lists of directors of the nitrate companies which Harvey and North subsequently formed on the basis of the properties they had acquired in Tarapacá: he remained a banker all his life, staying with the Bank of Valparaiso until 1886,[136] and then becoming manager of another bank in Iquique in 1888.[137] Dawson seems, indeed, to have been the Lepidus of the triumvirate.

Yet, although North and Harvey were, by 1882, the undisputed owners of rich nitrate-fields in Tarapacá, their wealth was still potential rather than actual. The nitrate industry did, indeed, recover quickly from the effects of the War of the Pacific, aided by high demand for the fertilizer in Europe, and exports in 1882 reached 492,000 metric tons, compared with 359,000 metric tons in 1881.[138] At the same time, however, increased production to meet a temporary rise in demand continued long after that demand had been met, and there was no corresponding growth of the world market. Moreover, a new method of refining the raw material from which nitrate was extracted, the Shanks process, was then being introduced, and this promised higher output still at lower cost.[139] To prevent a glut of nitrate, therefore, which would inevitably reduce prices and cut

---

[135] Billinghurst, loc. cit., p. 50; Ramírez, loc. cit., pp. 22–3; Keith Griffin, *Underdevelopment in Spanish America: An Interpretation* (Cambridge, Mass., 1969), p. 142. Griffin cites one Chilean author who is quoting another who does not give his source to say that the nitrate industry is an example of foreign control of an enterprise with domestic capital and without any inflow of capital from outside. This may well have been how North and Harvey acquired the nitrate *fields*, but a nitrate field is not a nitrate *works*.

[136] *The South American Journal*, 3 April 1886.

[137] See below, pp. 60–63.

[138] Hernández, *El salitre*, p. 174.

[139] Donald, 'History of the Chile Nitrate Industry', pp. 195–216, gives a detailed account of the Shanks process.

profits, producers turned to a temporary solution which would be invoked time and time again in the history of the natural nitrate industry—the formation of a producers' combination, whereby fixed production quotas for each *oficina* were agreed among them until world supply and demand again moved into equilibrium.[140] The first such combination was established in 1884, by which time John Thomas North was already on the way to assuming, as he would, the crown of 'the Nitrate King'.

[140] See J. R. Brown, 'Nitrate Crises, Combinations, and the Chilean Government in the Nitrate Age', *HAHR*, xliii (1963), pp. 230–46, *passim*.

II

THE KEYS OF NORTH'S KINGDOM

The Nitrate-fields of Tarapacá

In 1882 John Thomas North returned to England to settle his
family and to embark upon the critical stage in the establishment of the partners' fortunes, the floating of British public companies to exploit the nitrate-fields of Tarapacá. It was no easy
task, at least on paper, for North was little known in his own
country, except to a few individuals connected with that small
number of British business houses active on the Pacific coast of
South America. But one of his contacts proved decisive. This was
John Waite, a partner in the important Liverpool merchant
house of William and Jno. Lockett, who had been entertained
by North at Pisagua in 1877 when on a business trip to Peru.
The meeting was fortuitous, but its outcome was crucial to
North's advancement: greatly impressed by North's hospitality, and very few people were not, Waite invited North to look
him up and meet his partners when he should return to
England.[1] This North did in 1882, with the title-deeds of the
Pampa Ramírez *oficina* in his pocket, and a proposition to the
Locketts that these should become the basis of the first British
limited liability company formed to work the nitrate-fields and
to ship and market the fertilizer.[2] With the backing of Locketts',
the Liverpool Nitrate Co. Ltd was registered at Somerset
House on 3 February 1883, with a paid-up capital of
£150,000, divided into 6,000 shares of £25 each.[3] Locketts'
position in the commercial and financial circles of Liverpool
gave North the entrée he needed to an important body of
businessmen, for, apart from the Lockett, North and Harvey

---

[1] R. C. Lockett, *Memoirs of the Family of Lockett* (London, 1939, privately printed),
pp. 104–5. I am indebted to Mr Richard Lockett for this reference.

[2] Loc. cit.

[3] Ibid., p. 109. See also *Burdetts Official Intelligence* (14 vols., London, 1882–96),
vi (1888), pp. 694–5. This publication is a more comprehensive survey of investment than the *Stock Exchange Official Year Book* for the years it covers and has been
used instead of the latter.

families, the major shareholders in the Liverpool Nitrate Company came from prominent commercial, shipping and banking concerns in that city.[4]

Meanwhile, that well-qualified engineer, Robert Harvey, who had also returned to England in 1882, was put in charge of the technical operations, asked to prepare plans for the exploitation of the grounds six months before the company was floated, and authorized to contract for machinery. Boilers, tanks, rolling-stock, engines, pumps and tools were ordered from firms in England, while the Tarapacá foundry of North, Humphrey and Dickinson at Iquique supplied the crushing machine.[5] Harvey arrived at Iquique on 15 May 1883, with a number of English artisans recruited to install the plant, though the imported machinery only reached Chile in December. Nevertheless, within a year, the *oficina* Ramírez was capable of a monthly output of 6,000 tons of nitrate, though limited to half that production by the combination agreement.[6]

With the Liverpool Nitrate Company, North was launched on the spectacular career which earned him the title of 'the Nitrate King'. For, despite the limitations of the combination, the company prospered, paying dividends of 26 per cent in 1885 and 20 per cent in 1886.[7] North, as Chairman—Harvey was one of the Directors—took much of the credit, and, by the time the combination collapsed in December 1886, he had already founded two more companies, the Colorado Nitrate Company in 1885 and the Primitiva Nitrate Company in 1886.[8] These companies also had the backing of the Locketts and, indeed, were run from the same office in Liverpool as the

[4] Lockett, op. cit., p. 110, gives a list of names which includes the important business-house of Brocklebank and the shipping firm of Harrison.

[5] Robert Harvey, *Machinery for the Manufacture of Nitrate of Soda at the Ramírez Factory, Northern Chili*, a pamphlet reprint of an excerpt from the minutes of the *Proceedings of the Institution of Civil Engineers*, lxxxii, Session 1884–5, Part iv (London, 1885), pp. 3–4. It is interesting to note that the contract for rolling-stock went to John Fowler & Co. of Leeds, the very firm which North joined as an apprentice in 1863, and which first sent him to Peru in 1869. See above, p. 23.

[6] Harvey, op. cit., p. 3. See above, pp. 30–1, for the establishment of the combination.

[7] Chilean Consul to Ministro de Hacienda, London, 8 February 1889. *Fomento de la Industria Salitrera* (Santiago, 1889), pp. 127–8.

[8] J. F. Rippy, 'Economic Enterprises of the Nitrate King and his Associates in Chile', *Pacific Historical Review*, xvii (1948), p. 460.

first concern.[9] Their shares moved less spectacularly than those of the Liverpool Nitrate Company in the mid-eighties, but were, nonetheless, highly remunerative, the ordinary shares of the Colorado company, valued at £25, realizing dividends of from 10 per cent to 15 per cent in these years, and the £5 shares of Primitiva averaging 10 per cent.[10]

But it was the collapse of the restrictive combination at the end of 1886 which saw the real boom in nitrates on the London Stock Exchange, and with it North's emergence as a figure in the City. The combination collapsed because of disagreements among producers, and because world demand for nitrates was increasing in the later 1880s.[11] The larger and more efficient companies, such as the Liverpool Nitrate Company, with its modern plant, had come to rely on their capacity to produce more cheaply than the smaller ones to secure a favourable position in the world market.[12] And, secondly, the market for nitrates expanded: in 1887, continental Europe, and notably the sugar-beet fields of France and Germany, imported over 245,000 tons, compared with 56,000 tons by Great Britain and 30,000 tons by the United States, but in 1889 these markets imported 370,000, 69,000 and 37,000 tons of nitrate respectively.[13]

In these buoyant circumstances, nitrate shares were in great demand on the London Stock Exchange when a number of new companies were floated during 1888 and 1889. By this time, London had supplanted Liverpool as the centre for nitrate dealings, since the City had begun to realize from 1887 that the industry offered ample scope for the favourable utilization of joint-stock funds.[14] By the middle of 1888, it was reported that 'the nitrate industry is now well-represented on the Stock Exchange, thanks to the exertions of a small but powerful group of company promoters'.[15] Prominent among these were North and Harvey who were the chief promoters of the San Jorge and

---

[9] *Memoirs of the Family of Lockett*, p. 110.
[10] *Fomento de la Industria Salitrera*, pp. 128–9.
[11] See Brown, 'Nitrate Crises', op. cit., pp. 233–4.
[12] Semper and Michels, *La Industria del Salitre*, p. 141.
[13] *The Economist*, 6 July 1889. Figures are for the year ending 30 June.
[14] See *The South American Journal*, 1 October 1887.
[15] *The Economist*, 7 July 1888.

San Pablo Nitrate Companies in 1888, and the San Donato and Paccha and Jazpampa Companies in 1889.[16] Other promoters and financiers, some of them associated with these concerns, floated other companies to engage in the nitrate business. W. MacAndrew was a leading promoter of the London Nitrate Company in 1887, the Santa Luisa Company in 1888, and the Lautaro Company in 1889, and was soon to be associated with North in other enterprises in Tarapacá.[17] F. H. Evans, a Member of Parliament for Southampton, was a director of the Santa Luisa and Lautaro Companies, and a leading promoter of the Tamarugal Company, founded in 1889, while another Member of Parliament (for West Bromwich), E. Spencer, equally active in similar promotions, also linked his fortunes to North's.[18]

There was thus created, first in Liverpool, then in London, a society of businessmen interested in nitrates of which North became the recognized head: it was his dynamic personality, business capacity and brilliant example that captivated investors and greatly contributed to the rapid growth of a new network of economic interests. Even those who had their suspicions of North's business methods, could not deny his impact:

> Put Colonel North's name on a costermonger's cart [said *The Financial News* in May 1888], turn it into a limited company, and the shares will be selling at 300 per cent premium before they are an hour old. . . North is a Pactolus among promoters. Whatever he touches turns, if not to gold, at least to premiums.[19]

Another commentator wondered whether North's success was the result of witchcraft or luck 'or may be, and probably is, an unusually keen perception of facts, combined with an extraordinary astuteness'.[20] Nor could representatives of long-established British business houses on the Pacific coast of South America altogether deny North's possession of these qualities, though they expressed a justifiable pique at the rise of the

---

[16] Data from *Burdetts Official Intelligence*, vii (1889) and viii (1890).

[17] Ibid. See also below, pp. 47–8.

[18] Data from *Burdetts*, loc. cit. See also below, pp. 95, 103.

[19] *The Financial News*, 23 May 1888. For the paper's antagonism towards North, see below, pp. 65–9, and for North's acquisition of the title of Colonel, p. 41.

[20] *The South American Journal*, 13 October 1888.

parvenu. 'Colonel North', wrote Stephen Williamson, '[is] a regular charlatan, tho' a shrewd one. He is the greatest man in England at present except perhaps Gladstone! Such is our nonsensical (?) worship.'[21] Another prominent figure in the City, whose family name was almost synonymous with British enterprise in Chile, also recognized North's ability in a similarly ironical vein:

. . . North did seize [wrote Herbert Gibbs] what has turned out to have been a golden opportunity and, adding success to success he has made an enormous fortune under our very nose, in our own country, and at our own business in which we have hardly participated at all. The result is that the gallant Colonel has completely eclipsed us in the nitrate business and whatever he touches is dashed at by the public and driven to a premium immediately. . . North is considered in London as the introducer of Nitrate into Europe and the owner of nearly all the Nitrate Works!![22]

These were realistic opinions, but they contained doubts, and the doubts soon grew into positive distrust, and distrust into outright hostility.

Meanwhile, however, North in the mid-1880s basked in the sunshine of public favour and worked hard to keep himself there. He was now a very wealthy man, though the basis of his fortune was much less the actual success of his companies and the dividends he secured from his holdings, together with such directors' fees as came his way, than the immense capital gains that he and Harvey secured through the sale of assets to the companies they founded, most of which were grossly overcapitalized. Thus, the certificates of the *oficina* of Santa Ramírez, bought by Harvey and North for £5,000 when their nominal value was £13,750, were sold to the Liverpool Nitrate Company on its formation in 1883 for £50,000, a clear profit to North and Harvey of nine times their original outlay.[23] Moreover the company itself was capitalized at more than double the sale price.[24] What the two were originally paid for other

[21] Stephen Williamson, Liverpool, to W. R. Henderson at Valparaiso, 21 February 1889. Balfour Williamson Papers, Letter Book No. 3. Copy. Letter No. 118.

[22] Herbert Gibbs, London, to W. Smail at Valparaiso, 28 November 1888. AAG, MS. 11,042. Vol. 2, p. 619.

[23] Semper and Michels, *La Industria del Salitre*, p. 138.

[24] See above, p. 32. Cf. Rippy, *British Investments*, p. 63.

certificates is not known, but, given the high capitalization figures of the other companies they floated, it is a fair assumption that the purchase price charged to the companies was comparable: the *oficinas* of Buen Retiro and Jazpampa, for example, passed into their hands as rather small concerns, by virtue of their purchase of the appropriate certificates, but when North founded the Colorado Company in 1885 to work Buen Retiro, the purchase price was put at £18,000, out of an authorized capital of £200,000.[25] The inflation of securities, in order to work them off on an unsuspecting public, did not, however, go unnoticed. *The Economist*, true to its traditional scepticism about 'investment booms, blind capital . . . and all other kinds of doubtful promotion and speculation',[26] was already wondering about the nitrate fever by the middle of 1888:

It is a moot point [the paper said] as to how far the securities oi these undertakings are held by the public, for, although industriously puffed, there is reason to believe that they are still largely in the hands of the promoters, who are seeking to work them off upon investors.[27]

Somewhat later, a highly respected British businessman, well known in Chile, angrily expressed his own opinion of these tactics, though this time it was not North who was involved:

Some of our neighbours [wrote Stephen Williamson] it is said have made fortunes by means of wild speculations in nitrate and issues by Companies palmed off upon the public—some of which . . . are manifest swindles [illegible]. That Coy [*sic*] the people say they acquired for £47,000. . . Did the Sellers even get that? I question it and think it was practically worthless. Well . . . the Syndicate have agreed to spend '*about*' £29,000—and *then* the concern is

[25] *Burdetts Official Intelligence*, vi (1888), pp. 652–3, gives the purchase price, Bermúdez, *Historia del Salitre*, pp. 420–1, the story of the *oficinas*. According to Billinghurst, *Los capitales salitreros*, p. 50, North and Harvey paid £22,000 for the certificates of the *oficina* Peruana, against a real valuation of £40,000. But this comparatively high price was owing to the fact that the holders of the bonds, the firm of Folsch & Martin, held on to them until July 1882, by which time the Chilean decision to return the industry to private hands had been made.
[26] Sir John Clapham, '*The Economist* as a Source for the Historian', in *The Economist, 1843–1943* (Oxford Univ. Press, 1943), p. 42.
[27] *The Economist*, 7 July 1888.

floated to the public by Mr. MacAndrew and others for £200,000—
out of which £20,000 will be kept as working capital the rest will go
into the pockets of Macandrew and that [blank space]. What a
swindle. The shares went at once to a premium! What a day of
reckoning there is in store. Nitrate is an article easily produced. It
can easily be made to be in large oversupply. Price drops from £10 to
£9—then to £8—then to £7. . . Then how will Nitrate Coys [sic]
shares stand?[28]

It was a good question. North, however, was a gambler, and he
well knew, as did his colleagues such as Harvey and Mac-
Andrew, that so long as boom conditions in nitrate lasted, so
long as dividends, however temporarily, were spectacularly
high, the investing public would also gamble its money in
pursuit of the great fortunes apparently made by the nitrate
capitalists. But it was not simply a matter of making a fortune
which would impress the public at large: it was also a question
of spending it in such a way that the image of North would be
constantly before the public, as a self-made man, enriched by
initiative, an example to all of how to make money and of what
could be done with it.

It was a role into which North entered with natural zest. He
was a born actor and a consummate showman. Like many men
of comparatively humble origins who attain to great wealth,
North sought to dazzle with ostentation, and his projection of a
public image to inspire confidence in his promotions was really
the key factor in his success. If he was to be called 'the Nitrate
King', he would spare no pains to justify his title. At vast
expense, he bought a large mansion at Avery Hill, Eltham,
Kent, near enough to London for business but sufficiently rural
for staging house parties and other entertainments for his City
friends and their families. The mansion was renovated and
made into a showpiece.[29] Italianate in style, it stood in spacious

[28] Stephen Williamson, Liverpool, to W. R. Henderson at Valparaiso, 14
December 1888. Balfour Williamson Papers, Letter Book No. 3. Copy. Letter
No. 100.

[29] The cost of renovation landed North in a lawsuit, since the architect entrusted
with it claimed, in 1891, that he had not been paid £2,718 which was due to
him, and brought an action to recover it. North, who had spent, it was said, some
£200,000 on Avery Hill, contested the action, alleging that the estimate had been
grossly exceeded and the work unduly delayed. North lost the action and was
rebuked in court by the Lord Chief Justice for flippancy. Newspaper cuttings

parkland, the large cupola on its roof visible for miles around, while at the entrance to the park itself, two huge gates of wrought iron bore the monogram 'N', ornately chased. Timber used in the reconstruction was specially shipped from South America, and at the entrance to the main hall, which also had an Elizabethan musicians' gallery, stood two large gates of decorative ironwork, reputedly seized from the cathedral of Lima by Chilean troops in the War of the Pacific. Outside, in addition to gardens, orchards, stables and kennels, there was a further reminder of the scenes of North's early labours, a vast conservatory of glass and iron, stocked with South American flora. Avery Hill became the social centre of the nitrate society, and the country seat, but fifteen miles from London, where North enjoyed playing the country squire and freely made his mansion available for a variety of philanthropic purposes:[30]

> Colonel North [said a local paper] is not only enormously rich, but he is a man of extremely generous disposition, and his happiest moments seem to be those when he is spending some portion of his wealth in giving pleasure to others... The five or six hundred children from the Westminster backstreets who visited Avery Hill the other day enjoyed a treat which will stick in the memories of most of them for many a year ...[31]

At Christmas time, virtually the entire population of Eltham was invited to the house; a great ox was roasted and eaten and children were given fruit and sweets and other gifts.[32] Accounts of North's good-natured benevolence were legion. Sometimes, the circumstances were conspicuous, as in 1888, when destruction threatened the abbey of Kirkstall, near his birthplace, Leeds. North paid £10,000 for the building and presented it to the city, as well as a sum of £5,000 to Leeds Infirmary, and numerous other gifts to the City Art Gallery, local schools and

---

(unidentified) dated June 1891, included in a card of cuttings on North in the Library of the Borough of Woolwich. I am indebted to the Librarian, Mr C. H. Turner, for drawing my attention to this item.

[30] Data from *The South American Journal*, *The Pall Mall Gazette*, *The Sidcup and District Times*, *The Leeds Mercury* and *The Yorkshire Post*. Much of the original character of the building and estate has been retained, despite bomb-damage during the Second World War. In 1904, North's family sold the entire estate to the London County Council, and it is now the Avery Hill College of Education.

[31] *The Sidcup and District Times*, 20 July 1888.

[32] Letter from Mr H. S. Backett of Sevenoaks, Kent, to the author, 24 August 1963.

other institutions.[33] For these services, on 25 January 1889 he was installed as the first Honorary Freeman of the City of Leeds.[34] 'With him', said *The Chilean Times*, 'hospitality almost amounts to a vice',[35] and while North undoubtedly benefited from reports of his benevolence, all the evidence suggests that it sprang from his expansive nature as much as from less attractive motives.

Another aspect of North's ebullient character was his sporting instinct, and this was a further route to general popularity.[36] A bloodstock stud of racehorses was established at Avery Hill, and North himself had many successes on the turf.[37] He took an interest, also, in hare coursing, one of his greyhounds, Fullerton, winning the Waterloo Cup, the championship award for the sport, three times in succession.[38] He was no less widely-known as a devotee both of boxing and cricket.[39] This patronage of the sports was undoubtedly a useful means of keeping North's name before the public; it was probably also an avenue to those sections of high society which had similar interests.[40]

In the last two decades of the nineteenth century, North was an important figure in the social life of his adopted county, Kent. His interests here were wide: he was Master of the West Kent Hunt, and Chairman or President of a number of societies in south-east London, such as the London Suburban Railway Officials Association and the Society of Railway Engineers and

[33] *The Leeds Mercury*, 6 May 1896.

[34] Ibid. See also *The Yorkshire Post*, 27 October 1953. The City Art Gallery at Leeds owns two splendid drawings of North done by the contemporary artist of *Punch*, Phil May.

[35] *The Chilean Times*, 23 March 1889.

[36] See, for example, contemporary pen portraits of North in *Baily's Magazine of Sports and Pastimes*, vol. LII, No. 354 (August 1889), pp. 73-5, and in *Vanity Fair*, 2 November 1889.

[37] See *The Victoria County History of Kent*, i (London, 1908), p. 499.

[38] Fullerton was passed to a taxidermist on his death, and stood for over thirty years in the Natural History Museum as the archetypal representative of his breed.

[39] The great Gloucestershire and England cricketer, Dr W. G. Grace, dedicated his autobiography to North. W. G. Grace, *The History of a Hundred Centuries* (London, 1895).

[40] *The Sidcup and District Times*, 14 December 1888, reported that North would shortly accompany Lord Randolph Churchill on a visit to South America, adding that Lord Randolph was going there 'in the hope of making a little money, of which he stands in need owing to recent turf and other losses, and Colonel North will show his lordship how to do it'.

Firemen. In 1888, when the Masonic Fraternity of Kent presented a piano to Princess Alexandra on her silver wedding anniversary, it was North who was chosen to make the presentation. It was his money, too, that secured him the honorary title of Colonel: he founded and equipped a Regiment of Volunteers at Tower Hamlets and allowed them to use his estate for their training and summer camps every year. His honorary title, of which he was inordinately proud, was another useful acquisition in his rise to social eminence.[41]

By mid-1888, Colonel North, 'the Nitrate King', had made his mark in London society, and there was no more popular figure in the City. People were captivated by the story of his career, and those who followed his advice and invested in nitrates in the 1880s had a more material interest in him. His social activities, his sporting interests, his widely-known philanthropy, all contributed to his business success, for the fact that so bluff and blunt a figure could rise to rub shoulders with the aristocracy, and largely through his own efforts, inspired confidence in his promotions and set an example which many were eager to follow. Among his friends and acquaintances could be counted such leading Conservative figures as the Marquis of Stackpole, Lord Dorchester, Sir Ellis Ashmead-Bartlett and Lord Randolph Churchill.[42] It was Lord Randolph, indeed, who presented North to the Prince of Wales at one of the many dinner parties they attended together.[43] And North also counted among his business colleagues the head of the best-known banking house in Europe, Nathan Rothschild.[44] To the gossip columnists of the press, North's social activities were an unending source of anecdote and rumour; and there is no evidence that he ever discouraged them.

The projection of a colourful image was all in keeping with

[41] Data from *The Sidcup and District Times*, *The Pall Mall Gazette* and *The South American Journal*.

[42] See *The South American Journal*, 22 December 1888. Lord Randolph Churchill held shares in some of North's companies.

[43] Ibid. See also *The Sidcup and District Times*, 28 December 1888.

[44] The only manuscript letter to North from a business colleague which I have been able to discover was from Rothschild, accompanying a gift for North's daughter, Emma, on her coming-of-age in 1889. Rothschild to North, London, 10 October 1889, in the possession of Mrs V. Proctor, to whom I am indebted for this citation.

North's own character, however much it may have aided his business activities, and it was never more in evidence than at the company meetings over which he presided. The meetings were as short as he could make them, and throughout the proceedings North himself, like Mr Melmotte in *The Way We Live Now*, irradiated confidence and calm, turning awkward questions aside with good-humoured skill, and employing a variety of devices to keep investors happy.[45] The most successful of these was to offer to buy out himself any worried stockholder, an offer which usually sent up the price of shares substantially.[46] At the game of bluff, North was a master, and no one knew better the art of taking calculated risks.

In the last analysis, however, an admiring and trusting public would only retain its confidence in Colonel North's promotions if his optimistic predictions were borne out, and there were clear limits to his capacity to maintain his position by bluff and showmanship alone. Already in 1888, informed opinion was uneasy about the proliferation of companies formed to produce nitrate, a product whose demand inelasticity had already been demonstrated in the early 1880s, when the first restrictive combination had been formed. To some, it now seemed that the circumstances surrounding that development were about to be repeated, and both public and private fears for the future of nitrate increased.

. . . the present nitrate 'boom' [said *The Economist*, early in 1889] presents some features which are far from satisfactory. New ventures are constantly springing up and if they are to be successful, the supply of nitrate must be practically unlimited. In this case, how do the older companies stand, whose shares command such immense prices? On the other hand, if the supply of nitrate which can be profitably worked is comparatively limited, what can be thought of the prospects of all these new undertakings?[47]

The day before this comment appeared, Stephen Williamson an old 'nitrate hand' himself, wrote to his manager in Valparaiso in precisely the same terms:

[45] See, for example, reports of company meetings in *The South American Journal*, 31 March 1888, 7 July 1888, 15 December 1888, 31 December 1888.

[46] See, for example, reports of company meetings in *The Economist*, 3 August 1889; *The South American Journal*, 6 April 1889, 21 December 1889.

[47] *The Economist*, 12 January 1889.

We dislike these nitrate speculative Companies and fear disaster ere long overtaking many of them. . . Nitrate is somewhat firmer for near cargoes. Distant cargoes are, however, considerable [?] and we look for a very marked decline. With all these schemes being floated it is certain to be overdone in the course of time.[48]

A month later he was even more emphatic:

You ask what is to happen to us with all these new English Nitrate Companies. Well, new developments constantly take place . . . We will see more clearly a little later—& [sic] in the meantime I look with great disquiet and apprehension *for the shareholders* on what is being done. . . My fear is this: nitrate is *easily* produced. It is easy to *over*-produce. So soon as that happens down go prices to a low point. In order to pay high dividends and show a fair result on the extortionately high capital of these concerns they will try to produce heavily and then we may see trouble—it may end in the formation of another 'Trust' to limit production—but that will not now be so easy.[49]

Easy, it would certainly not be, for a new factor had now entered into the nitrate equation. The Chilean government had benefited enormously from the rapid expansion of the nitrate industry from the mid-1880s, and it now depended heavily on export duties on nitrate for government income: whereas in 1882, the amount contributed by such duties to the national exchequer was nearly 27 per cent of all income, by 1888, the figure had risen to 41 per cent, and by 1889, to over 45 per cent.[50] It was on the basis of this windfall wealth that the government, in the late 1880s, embarked upon a large and varied programme of public works, employing many people, and designed to improve Chilean communications, port facilities, educational provision and the like.[51] These policies were to a considerable extent sponsored by the Chilean President, whose government, it was reported, could not 'allow a falling in

[48] Stephen Williamson, Liverpool, to W. R. Henderson at Valparaiso, 11 January 1889. Balfour Williamson Papers. Letter Book No. 3. Copy. Letter No. 110.

[49] Same to same, 21 February 1889. In ibid., Letter No. 118.

[50] Hernández, *El salitre*, p. 177.

[51] See below, pp. 71ff., for a fuller discussion of this question. The best account to date is Ramírez, *Balmaceda y la contrarrevolución, passim.*

revenue from the nitrate business'; 'any curtailment of production causing a loss of revenue would be met by a corresponding increase in duty on exports'.[52] The fact of the matter
was simply that the market for nitrate was not a stable market,
particularly since the agricultural industry, the chief con-
sumer, was affected by vicissitudes which could hardly be
predicted. This natural instability had been compounded in
the 1880s by a rapid increase in production which was not met
by a proportionate demand: thus, whereas in 1886, almost 10
million *quintals* had been produced in Chile, in 1887 the figure
rose to over 15 million *quintals*, and by 1889 output was to reach
the unprecedented figure of over 20 million *quintals*.[53] And it
was the formation of the large number of new joint-stock
companies in London, not least by North, which had created
this situation. Their shareholders naturally expected to reap
dividends comparable to those realized by North's earlier
ventures, such as the Liverpool Nitrate Company, and the
companies were thus greatly tempted to produce at full
capacity, despite the deterioration of a world market now close
to saturation.

In the long run, increased world consumption of nitrate was
clearly the only solution to the problem which would satisfy
both the Chilean government and producers alike, and,
accordingly, in 1888, a propaganda campaign was instituted to
extend the market in nitrate.[54] In December 1888, the Chilean
Ministro de Hacienda sent out a circular to all Chilean con-
sulates requesting information on the present consumption of
nitrate in their districts and on the scope which was offered for
increasing its use.[55] At this time also the Chilean government
began to pay far more attention than hitherto to the nitrate
industry as a whole.[56] Increasing the size of the world market
for nitrate, however, was clearly a long-term undertaking, of

[52] Consul-General Newman to Lord Salisbury, Valparaiso, 19 January 1889.
Report on the Nitrate Industry of Chile in the Year 1888. *Miscellaneous Series of
Trade Reports No. 31. Accounts and Papers Vol. lxxvii* (1889).

[53] Semper and Michels, *La Industria del Salitre*, p. 328.

[54] Ibid., p. 141.

[55] Ministro de Hacienda to Chilean Consuls, Santiago, 15 December 1888.
Fomento de la Industria Salitrera, pp. 4–6.

[56] See below, pp. 79 ff.

which the results would not be apparent for some time. Meanwhile, the problem was urgent, and there seemed no answer to it but the revival of the idea of a combination among producers to restrict output until stocks were reduced, and world consumption caught up once again with production. That this would bring the foreign nitrate capitalists, and notably North, into conflict with the Chilean government became obvious in 1889, and by that time also other issues between them were reaching a critical juncture.

The Nitrate Railways

The railway which linked the nitrate-fields to their commercial outlets on the Pacific coast had had a chequered history even before it became associated with the name of North.[57] In June 1868, the Peruvian government granted a concession to the Peruvian firm of Montero Brothers for the building of a railway to link the port of Iquique with the nitrate-ground of La Noria near the Bolivian frontier, giving the concessionaires exclusive possession of the line for twenty-eight years, prohibiting the construction of any other line between the stipulated points during this period, fixing maximum freight charges, and granting Monteros permission to transfer their rights to third parties, provided the government gave its consent. A second concession, of May 1869, and on similar terms, gave Monteros the right to build and operate a line from the port of Pisagua to *salitreras* in Tarapacá, and yet a third, in October 1871, permitted them to link the two lines and extend the section from La Noria to the Bolivian frontier. The final grant, however, fixed the term of exclusive privilege at twenty-five years, and asserted the government's prerogative to annul the concessions if the works were not begun at the stipulated times or whenever work was interrupted for more than a year.

[57] There is a considerable literature on the Nitrate Railways. This account o their early history is based on five volumes of material in the Foreign Office archives, *Correspondence Relating to Nitrate Railways, 1889–1903*, F.O. 16/266–8, 298, 317. Two important articles are Joseph R. Brown, 'The Chilean Nitrate Railways Controversy', *HAHR*, xxxviii (1958), pp. 465–81, and Fernando Silva Vargas, 'Los Ferrocarriles Salitreros de Tarapacá durante el Gobierno de Santa María', *Estudios de Historia de las Instituciones Políticas y Sociales*, i (Santiago, 1966), pp. 43–120.

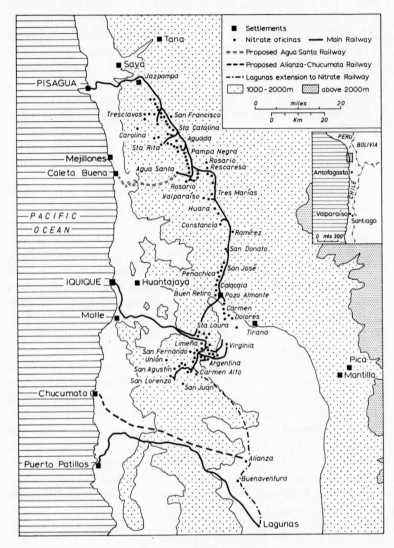

Tarapacá: the Nitrate Railways

Between 1868 and 1875, Montero Brothers built the Iquique and Pisagua lines, but the line from La Noria to the Bolivian frontier was never begun. To finance construction a loan was contracted in London in 1872, but the sum of £1,000,000 proved insufficient, and in 1873 an additional £450,000 was secured, both sums being guaranteed by a mortgage on the lines. At the same time, Montero Brothers transferred most of their rights to a company registered in London on 24 January 1874, as the National Nitrate Railways Company of Peru. The Monteros retained a large block of shares in the new company, and also specifically excluded from the deal their rights in the line to the Bolivian frontier, not yet built, and in a line further south, linking the nitrate fields of Lagunas to the tiny port of Patillos. For one reason and another, the transfer took a long time, nor was it until 10 February 1879 that the Peruvian government itself approved it, and then only under the stipulation that:

the foreign Companies . . . shall not in any question which may arise with the Government by reason of the rights and obligations arising out of the original concessions, have recourse to any other laws or tribunals than those of the Republic, and shall not in any case or circumstances be permitted to resort to diplomatic means . . . [58]

When the War of the Pacific broke out between Chile and Peru, the Chilean forces used the railway for the transport of troops and supplies.[59] On 27 May 1881, however, the lines were returned to the Railways Company, but the company being unable to meet its obligations under the mortgages of 1872 and 1873, further reorganization took place, and on 24 August 1882, a new company, the Nitrate Railways Company Ltd, was registered in London with a capital of £1,200,000.[60] Monteros still retained some 9,000 shares, nominally worth £100 each, in the new company.[61] Among the twelve directors were W.

---

[58] *Translation of the Decree of the Peruvian Government of the 10th February 1879* (Canterbury, n.d.), p. 3. Pamphlet printed for the Nitrate Railways Company enclosed in F.O. 16/286.

[59] Sir C. R. Markham, *The War between Chile and Peru*, p. 150.

[60] Agustín Ross, *Memorandum on the Nitrate Railways of Tarapacá* (London, 1891), p. 9.

[61] Silva Vargas, op. cit., p. 50.

MacAndrew and Melton R. Pryor,[62] staff artist of the *Illustrated London News*, who later became a great friend of Colonel North, and whose name will recur in this narrative.

The company did not really flourish in the early 1880s and, indeed, in 1886 it ended the year with a deficit of £5,197 and paid no dividends to its shareholders. But the great increase of traffic on the lines in the years following the collapse of the first nitrate combination enabled it to announce a dividend of 10 per cent on ordinary shares early in 1888, and in September of the same year a dividend of 15 per cent on deferred shares.[63] In 1889, it paid dividends of 25 per cent on ordinary shares, and in both 1890 and 1891 dividends of 20 per cent.[64] In retrospect, it rather looked as though the remarkable upturn in the company's fortunes coincided with the advent of Colonel North to the Board of Directors, for it was in 1888 that he became not only a Director but also Deputy Chairman, becoming Chairman of the Board in 1889.[65] He secured this position by virtue of the fact that in April 1887 he had purchased from the Monteros 7,000 of their shares in the Nitrate Railways Company, paying £14 a share.[66] Since the shares were nominally worth £100 each, the price that he paid was some reflection of the low esteem in which they were then held, and there were other strong reasons why it may have seemed at the time that North had made his first mistake.

Throughout its history, the Nitrate Railways Company had relied on its monopoly of transport in Tarapacá: controlling the railway linking the ports of Iquique and Pisagua, together with the branch lines connecting the *oficinas* with the main line, the company was able to charge high freights on nitrate shipments which almost all producers had to pay. Only one works of any size, run by the Agua Santa Company, registered in Chile but mostly controlled by the British firm of Campbell, Outram and Company, was so situated that it could challenge the railway

[62] *Burdetts Official Intelligence*, ii (1883), p. 809. For MacAndrew, see above, p. 35.
[63] Chilean Consul to Ministro de Hacienda, London, 8 February 1889. *Fomento de la Industria Salitrera*, p. 131.
[64] Letter in *The Economist*, 30 April 1892.
[65] *Burdetts Official Intelligence*, vi (1888), p. 514, vii (1899), p. 550.
[66] Silva Vargas, op. cit., p. 50. The Lockett and Grace interests were associated with this purchase.

monopoly.[67] The distance from its *oficina* to the port of Caleta Buena was only twenty miles, whereas the distance from Agua Santa to Pisagua by rail was over fifty miles: since the Railway Company's freight charge was 9¾d. for every *quintal* of nitrate carried per mile, to a maximum chargeable distance of forty miles,[68] the Agua Santa Company chose to take its nitrate to the coast by a cart road to Caleta Buena so long as the railway monopoly survived. The other producers, however, were obliged to accept a tariff they regarded as excessive, and before Tarapacá became part of Chile, but on the assumption that, as a result of the War of the Pacific, it would, they requested the Chilean government to compel the Railways Company to reduce its charges.[69] And in 1881, concessions to construct other lines were solicited by Campbell, Outram and other companies.[70] On 15 May 1883 the Chilean government nominated a special commission to consider this question, but, although this reported in favour of new concessions on 8 January 1884, the government held its hand, since the peace Treaty of Ancón was not yet ratified.[71]

During the years of the Santa María administration in Chile, 1881–86, pressure on the government to declare the Montero concessions invalid grew in volume and intensity, and the matter became one of great public debate.[72] And more powerful arguments than the solicitations of nitrate producers had appeared. The high tariff of the Nitrate Railways Company was a factor tending to hinder the fullest exploitation of the nitrate industry, from which Chile was now deriving an increasing proportion of government revenue. Yet it was only after long Congressional debates and strong attacks on the government that action was finally taken when, on 29 January 1886, a government decree declared the original concessions

[67] Castle, *Sketch of the City of Iquique*, p. 34.

[68] Billinghurst, *Estudio sobre la jeografía de Tarapacá. Appendix* (unpaginated).

[69] Herbert Griffin to St John, Iquique, 5 December 1879. F.O. 177/164. Misc.

[70] A. Titus, *Monografía de los Ferrocarriles Particulares de Chile* (Santiago, 1910), p. 28. See also, Silva Vargas, op. cit., pp. 51–2.

[71] Castle, op. cit., p. 34. Cf. Brown, op. cit., p. 467.

[72] Silva Vargas, op. cit., provides a detailed account of these years, based on much original material.

annulled on the grounds of non-fulfilment of contract.[73] Economic expediency rather than legal principle was the reason for government action.

Thus began an extraordinarily complicated and drawn-out controversy. The company appealed to the Chilean courts, and the case proceeded from one level of judicial competence to another, and eventually to the Chilean Council of State in 1889: the Supreme Court having declared that annulment of the concessions could not be an administrative act which deprived the company of the right of juridical appeal, the Council took the opposite view, asserting that an ordinary court of law had no jurisdiction over the company's petition.[74] The case, therefore, became by 1889 a subject of conflict between the government and the judiciary, and a constitutional issue of some significance.

It was then, at a time of some uncertainty for the Nitrate Railways Company, that North took over the direction of its affairs in the late 1880s. Its monopoly of railway transport in the nitrate regions had been challenged, not only by many nitrate producers, but also by the Chilean government itself, and the company's future status was clearly in some doubt. Yet North had gone ahead, purchasing the Montero shares in the company to secure a leading position as a stockholder, and assuming the chairmanship of the Board of Directors in 1889. North, however, was a gambler, and it probably seemed a reasonable bet, either that the Supreme Court's insistence on the competence of the judiciary to give the final ruling would prevail and that the company would win in the courts, or that at the very least, the complicated dispute would take so many years to unravel that the profitability of the company would be long maintained by the *de facto* continuance of its monopoly and high freight charges on nitrate cargoes.

This was indeed a gamble, but the stakes were high. And they were not confined to the Nitrate Railways, though the transport

---

[73] J. M. Yrarrázaval, *El Presidente Balmaceda*, i, 299–301, 305. See also the same writer's 'La Administracion Balmaceda y el Salitre de Tarapacá', *Boletín de la Academia Chilena de la Historia*, No. 47 (1952), pp. 60–3. The argument of 'non-fulfilment' related to the line to La Noria.

[74] See Brown, op. cit., *passim*, and, a more detailed account, Blakemore, 'The Chilean Revolution of 1891', op. cit., pp. 63 ff.

monopoly in Tarapacá was the key to wider possibilities which North and his associates envisaged when they bought the Montero shares. At that time, North explained his purpose to the directors of Antony Gibbs, whose London office informed its managers at Valparaiso and Iquique what he intended to do:

... this is only the beginning of a grand scheme which is being hatched of bringing out the whole Nitrate business as a Company, his idea being to use his power in the Railway as a lever to make all the producers, especially the small ones, to come into the Company. He would virtually say this: 'My interest in the railway is so great that I will never permit another combination to be formed to restrict production; you small people cannot live with open competition therefore you will be ruined. As, however, I am a benevolent man, I will suggest to you a way of escape, and that is to try and have a general company formed that will take your oficinas over.' If, however, they refuse, Mr. North proposes to arrange with the Banks to sell the oficinas to him as they foreclose on them—as they will do after a period of open competition.[75]

Gibbs were in two minds about the matter: North was then rising to a crest of business success and public esteem as a man with the enthusiasm and ability to get what he wanted; this, they had to weigh against the likely reaction of the Chilean government and the other producers to the scheme, and they did not like North's hints that, if they would not come in, the important banking house of Barings would be perfectly willing, if not eager, to do so. Though they did not fully believe 'this part of the story, but imagine that it was introduced to make us keen', they concluded that 'a powerful and determined attempt will be made . . . and it is for us to consider carefully whether we should oppose it or ride in on the top of it'.[76] For the moment, they would 'wait and see'.

The idea was typical of North's grandiose schemes. He proposed to raise a share capital of £5,000,000, and he and Robert Harvey had valued all the *oficinas*, ready for the grand takeover. But Gibbs's caution was justified, for within a month of this approach by North, their London house reported that the scheme had run into difficulties: although North and his

[75] Antony Gibbs, London to Valparaiso and Iquique, 6 May 1887. AAG, MS. 11,471. Vol. 26.   [76] Ibid.

associates had 'presented themselves with Bank of England notes to the amount required, either sufficient shares were kept back to prevent their having a majority of the votes, or the voting power of the shares themselves were in some way withheld; anyhow the purchase was not there completed'.[77] What actually happened it is impossible to say, but it is a fair assumption that if he could not secure complete control there and then, North would not have been interested further at that moment. And he could afford to wait for a more propitious opportunity. So long as the legal wrangle over the company's privileges continued in Chile, the monopoly would be maintained, freight would continue to flow, and dividends were assured. The law's delays, perhaps more notorious throughout Latin America than anywhere else, gave him ample time to think and work in other directions. Not until 1889, when the Council of State supported the cancellation of the monopoly made by the Chilean government in 1886, was the issue of the Nitrate Railways again thrust to the forefront of North's preoccupations.

In addition to the main railway line running from Iquique to Pisagua along which were strung, like pearls on a necklace, the richest *oficinas* of Tarapacá, there was another line further south in which North was greatly interested. This was the Patillos railway which linked that port to the Lagunas nitrate-fields, and which, like the main line, was first associated with Monteros Brothers. As already noted, Monteros retained their rights in this line when they transferred the rest to the Nitrate Railways Company, but it had not been built by them. Under agreements between Monteros and the *Sociedad Salitrera Esperanza*, made in 1871 and 1872, the latter had constructed the railway for Monteros in return for monthly payments to *Esperanza* and satisfactory arrangements on freight costs and quantities of nitrate shipped by *Esperanza*, which owned the nitrate-grounds.[78] In 1876, the owners of *Esperanza*, however, sold their *oficina* to the Peruvian government, and they tried to sell the railway as well, but a legal action by Monteros frustrated this, and in

[77] Antony Gibbs, London, to Valparaiso and Iquique, 21 May 1887. AAG, MS. 11,471. Vol. 27.
[78] Silva Vargas, op. cit., pp. 58–9.

1878 Monteros's rights in the railway were confirmed. For their nitrate properties, the owners of *Esperanza* were paid in Peruvian government bonds, and in November 1881 these were sold to a group of Chileans, prominent among whom was a certain Eduardo Delano, whose property rights in the nitrate-fields were recognized a year later by the Chilean government.[79]

The significance of the Lagunas nitrate-field and the Patillos railway was simply this: together, they constituted a formidable barrier to the erection of any monopoly of nitrate production and transportation in Tarapacá, should control of both Lagunas and the Patillos railway remain in hands other than those which held the predominant position further north. The railway line, still held by the Monteros, was independent of the Nitrate Railways Company, while the Lagunas field, owned by Delano and his associates, was potentially sufficiently rich to become a major producing region.[80] North recognized the possible threat to his plans, and took steps to see that it did not materialize. The task was a formidable one, since North would have to deal with both the Monteros and the Delano groups, and he might also have to reckon with the Chilean government, which was unlikely to turn a blind eye to private negotiations of such public significance.

His first objective was the Patillos railway, owned by the Patillos Railway Co. Ltd, which had been registered on 9 December 1882, with a capital of £100,000 in 10,000 shares of £10 each. Of these shares, members of the Montero family held all but four, the other owners, of one share each, being Melton R. Pryor, C. Barclay, A. G. Kendall and H. J. B. Kendall. But the majority shareholder, J. M. Montero, then placed 5,025 shares with the International Financial Society Ltd, and on 1 July 1887, these were transferred to the names of J. T. North, R. R. Lockett and M. P. Grace, curiously enough all directors of the Nitrate Railways Company. Before this transaction took place, however, on 19 April 1887, North obtained an option on 5,001 of the total of 10,000 shares which, on 9 February 1888, were put into the joint names of North,

[79] Ibid., p. 60.

[80] Annual production of nitrate from Lagunas rose from 360,000 *quintals* in 1882 to over 1,500,000 *quintals* in 1900. See tables on p. 281 and p. 303 of Semper and Michels, *La Industria del Salitre.*

Lockett, Grace and H. J. B. Kendall, a further 24 shares being ascribed to Kendall alone.[81] The precise reasons for these complicated manœuvres are not clear, but it may well be that North saw some advantage in associating Kendall with the move as an original shareholder in the Patillos company who had no connection with the Nitrate Railways company, and whose name, therefore, along with those of other minority shareholders, might cloak his true purpose. If this was so, and it is conjectural, the plan misfired, for it was certainly known to Antony Gibbs in May 1887 that North and his associates had obtained 'some sort of control, by means . . . of the call of the shares, over the Patillos Railway'.[82] Gibbs, indeed, feared that North intended to use the Patillos railway, as he did the Nitrate Railway itself, to impose high freight rates on nitrate shipments, 'to bleed us', as one of the partners put it, 'in the South as he is doing in the North'.[83] The 'Nitrate King', however, had no such intention: his main concern in controlling the Patillos railway was, in fact, to keep it closed.

The second problem lay in the Lagunas nitrate properties, which North also needed to secure in pursuit of a monopoly of production, and he moved to deal with that issue also. In September 1887 he bought from the Delano group the northern Lagunas properties for £111,000,[84] and a year later formed the Lagunas Syndicate, capitalized at ten times that figure.[85] But, if it seemed at the time that he was going from strength to strength, appearances were deceptive. The Chilean government was closely interested both in the Patillos railway and in the Lagunas *salitreras* and, as events were to reveal, it was not disposed to allow North to pursue his own interests unhindered. In the first place, the government had its own claim on the Patillos railway and, secondly, it had its own opinion on the transfer of the Delano holdings in Lagunas. For the moment, in 1888, no action was taken, but that it could be taken was a

[81] *The Railway Times*, 8 January 1898.

[82] Antony Gibbs, London, to Valparaiso and Iquique, 6 May 1887. AAG, MS. 11,471. Vol. 26.

[83] Herbert Gibbs to Mr Smail, London, 28 November 1888. AAG, MS. 11,042. Special Out-Letter Book, Vol. 11.

[84] *The Railway Times*, 8 January 1898.

[85] Rippy, *British Investments*, op. cit., pp. 60, 63.

permanent threat to North's consolidation of his holdings in Tarapacá. At that time, the case of the Nitrate Railways' monopoly was still under consideration by the Chilean courts and, indeed, on 11 August 1887 the Supreme Court of Second Instance in Chile had given a judgement favourable to the company, declaring that the Chilean government itself was a party to the case and that the right of adjudicating contentious matters belonged exclusively to the courts.[86] The government's reply, four months later, took the form of a note to the court from the Minister of Industry and Public Works, contesting this view, and declaring that the relevant documents should be sent to the Council of State as the appropriate body called upon to decide questions of competence between the executive power and the judiciary.[87] Another three months elapsed before the Supreme Court replied to this move, when, in a comprehensive and lengthy document, it reiterated its earlier opinion, but agreed with the decision to remit the matter to the Council of State.[88]

Thus, throughout 1887 and 1888, when North was pressing forward with both the Patillos railway and the Lagunas nitrate-fields, no final decision had been reached over the future of the Nitrate Railways, the lynch-pin of all his operations in Tarapacá. If the company won through, these deals would be well worth the expense and trouble they had entailed, but, if not, North's painstaking efforts might well come to nothing. The Chilean government might well feel confident of a favourable decision from the Council of State since, under the Chilean constitution, that body was appointed by the President. But, whatever the final outcome, both North and the Chilean government had other weapons in reserve. Meanwhile, North was quite prepared to pursue other ventures which would consolidate his existing interests.

[86] *Translation of the Judgement of the Supreme Court of Second Instance, 11 August 1887* (Canterbury, 1889), *passim.* Enclosed in F.O. 16/286.

[87] *Translation of Note addressed by the Chilean Government to the Supreme Court and the Reply thereto* (Canterbury, 1889), *passim.* Enclosed in F.O. 16/286.

[88] Ibid. By the terms of the Chilean constitution the government was fully justified in referring a dispute between the executive and the judiciary to the Council of State. See *Constitución política de la República de Chile de 25 de mayo de 1833 con las reformas efectuadas hasta el 10 de agosto de 1888,* Article 95, v, p. 45.

The Tarapacá Waterworks Company Limited

Control of water-supplies in the desert regions where the nitrate
works were situated had already played a significant part in the
founding of North's fortunes.[89] Now, his reputation in England
established through the formation of nitrate companies, North
moved to consolidate his position in this critical business. At the
end of September 1888 there was registered in London the
Tarapacá Waterworks Company Limited, with an authorized
share-capital of £400,000 in 40,000 shares of £10 each. Robert
Harvey was the chairman of the board, and its other members
—all well known on the Pacific coast—were North himself,
G. A. Lockett, H. B. James, G. M. Inglis and F. F. Reed. The
company's stated objectives were to supply water to Iquique
from the springs of Pica, and to take over North's existing
interests in water-supply in Tarapacá.[90] Its formation, however, was simply the culmination of a long campaign by North
to monopolize the province's water, a campaign in which he
had succeeded in frustrating, by a series of manœuvres, the
attempts of other concessionaires to establish water companies
in Tarapacá.

In January 1883 a certain engineer, Dixon Provand by name,
had organized a company in Valparaiso to utilize a type of
distillation plant in Iquique which he had invented for con-
verting sea-water into drinking-water.[91] This was so successful
in undercutting the price of fresh water produced by North's
own condensers and that carried by his tankers from Arica
that North was obliged to take action: how he did so is not
clear, but, within two years of the establishment of Provand's
Compañía Proveedora de Agua, he had secured a share-holding in
the company and a contract both to rent its equipment and to
secure the company's concession to operate in Iquique on an
eight-year lease.[92] In January 1885, however, another threat
to his position loomed up when a Scotsman, Thomas Hart,
obtained from the Chilean Congress a concession to carry
water from the springs of Pica to the town of Iquique by pipeline. Hart returned to Scotland in 1886, to organize a company

[89] See above, pp. 25–6.
[90] *Burdetts Official Intelligence*, vii (1889), pp. 1312–13.
[91] Ramírez, *Balmaceda y la contrarrevolución de 1891*, p. 46.   [92] Ibid.

to carry out the proposed works, and in that year the Iquique Water Company Limited was founded in Glasgow, with a capital of £350,000 in £10 shares, 31,900 of which were available to the public.[93]

The company's prospectus was a detailed description of all the factors which were relevant to its promotion—Iquique's need for water at a reasonable price, the quality and volume of the water at Pica, the equipment to be used and, above all, the company's likely prospects on the terms agreed for the Hart concession:

... the company is entitled to charge for the water at the rate of two cents a decalitre, or nearly one cent per gallon, which is about 50 per cent less than is being paid at present in Iquique, but which is sufficient to yield, assuming the extremely moderate consumption of 208,000 gallons per day, a return of 26 per cent on the proposed capital... In order, however, to encourage the demand, and at the same time to prevent all chance of competition, it is proposed to sell the water in Iquique at one-half cent per gallon.[94]

Here, indeed, was a threat to North's interests in water-supply, since he was then charging so much more for the only available potable water in Iquique, and he was not the man to take such a challenge lightly.

His first tack was to cast serious doubt on the Glasgow company's claims in the eyes of the public. The Liverpool and Colorado Nitrate Companies were already floated, and North was sufficiently established as an entrepreneur who knew what he was talking about, particularly if it were those far-away regions where he had lived so long. Through the *Money Market Review*, he launched his counter-attack on the proposed Iquique Water Company, only a few days after its prospectus had been issued, in a long letter which dealt, point by point, with the company's claims. The crucial points he made were not exactly designed to bolster investors' confidence in the proposed company:

I am now [he said] actually supplying Iquique with water at a half-cent per gallon at the current rate of exchange, which is about 25d per dollar, being nearly one-third less than the Company's

[93] *The Financial News*, 4 June 1888.   [94] Ibid.

proposed charge. . . The estimate in the prospectus of the quantity required for the town of Iquique is greatly in excess of the real consumption. At this moment I have two water-carrying vessels laid up at Iquique, the demand for water having so largely fallen off, and there are several water-condensing machines which have been idle for many months.

But the real sting was in the tail:

The estimates of profits given in the prospectus are based upon the assumption that the entire supply will hereafter be taken from the new company. It must be obvious that they will not escape competition with those who have hitherto supplied the locality, and to the satisfaction of their customers.[95]

This letter began a long and heated discussion in the commercial press, between the supporters of the Glasgow company and those of North, in which the Colonel contributed a long account of the springs at Pica, decrying their potential, and reiterating his previous arguments.[96] But, before the Glasgow company could actually be launched, the concession on which it was based passed into other hands when, in 1887, the original concessionaire, Thomas Hart, died, and his widow sold it to North himself![97] With this event, it appeared that the water-supply to Iquique was firmly in his hands, and all that remained was to organize the appropriate public company, to which he could sell his assets for large capital gains, though still retaining a share-holding interest.

The Tarapacá Waterworks Company was the eventual outcome, and the benefits accruing to North from its formation were very considerable. In the first place, he sold the company his Pica concession for £25,000—£10,000 in cash and the rest in shares; his lease from the *Compañía Proveedora de Agua*, due to

---

[95] *Money Market Review*, 27 February 1886.

[96] *The Financial News*, 4 June 1888, printed a number of letters which had previously appeared in other journals.

[97] Ramírez, *Balmaceda y la contrarrevolución*, p. 46, states that Hart's widow received £1,000 from North for the concession. It appears, however, that, in addition, Mrs Hart stipulated as one of the terms of sale that her nephew, one Alexander Cochrane, should have the contract for laying the pipeline, and left the bulk of the money she was to receive as a guarantee for his fulfilment of it. His incompetence, however, led to his legal dismissal and the ruin of his kind-hearted, but misguided, aunt. R. C. Lockett, *Memoirs of the Family of Lockett*, p. 113.

expire in March 1892, cost the new company over £4,000 and, most significant of all, as part of the deal, the rest of his water business in Tarapacá, based on condensers at Iquique and the tankers plying from Arica, was transferred to the Tarapacá Waterworks Company for the princely sum of £100,000. Finally, until the pipelines were laid from Pica to Iquique, North was to operate the whole water business for one-third of the profits.[98]

This extraordinary coup did not pass unnoticed, and neither did other curious features of the transaction. As *The Financial News* maliciously and gleefully pointed out, the prospectus of the Tarapacá Waterworks Company bore a striking resemblance to that put out two years before by the ill-fated Iquique Water Company, even in its phraseology, and North's opinions of the company's prospects had performed a remarkable volte-face:

> The difference between the two concerns is this [the paper said] that whereas the Iquique Company proposed to enter into competition with the existing organizations for the supply of water, the Tarapacá scheme buys up the inferior sources of supply for four times the sum paid for the Pica concession.[99]

But, however embarrassing such attacks might be to North himself, his bluff and genial character was quite capable of defeating them, provided, of course, that the new company was a success. For it to be so, however, on the basis of a monopoly which he had worked so hard to secure, depended on two things: the acceptance in Chile of the state of affairs the company proposed to arrange, and the ability of North and the Tarapacá Waterworks Company to ward off any future attack on their privileged position as water-suppliers in Tarapacá, as successfully as North himself had dealt with both Dixon Provand and the Iquique Company. Towards the end of 1888, a small cloud appeared on the horizon of North's hopes, when a certain Carlos Wüth solicited the Chilean Congress for permission to supply Iquique and some nitrate *oficinas* with water, and was supported in his application by the Chilean President.[100] And the new company still had to persuade the

[98] *Burdetts Official Intelligence*, vii (1889), pp. 1312–13.
[99] *The Financial News*, 4 June 1888.   [100] Ramírez, *Balmaceda*, p. 47.

municipality of Iquique to accept its terms for supplying water. It rather looked, at the end of 1888, that the following year might be a very interesting one for yet another enterprise of North's in Tarapacá. But, for the moment, with the colossal capital gains he had, or would acquire from water, 'the Nitrate King' had every reason to be pleased.

The Bank of Tarapacá and London Limited

Busy as North had been, in 1888, with his nitrate-fields, his railways and his waterworks in the distant province of Tarapacá, he had not finished yet. In mid-December, the commercial press of London carried news of yet another enterprise to be launched in North's name—the Bank of Tarapacá and London Limited.[101] The foundation of a bank was, in many ways, simply a logical extension of North's existing concerns: these now had a considerable turnover of business and often required local credit for further operations, but the existing facilities were both inadequate and expensive.[102] Moreover, North had at hand a most experienced banker who had the great advantage of knowing the desert regions and the business community of Iquique, namely John Dawson, and it was, indeed, with Dawson that the matter was discussed before the Bank was launched.[103] Once again, the firm of Lockett added the prestige of their name to North's enterprise, and it was R. R. Lockett and North together who worked out the project in detail in the summer of 1888.[104] Their other allies as promoters were all well-known City men, the chairman of the Board being William Fowler, also then chairman of the largest discount house in London, the National Discount Company.[105]

---

[101] *The Standard*, 17 December 1888; *The Economist*, 22 December 1888. North had, in fact, announced the Bank a month before, at a banquet given in his honour by business friends in Liverpool. *The South American Journal*, 17 November 1888.   [102] *Memoirs of the Family of Lockett*, pp. 113–14.

[103] Dawson was actually negotiating for the purchase of a site for the Bank in Iquique in October 1888. Papers in Mr Dawson's Letter File, 1888–9. Archives of the Bank of London and South America Ltd, University College Library London. Subsequently cited as BOLSA Archive.

[104] *Memoirs of the Family of Lockett*, p. 114.

[105] David Joslin, *A Century of Banking in Latin America: Bank of London and South America Limited, 1862–1962*, p. 177.

Finally, with N. M. Rothschild and Sons as the London bankers, the new concern was launched at the end of 1888, apparently in an aura of high respectability, given the names of those associated with it.

The Bank's capital was authorized as £1,000,000 in 100,000 shares of £10 each, of which, the prospectus announced, it was not intended to call up at present more than £5 per share, adding that 'no promotion-money or consideration in any form has been or will be paid, and no Contracts have been entered into with anyone in relation to the formation of the Company'. There followed the usual instructions to prospective shareholders on the procedure to be followed in applying for shares, and the opening of the subscription list was announced for 18 December 1888.[106] In fact, however, the lists were open for such a short time and so many interested members of the public were unable to obtain prospectuses and could not, therefore, apply for shares, that suspicion of unfair practices was aroused:

> ... it is said [reported *The Economist*] that considerable amounts were offered for the prospectuses, and that for days before its issue the offices of the leader of the group were visited by crowds of premium-hunters, who were anxious to get the chance of applying for shares.[107]

Suspicion was one thing, proof another, and the paper was not to know that as early as November, if not before, John Dawson in Iquique was busily allocating shares, at North's behest, to a number of favoured individuals who, early in 1889, were to be asked by Dawson to give power of attorney to North and Lockett, authorizing them to sign applications for the allotment of shares.[108] More than that: when the prospectus was actually despatched from London to Dawson, almost a week *before* the lists were opened in the City, it went with the message that 'the Capital is privately applied for, including the amount reserved for the coast, very much in excess of what is asked for'.[109]

---

[106] *The Standard*, 17 December 1888.

[107] *The Economist*, 22 December 1888. The paper added that if the rumour was true, Stock Exchange rules had been seriously infringed.

[108] Correspondence in Dawson File, BOLSA Archive.

[109] B. Depledge, London, to Dawson at Iquique, 12 December 1888, in ibid.

Another communication, sent but three days later, contained the bland statement that:

the Prospectus contained in Colonel North's communication to you of Wednesday last, via Panama, was not one actually issued to the public. The only difference, however, consists in the alteration of the date of opening the list of subscribers.[110]

Since the flotation of a *public* company was the subject under discussion, clearly the difference was quite a significant one.

At any rate, the Bank was launched, and the capital was called up to the tune of £500,000 by mid-1889.[111] Already in October 1888 Dawson had secured from the Banco de Santiago an agreement that its branches in Santiago, Valparaiso, Concepción and Los Andes would accept bills drawn on the Bank of Tarapacá, in return for the Bank of Tarapacá acting as its agents in Iquique and Pisagua.[112] Agents for the Bank were also appointed in New York and Hamburg, both prestigious names in their own countries—W. R. Grace and Sons and the Norddeutsche Bank—and arrangements were made for the Chilean branches to draw on Rothschilds.[113] North himself, meanwhile, had become Deputy Chairman of the Board of Directors and seemed, at the end of 1888, to have stuck yet another feather in his cap.[114]

But, again, it was not quite plain sailing for the enterprising Colonel. Apparently, all the careful planning which had gone into the founding of the Bank had been put into operation before official permission for it to operate in Chile was secured, and this was still the situation.[115] With so many of his newly-formed concerns—the Bank, the Waterworks and the Nitrate Railways—possibly under something of a cloud in Chile itself, the time had clearly come for North personally to return to the

---

[110] Same to same, 15 December 1888, in ibid.

[111] Joslin, *A Century of Banking*, p. 177.

[112] O. Prieto Goni, Valparaiso, to Dawson at Iquique, 24 October 1888. Dawson File, BOLSA Archive.

[113] Joslin, *A Century of Banking*, p. 177.

[114] 'When North does get into the House of Lords I suppose his title will be Baron North of Tarapaca', wrote one of the recipients of Bank shares in Chile. J. Woodsend, Valparaiso, to Dawson at Iquique, 14 November 1888. Dawson file. BOLSA Archive.

[115] Joslin, loc. cit.

scene of his earlier labours, to bring his own considerable gifts
to bear on a solution to these problems. He had not been in
Chile since 1882, for the intervening years had been fully
occupied in putting nitrates and nitrate interests on the London
Stock Exchange, and in establishing his own standing in business
and society. And there were other good reasons for a visit to
Chile in 1889. In the first place, the impression was growing
abroad that President José Manuel Balmaceda, who had taken
office in 1886, had his own views of the penetration of Tarapacá by British capital and enterprise, and it might, therefore,
be useful for the virtual embodiment of that penetration, John
Thomas North, to see for himself what was afoot in Chile. And,
secondly, after his brilliant early successes, North's more recent
activities on the Stock Exchange were exciting increasingly
critical comment from parts of the British commercial press.
He had worked very hard in the last few years to secure the
confidence of the investing public, and if that confidence were
not to wane, some dramatic gesture in typical style was needed
at this juncture. With his great gift for showmanship, 'the
Nitrate King' saw in a highly-publicized visit to Chile a golden
opportunity to solidify his interest abroad and consolidate his
position at home. For if, indeed, his interests were under
attack, North was not the man to stand idly by and do nothing
to prevent it.

The Nitrate Provisions Supply Company and Other Interests

The towns on the seaboard of Tarapacá and the nitrate *oficinas*
which lay inland beyond the coastal range of low mountains
were essentially artificial communities, dependent on outside
sources of supply for everything they used and consumed. It
probably seemed logical to North, therefore, that since his
interests embraced nitrate of soda itself, communications, banking and water-supply, he might profitably add to these undertakings by forming yet another company to trade in that barren
region in general merchandise, importing from other parts of
Chile and from abroad stores of all kinds to supply the *oficinas*
and ports. Hence, in 1889, the Nitrates Provisions Supply
Company was floated on the London Stock Exchange, with an

authorized capital of £200,000, and with Robert Harvey as
chairman of the Board.[116] Like nitrates and water, this interest
was by no means a novel undertaking for North: his earlier
activities with Maurice Jewell had been precisely in this line
of business.[117] He now had, however, much more behind him,
and not least the support and business co-operation of prominent shipping concerns in Liverpool, of which, for him, the house
of Lockett was certainly the most important.[118] Their ships
were very active in the West Coast trade, one of them, indeed,
being the *John Thomas North*.[119]

Locketts were also associated with North in many other
ventures, though not in Chile itself. These included collieries
in Wales, owned by the eponymous company, North's Navigation Collieries, tin mines at Maravillas in Bolivia, quicksilver
mines at Ripanji in Serbia, and a gold mine, Spes Bona, in
South Africa. But all these concerns, including—despite its
name—the gold mine in South Africa, were failures, and all
were abandoned or sold.[120] North had, however, one other
major concern in Chile which was far from being a failure:
this was the Arauco Railway Company Limited, founded in
1886, of which North was chairman and a major shareholder,
a company formed to run coalfields in the southern Chilean
province of Arauco and construct and run railway lines
associated with them.[121] Yet it was nitrates, and really nitrates
alone, which had made North's name on the Stock Exchange,
and no one in the City of London could be ignorant of the fact.

[116] *Burdetts Official Intelligence*, viii (1890), pp. 860–1.

[117] See above, p. 24.

[118] See *Memoirs of the Family of Lockett*, pp. 124 ff.

[119] Ibid. Appendix 'Wm. & Jno. Lockett's Ships', pp. 130–8. The *John Thomas North* is commemorated in a poem by John Masefield. Lockett, *Memoirs*, p. 138. North himself is also commemorated in the poem 'Balmaceda' by the Chilean poet and Nobel prize-winner, Pablo Neruda.

[120] Lockett, *Memoirs*, p. 116. The partnership of Lockett and North was not merely a business one. In 1891, North's daughter, Emma, married George Alexander Lockett.

[121] *Burdetts Official Intelligence*, vii (1889), pp. 500–1. For a detailed description of the company's properties and operations in 1889, see William Howard Russell, *A Visit to Chile and the Nitrate Fields of Tarapacá* (London, 1890), pp. 46–66.

III

THREATS TO NORTH'S THRONE,
1889–1890

North and the British Commercial Press

The flamboyant rise of 'the Nitrate King' naturally attracted a good deal of public attention, as, indeed, it was intended to do. No one knew better than North the value of publicity in the launching of joint-stock companies, and his own particular brand of public relations consisted largely of selling his promotions by selling himself. The image he constantly projected was that of a self-made man whose native intelligence and bluff personality had secured him a very large fortune: others who also wished to get rich could do a lot worse than give him their trust, since he clearly knew what he was about. The mark he was making in London society in the late 1880s was merely the latest chapter in the captivating story of his career, and the ease with which shares in his promotions were taken up is the best evidence of the success of his methods.

But the applause was by no means universal. To some commentators, North's very success was suspicious, and to those who were better informed about nitrates than the average investor there were more fundamental questions to be answered about the long-term prospects of an industry and trade which had experienced so rapid a boom under North's genial guidance. Two papers, in particular, of considerable influence in business and financial circles, maintained a watchful eye on North's affairs, and did not hesitate to express their opinions in a forthright fashion, though in markedly different styles. *The Economist*, however, unlike *The Financial News*, confined its attention to North's companies and the nitrate industry's position; *The Financial News* was no less concerned to enlighten the general public about the Colonel himself.

Early in 1888, when the nitrate interests were beginning to establish themselves in London, *The Economist* was already reminding the public that the past history of the nitrate industry, with its record of boom and slump, was not one to inspire confidence. Referring to the 'wild speculation' then taking place in Nitrate Railways shares, it pointed out that the increased prosperity of the railway line in 1887, which had resulted in share prices doubling in a week, was due entirely to the restricted output; and what producers had done before they might well do again.

It is a question, therefore, whether the public had not better leave the shares alone for the enjoyment of those inside manipulators who have so far had such excellent success.[1]

But the rapid launching of new nitrate companies during 1888 turned *The Economist*'s attention to the industry as a whole, and, while it recognized that the world market position had recently improved:

As regards the future [it declared] it may be pointed out that the present stocks are not excessive, but there is every probability of the supplies being greatly increased, and increased possibly in excess of the demand. Hence the future of the existing nitrate companies is by no means clear, and investors would do well to be cautious in dealing with them.[2]

This warning was persistently repeated. Commenting in September 1888 on a general, speculative rise in share values on the Stock Exchange, *The Economist* singled out the nitrate industry for particular attention, and urged the public to leave the companies' securities alone 'to the cliques which are so busy manipulating them'.[3] The paper was very worried by the fact that the extraordinary rise in the shares of the nitrate companies was based less on past results than on prospective dividends, alleged to be likely to reach 100 per cent in some cases, a result which seemed to *The Economist* to be most unlikely in view of the world market situation.[4]

---

[1] *The Economist*, 14 January 1888. It may be relevant to note that at precisely the same time the paper was much concerned with the world market position of another primary material, copper. Here, too, universal over-production had resulted in the formation of a syndicate to limit the supply, but this had limited success, and share prices fluctuated enormously. See *The Economist*, 3 and 31st December 1887, 14 and 28 January, 25 February, 24 March, 28 April, 19 May, 9 June 1888, for full and detailed reports and comments.

[2] Ibid., 7 July 1888. Cf. above, pp. 37-42.

[3] Ibid., 22 September 1888.   [4] Ibid., 17 November 1888.

Yet, before 1889, *The Economist* refrained from mentioning Colonel North by name, and confined itself to warnings about the new companies generally in the light of its knowledge of the nitrate market.[5] *The Financial News* was not so obligingly reticent, and throughout 1888 it kept up a running battle against 'the Nitrate King' and all his doings, in a series of witty and provocative articles which were designed to discredit the man himself as well as to cast doubt on his promotions. A favourite target was the Nitrate Railways Company, whose sudden prosperity, after years of stagnation, was based, the paper said, on the 'exceptional and artificial' character of the current nitrate boom:

The big traffics [*sic*] on which the shares have been boomed began about twelve months ago with the breaking up of the Nitrate Ring, which had previously restricted the output. . . Europe is . . .being treated to a deluge of nitrate, and experienced importers are beginning to be nervous about how long the market will be able to bear the strain. . . The railway has but one string to its bow, and it has been stretched almost to breaking. A collapse in the nitrate market . . . would send this pet rocket of Colonel North's tumbling like a stick.[6]

Subsequent editorials continued the attack almost day by day, and much more unflattering remarks were made: in one column entitled 'The Wabash of South America', a pointed comparison was drawn which all followers of share movements could be expected to understand:

We should be sorry [said the paper, ironically] to hurt the Colonel's feelings by suggesting that he is the Jay Gould of that salamandrine region [South America], but it is not our fault if the ideas of these two illustrious financiers have a strong family resemblance. Of the two, Colonel North appears to be the more successful balloonist. Jay Gould raised the eyelids of the British public pretty considerably,

[5] Early in 1889, however, *The Economist* attacked the promoters of the Tarapacá Nitrate Company in a rather genteel way for forming a company capitalized at £160,000 which was *hoping* to acquire nitrate-fields: 'to sum up, we have a few gentlemen who, on account of their staking £500, quietly ask the public to supply them with £160,000, in order to buy a nitrate property . . . and reserve to themselves as remuneration . . . no less than one-fourth of the profits when 15 per cent is paid to the shareholders'. *The Economist*, 12 January 1889. This was the company against which Stephen Williamson inveighed so bitterly. See above, pp. 37–8.

[6] *The Financial News*, 23 May 1888.

but he was not clever enough to get £28,000 per mile out of them for Wabash, or even for Missouri, Kansas and Texas. Whatever the merits of nitrate may be as a fertiliser, there can be no question that it has raised a big crop in Tower Hamlets . . .[7]

North and 'his merry men', it was alleged, were disposing of their stock in the Nitrate Railways Company by promises of high dividends, while the artificially-high share prices were sustained by the temporary boom in nitrate production and carriage.[8] But the crash must come, and 'the heaven-born fools who are relieving Colonel North of his Nitrate Railways shares at three times their value' would soon realize how absurdly over-capitalized was the 'single-track tramway traversing moor and mountain in Tarapacá'.[9]

An equally devastating attack was launched against the Tarapacá Waterworks Company, and it was, indeed, *The Financial News* which retailed the detailed story of North's manœuvres to obtain the exclusive concessions on which it was promoted.[10] In its treatment of this subject, the paper's sarcasm reached new heights:

The latest good story about our friend Colonel North is that he was heard lamenting there were not more elements in nature than air, earth and water, as they were such nice things to finance. In Tarapacá he has made himself master of all the existing elements. With his Nitrate Companies and Nitrate Railways he controls all the saleable earth in the province. With his sea-water condensers, his water barrels and his Pica concession he monopolises the drinking materials. It is generally understood that before the recent break in Nitrate Railways diverted his attention he was elaborating a scheme for placing the atmosphere of Tarapacá under the care of a limited liability company, with an airy capital of several millions sterling . . .[11]

Such attacks, however humorously made, were bound to sting, and at one stage North, apparently, threatened to sue *The Financial News* for libel.[12] But nothing came of the threat, and the Colonel had to rely on his own ability to counteract the

---

[7] Ibid., 24 May 1888. Jay Gould was the best-known speculator in railway shares in the United States, almost an exact contemporary of North's.

[8] *The Financial News*, 25 May 1888.   [9] Ibid., 26 May 1888.

[10] Cf. above, pp. 58-9.   [11] *The Financial News*, 14 June 1888.

[12] Ibid., 29 May 1888.

bad impressions which might have been created. In any event, while he had his detractors, he also had defenders in the press. *The South American Journal*, for example, was as consistent in its support of North as *The Financial News* was hostile, and, during 1888, it maintained an optimistic outlook on the prospects for nitrate shares.[13] Unlike *The Economist*, *The South American Journal* believed that the world nitrate market would expand sufficiently to absorb the increased output which would come from the operations of the new companies, and it looked forward confidently to 1889 as a year which would see yet even more impressive results than 1888.[14] As that year closed, however, both optimists and pessimists about nitrates in general and North in particular already knew that the press would not lack material on both subjects in the early months of 1889, for 'the Nitrate King' had already proclaimed his intention to go on progress through his distant kingdom.

President José Manuel Balmaceda, his Character and Policies[15]

At the time that North turned his thoughts towards his forthcoming visit to Chile, including the nitrate regions, President José Manuel Balmaceda was also contemplating a journey to Tarapacá, a province not yet visited by the Chilean head of state. Balmaceda was now a man of 50, and at the apex of an outstanding political career. A tall, commanding figure with a gift for oratory, he had served his country with distinction as congressman, diplomat, and cabinet minister and he had assumed the presidency precisely at that moment in Chilean

---

[13] See, for example, the issues of 9 June, 13 October, 17 November and 22 December 1888.   [14] *The South American Journal*, 5 January 1889.

[15] Balmaceda is a key figure in the modern history of Chile, and studies of his life and work are legion. Among the most important are: J. Bañados Espinosa, *Balmaceda: su gobierno y la revolución de 1891* (2 vols., Paris, 1894); R. Salas Edwards, *Balmaceda y el parlamentarismo en Chile* (2 vols., Santiago, 1914 and 1925); J. Rodríguez Bravo, *Balmaceda y el conflicto entre el Congreso y el Ejecutivo* (2 vols., Santiago, 1921 and 1926); J. M. Yrarrázaval, *El Presidente Balmaceda*; F. A. Encina, *Historia de Chile*, xix and xx, and H. Ramírez N., *Balmaceda y la contrarrevolución de 1891*. But the literature is enormous. See also Harold Blakemore, 'The Chilean Revolution of 1891 and its Historiography', *HAHR*, xlv (1965), pp. 393–421, for a discussion of some evaluations of Balmaceda and his policies. The account given in this book cannot be exhaustive, but provides, in part, an interpretation based on new material.

history when the country's international reputation was at its height. Foreigners were already persuaded that Chile was quite unlike her neighbours on the South American continent, and had long been so:

Respect for the law [said *The South American Journal*] and love of order have become so deeply rooted in the people that any interruption to the regular course in the transmission of the supreme authority of the Republic is a thing not to be dreamt of; in fact, it is a sheer impossibility.[16]

It was, of course, recognized that Chile was no democracy, and that the political benefits conferred by aristocratic rule carried with them social disadvantages.[17] But, at any rate, foreign loans were safe in Chilean hands and Chile was prompt to meet her international financial obligations.[18] And the country accepted immigrants:

welcoming such impulse as these foreigners gave to the trade and industry of the country, harbouring no envy or jealousy of the fortune these came to accumulate . . .[19]

When Chile decisively defeated the combined forces of Peru and Bolivia in the War of the Pacific, the seal was set on a reputation which clearly seemed to be the product of the country's distinctive qualities:

The military and naval triumphs of Chile have been conspicuously remarkable . . . but the true greatness of Chile is to be recognised in the industry of its people, in their respect for law, in their intelligent culture of literary and scientific pursuits, in their dedication to commerce and in their prosperous utilisation of the natural riches of a country possessing all the elements of national greatness.[20]

These sentiments, with their overtones of 'manifest destiny', were undoubtedly shared by Balmaceda, whose own public life

[16] *The South American Journal*, 28 February 1884.
[17] See *The Times*, 26 April 1880, for a long and interesting article on contemporary Chile, full of acute observation.
[18] *The South American Journal*, 22 January 1880, called Chile 'the Abdiel of South American finance—"among the faithless, faithful only she"'.
[19] *The Times*, 26 April 1880.
[20] *The South American Journal*, 24 April 1884. That Englishmen were not alone in the favourable evaluation of Chile may be seen from C. Wiener, *Chili et Chiliens* (Paris, 1888), and many other examples might be cited.

spanned the critical years of Chile's rise in international esteem. He had played a prominent part in that process himself, notably as Minister to Argentina in 1879, and subsequently as Foreign Minister in 1881: no other Chilean had done more than Balmaceda to ensure that Chile's victory on the battlefield would not be nullified at the conference table.[21] And when he assumed the presidency in 1886, it was with the conscious mission to lead his country to even greater heights, economically prosperous at home and deeply respected abroad, an ambition quite in accord with his own self-confidence.[22]

Balmaceda's programme for Chile's development was simple in conception: the proceeds of the export duty on nitrates, now the chief source of government income, were to be invested in public works and education, so that when that source declined as the nitrate deposits were diminished, Chile would have derived permanent benefit, and would possess other productive assets to take the place of nitrate.[23] This policy did not originate with Balmaceda,[24] but the rapid growth of income from nitrates in his presidency, and the personal inspiration he provided widened the scope and increased the pace of the development programme to such an extent that he could well be credited with the achievement.

In 1887, a new Ministry, that of Industry and Public Works, was created and, as the state's income increased, so did the proportion allocated to public works and to education. In the

---

[21] For this story, see Robert N. Burr, *By Reason or Force: Chile and the Balancing of Power in South America, 1830–1905* (Berkeley and Los Angeles, University of California Press, 1965), pp. 144–63; the same author's *The Stillborn Panama Congress: Power Politics and Chilean-Colombian Relations during the War of the Pacific* (Berkeley and Los Angeles, University of California Press, 1962), *passim*, and Geoffrey S. Smith, 'The Role of J. M. Balmaceda in Preserving Argentine Neutrality in the War of the Pacific', *HAHR*, xlix (1969), pp. 254–67. Balmaceda's nationalism was apparent in a circular on the War of the Pacific which he issued as Foreign Minister in which he spoke of 'Chile's civilising mission' in Tarapacá. Cutting from the *Diario Oficial* of Santiago, 25 December 1881, encl. in Pakenham to Lord Granville, Santiago, 27 December 1881. F.O. 16/213. No. 91. Diplomatic.

[22] See *Discurso de Su Excellencia el Presidente de la República al Apertura del Congreso Nacional de 1887* (Santiago, 1887), *passim*.

[23] Ramírez, *Balmaceda, passim*, is much the fullest account of this policy. The present narrative adds fresh detail.

[24] President Santa María (1881–86) had similar ideas. See Encina, *Historia de Chile*, xviii, 327–93, *passim*.

estimates for 1886, which totalled $33,733,002, the amount for public works was included in the sum of $10,263,344 allocated to the Ministry of the Interior, while $2,200,070 was earmarked for education.[25] Of a total estimated expenditure of $40,234,685 in 1888, however, the sum of $8,442,236 was assigned to the new Ministry of Industry and Public Works alone, while $5,957,436 was for education.[26] And in the estimates for 1890, totalling $67,069,808, no less than $21,000,000 was for industry and public works, while some $6,628,000 was to be spent on education.[27]

Education statistics themselves provide further and striking testimony of the development of Chile under Balmaceda. In 1886, Chile had 1,394 schools of all types with an enrolment of almost 79,000 pupils.[28] By 1888, there were some 1,450 schools, both public and private, and over 140,000 pupils,[29] and by 1890, after a period of reorganization, Chile possessed 1,097 state schools and 556 private schools, the total enrolment exceeding 150,000.[30]

The telegraphic and railway systems were greatly extended. In 1886, there were 150 telegraph offices in Chile;[31] there were 182 by 1890.[32] The amount spent by the government itself on extending and improving the railway network rose from over $4,000,000 in 1886 to over $7,000,000 in 1890.[33] Several important bridges, such as that over the River Bío-Bío, were built; the River Mapocho, running through Santiago, was canalized, and the great dry-dock at Talcahuano was completed. In addition, a large number of public buildings were

[25] *Lei de Presupuestos de los gastos generales de a administración pública para el año 1886* (Santiago, 1885). Not paginated.

[26] *Lei de presupuestos . . . para . . . 1888* (Santiago, 1887).

[27] *Lei de presupuestos . . . para . . . 1890* (Santiago, 1889).

[28] *Memoria del Ministro de Justicia, Culto e Instrucción Pública presentada al Congreso Nacional de 1887* (Santiago, 1887), pp. xxv–xxvi.

[29] *Memoria del Ministro del Justicia e Instrucción Pública . . . de 1888* (Santiago, 1888), p. xxxix.

[30] *Memoria del Ministro . . . de 1890* (Santiago, 1890), pp. 55–6.

[31] *Memoria del Ministro del Interior presentada al Congreso Nacional de 1888* (Santiago, 1888), p. xxxv.

[32] *Memoria del Ministro . . . de 1890* (Santiago, 1890), p. xvii.

[33] *Memoria presentada al Ministro del Interior por el Director-Jeneral de los Ferrocarriles del Estado en 1887* (Santiago, 1888), pp. 6–7, and *Memoria . . . de 1890* (Santiago, 1890), p. 4.

erected—hospitals, prisons, town-halls, and government offices. [34]

⟋ Balmaceda also sought to encourage foreign immigration. In July 1887, the Chilean Foreign Minister informed the British Minister to Chile that the government wished 'to engage emigrants from Great Britain to settle in the southern part of the Republic', [35] and early in 1888 a number of British families reached Valparaiso on their way south. [36] But their story was not a happy one, and, throughout 1888 and 1889, the Minister was kept busy by appeals for assistance from settlers who had found southern Chile very different from the potential paradise depicted for them by the Chilean colonization agent in England. [37] Nevertheless, between 1886 and 1890, almost 30,000 Europeans emigrated to Chile, and the colonization schemes, however unsuccessful in places, were yet another facet of Balmaceda's programme of development. [38]

Within Chile itself, however, and also abroad, that programme was not universally applauded, and there were a number of grounds—economic, political and personal—on which Balmaceda could be attacked. A substantial body of opinion had long held that what the Chilean economy needed above all was not so much a programme of public works as a deliberate and sustained policy to retire the inconvertible paper money which was the country's principal medium of exchange. [39] Summing up the consequences of the paper-money system in 1886, the British Minister declared:

the country should be solvent enough but it is flooded with dubious paper; the law prescribing a periodical destruction of forced currency notes is apt to be disregarded . . . whilst private banks of more

[34] See the *Memoria del Ministro de Industria y Obras Públicas presentada al Congreso Nacional de 1888* (Santiago, 1888), *passim*, and the corresponding volume for 1889 (Santiago, 1889), *passim*.
[35] Fraser to Lord Salisbury, Santiago, 28 July 1887. F.O. 16/248. No. 53. Diplomatic.
[36] Same to same, Santiago, 4 January 1888. F.O. 16/252. No. 8. Diplomatic.
[37] Letters in F.O. 16/250 and 253. Consular and Commercial, 1887 and 1888.
[38] Ramírez, *Balmaceda*, pp. 138-9.
[39] For the story of the establishment of the paper-money regime in Chile, see F. W. Fetter, *Monetary Inflation in Chile* (Princeton, 1931), pp. 1-43. The more technical study of R. E. Santelices, *Los Bancos Chilenos*, contains much relevant documentary material.

or less doubtful solvency have been allowed to go on issuing notes far beyond their proper means, and these have become merged in the general circulation under protection of the forced currency laws; foreign exchanges are ruinously speculative and fluctuate to such an extent as to render all mercantile transactions precarious ... the administration is not above suspicion of dealing tenderly with financiers, wealthy owners of raw produce, and persons largely interested in the export trade; and there have been fears lest the existing currency, instituted in a moment of necessity, should come to be maintained until it loses all value and all faculty of reconversion.[40]

Even before Balmaceda launched his ambitious programme of public works, informed opinion criticized expenditure on such projects so long as the currency remained unconverted: in 1885, the Chamber of Commerce of Valparaiso expressed concern at the fluctuating rate of exchange, the result, it believed, at least in part of 'the want of confidence caused by the Government in undertaking costly public works' with funds which could be used to build up a metallic reserve for retiring the paper money of the republic.[41] In October 1886 *The Economist* commented on the 'very unwieldy' paper currency of Chile, adding that 'unless ... radical measures are undertaken for the improvement of the currency ... it is likely to remain for a long time in a bad condition'.[42] Private views of individual businessmen dealing with Chile echoed these opinions:

Is paper money [wrote Stephen Williamson] a blessing or is it to be a curse to Chili? In the hands of ignorant people—who lose sight of the obligation to resume specie payments, it may be a curse eventually. . . On what sort of money is property valued—and held at present? . . . It is clear your resources should be accumulating in sterling money and you [are] always indebted to Chile so long as there is paper money.[43]

With Balmaceda's government concentrating its interest on vast public expenditures, it showed little interest in monetary

[40] Fraser to Lord Rosebery, Santiago, 17 June 1886. F.O. 16/244. No. 5. Commercial. Confidential.

[41] *The South American Journal*, 7 March 1885.

[42] *The Economist*, 9 October 1886.

[43] Stephen Williamson, Liverpool, to W. R. Henderson at Valparaiso, 20 October 1887. Letter in Folder No. 28, Balfour Williamson Papers.

reform.[44] 'The currency', complained *The Economist* in August 1889, 'is much depreciated and rates of exchange fluctuate in a way which is very damaging . . . the true magnitude of these evils, however, does not seem to be realized'.[45]

A policy of public works also had critics on political grounds, since the large numbers of new posts such a policy created were at the disposal of the government of the day. Balmaceda's predecessor had himself been attacked on this issue in connection with the extension of the state railways which, it was said, resulted in the creation of

a number of useless posts in which to place certain favoured individuals, friends and relations of the Government, who had rendered some party services, and who could not otherwise be so bountifully provided for, nor in any other manner be relied upon to continue them.[46]

Attacks of this kind by the political opposition to the government were clearly given more scope with the expansion of the public works programme under Balmaceda, though in the early years of his administration they were launched mainly by his implacable opponents, the clerical Conservatives.[47] Thus, the leader of the Conservative party, Carlos Walker Martínez, consistently opposed Balmaceda's projects of material development, arguing in Congress that money ostensibly voted for these

[44] The entire question, however, is complicated, and the literature is partisan. Cf., for example, Ramírez, *Balmaceda*, pp. 123–34, a highly favourable view of Balmaceda's monetary policies, and J. M. Yrarrázaval, 'El Gobierno y los Bancos durante la Administración Balmaceda', *Boletín de la Academia Chilena de la Historia*, No. 48 (1953), pp. 5–26, a very critical one. In 1887, Balmaceda did promulgate a law restricting the note issues of the banks, creating a bullion reserve in the Treasury and providing for the retirement of $100,000 paper money each month until the amount of paper in circulation reached no more than $18,000,000. Fetter, op. cit., pp. 53–6. The law, however, was largely ineffective. A stimulating modern view of the controversy, which suggests, however, that the basic research still requires to be done, is Albert O. Hirschman's essay on 'Inflation in Chile' in his fundamental work *Journeys Towards Progress. Studies of Economic Policy-Making in Latin America* (New York, The Twentieth Century Fund, 1963). See particularly pp. 170–2, and notes.

[45] *The Economist*, 31 August 1889.

[46] *The South American Journal*, 22 August 1885, quoting *The Chilean Times*.

[47] For the political parties in Chile at this time, see above, pp. 5–6, and below, pp. 77–8. Conservative hatred for Balmaceda derived from the fact that it was he, as Minister of the Interior in 1882–84, who had piloted through Congress the controversial religious reforms of the period.

purposes would, in fact, be used for political ends.[48] He also opposed the creation of a Ministry of Industry and Public Works on these grounds.[49]

Balmaceda had little to fear so long as these were minority opinions, and so long as his government enjoyed majority support in Congress. But it was absolutely essential to his programme to retain that support, and to avoid antagonizing important sections of political and congressional opinion. Given the highly fragmented and personalized nature of Chilean politics, however, this was a very difficult, if not impossible, task, as was clearly seen by one acute observer:

The President [reported the British Minister, in December 1886] as the natural consequence of his election, is hampered by personal engagements to individual partisans, and, in his inability to free himself from these entanglements, will probably be compelled to perpetuate the blunders and abuses of Don Domingo Santa María, govern personally with ... what can only be called hack administrations, and with all this disadvantage, undertake the same eternal conflict with public opinion that embittered the days of his predecessor.[50]

The 'eternal conflict' to which the Minister referred was the growing dichotomy between the juridical organization of government, enshrined in the constitution of 1833, and the presidential practices which had grown up around it, on the one hand, and, on the other hand, the increasing body of informed political opinion in Chile which sought drastic revision of both. The constitutional reforms of the autocratic charter of 1833 effected during the nineteenth century themselves testified to the strength of that opinion, and it is significant that the political reputation of such strong-minded presidents as Santa María and Balmaceda himself had been built, in part, on their advocacy, when in opposition, of constitutional reform.[51]

[48] See his *Balance del Liberalismo Chileno* (Santiago, 1888), a collection of extracts from his speeches in Congress during 1887-88.
[49] *Boletín de las Sesiones Extraordinarias de la Cámara de Diputados de 1887-1888* (Santiago, 1888), pp. 870-1.
[50] Fraser to Lord Salisbury, Santiago, 1 December 1886. F.O. 16/243. No. 104. Diplomatic.
[51] See J. and D. A. Arteaga Alemparte, *Los Constituyentes de 1870*, vol. II of the *Biblioteca de Escritores de Chile* (Santiago, 1910), pp. 2-25, 147-52.

Yet, once in power, both Santa María and Balmaceda were singularly reluctant to do anything which might detract from the enormous prerogatives of the presidency and, like almost all of their predecessors, they felt obliged to defend the constitution of 1833, as it stood when they assumed office.[52] The key to the situation was presidential control of the congressional majority, since a serious constitutional crisis could only arise if the executive and legislative powers ceased to see eye to eye. Consequently, throughout the century, successive presidents, armed with the wide powers conferred on them by the constitution, forestalled the possibility of having to deal with an antagonistic Congress by interfering in congressional elections to select the kind of Congress they desired.[53] This abuse of the system had come under increasing criticism, though it was not always easy to discover, in the confusion of Chilean party politics, which politicians were activated by genuine conviction and which were moved more by personal ambition. All oppositions can usually find an idealistic cause and couch it in disinterested language when they choose to do so.

Balmaceda had been elected President at a time of bitter controversy between the government and the opposition in Congress precisely over these issues, and was, in fact, put into office only through the government's use of electoral intervention and its arbitrary closure of congressional debate: the election itself saw 'a good deal of disorder and not a little loss of life'.[54] Balmaceda assumed office, therefore, with the intention of unifying the various Liberal groups by conciliation, in order to have the necessary backing in Congress for his ambitious programme, since the real opposition, the Conservatives, was very much a minority group. This policy succeeded initially.

[52] 'President Santa María', wrote the British Minister in 1886, 'has no idea of relinquishing any atom of the authority, regular or irregular, that may have been exercised by others in his place before him . . .' Fraser to Lord Salisbury, Santiago, 7 January 1886. F.O. 16/242. No. 2. Diplomatic. For Balmaceda's similar views, see *Discurso de su Excellencia . . . de 1887*, *passim*, and Maurice H. Hervey, *Dark Days in Chile. An Account of the Revolution of 1891* (London, 1892), pp. 89–92.

[53] The best account of this practice is Yrarrázaval, *El Presidente Balmaceda*, *passim*.

[54] Fraser to Lord Rosebery, Santiago, 19 June 1886. F.O. 16/242. No. 47. Diplomatic. One result of this situation was the defection from the Liberal party of a group of politicians who objected less to Balmaceda than to the method of his election. They formed the *Sueltos* or 'free-lance' party.

President Balmaceda's policy of conciliation [reported the British Minister in March 1887] has much strengthened his influence in the country and has gained for him the support of influential persons who had been driven into opposition by . . . his predecessor's rougher and narrower methods of administration.[55]

From 1886 to 1888, all went reasonably well, though three different ministries held office from September 1886 to June 1887, testifying to the President's perpetual problem of allocating portfolios to representatives of so many different groups, to their satisfaction as well as to his.[56] Then, in 1888, the policy of conciliation collapsed: under pressure from the Government Liberals, Balmaceda allowed intervention in the congressional elections in March; the existing cabinet resigned and, in its place, Balmaceda formed its successor entirely from the Government Liberals. He thus signified his abandonment of a conciliatory policy and, in so doing, alienated the other Liberal groups. The Nationals felt particularly aggrieved: they had given Balmaceda valuable support, and the idol of the party, Agustín Edwards, had held his seat in the cabinet for two years. In the following weeks, they were even more embittered as the Government Liberals tried to deprive them of representation on the Comisión Conservadora.[57] This split in the government ranks was of great significance: though the Government Liberals were strong in numbers, they were not correspondingly strong in talent, and the exclusion of the other groups deprived Balmaceda of the support of many outstanding public figures, and of the press which they controlled.[58]

So, by the latter months of 1888, the position of Balmaceda's government had been gravely weakened: the President was now disillusioned with his dream of Liberal unity, and in Santiago public opinion was becoming increasingly critical of his methods. On the other hand, the public works programme

[55] Fraser to Lord Salisbury, Santiago, 23 March 1887. F.O. 16/248. No. 32. Diplomatic. Confidential.
[56] For the detailed political history of this period, see Encina, *Historia*, xix, *passim*, and cf. Bañados, *Balmaceda*, 1, *passim*.
[57] For the Comisión Conservadora, see above, pp. 4, 6.
[58] The Nationals alone owned one-third of Chile's newspapers, including the outstanding national paper *El Mercurio*, owned by the Edwards family. Encina, *Historia*, xix, 64.

with which Balmaceda's name was associated had clearly
brought visible progress to Chile, and, if he could capitalize on
that, he might well strengthen his position nationally, if not
directly with the political parties. No other gesture by a Chilean
president would serve the purpose better than a much-publi-
cized and carefully-prepared visit to the northern regions of the
republic, territories purchased by Chilean blood and money in
a victorious war against hostile neighbours, a war, moreover,
in which Balmaceda's diplomatic contribution was well known,
and which was within the living memory of most Chileans. To
tour the northern provinces of Tarapacá and Antofagasta at
this particular time would serve not only the purpose of binding
them closer to the republic into which they had so recently
been incorporated: it would also divert attention from the
narrow political stage of Santiago, and give Balmaceda, that
eloquent orator, an ample platform to show himself, as President of the republic, concerned with the wider destinies of
Chile rather than with the petty squabbles of party politics.

There were, in addition, other good reasons for such a
journey at that particular time. Tarapacá's nitrates were the
financial basis of Balmaceda's programme, and the implications
of the rapid development of the nitrate industry, most of it
foreign owned, were now beginning to impinge on government
thinking much more positively than in the past.[59] Balmaceda
himself, indeed, had already hinted in a number of speeches
that he would like to see Chilean capital and enterprise play a
much greater part in national economic development. In his
first annual message to Congress, he had stated that his government would study what measures could be taken, as far as was
practicable, 'to nationalise industries which are, at present,
chiefly of benefit to foreigners'.[60] He did not specifically refer
to nitrates, but it is difficult to think of any other industry he
might have had in mind.[61] More significantly, at the opening
of the Santiago Exhibition on 25 November 1888, when the
idea of the northern tour may already have crystallized,
Balmaceda had asked:

[59] See above, pp. 43–5.   [60] *Discurso . . . de 1887*, op. cit., p. 9.
[61] Cf., however, J. M. Yrarrázaval, 'La Administración de Balmaceda y el
Salitre', pp. 53–4.

Why does the credit and the capital which are brought into play in all kinds of speculations in our great cities hold back and leave the foreigner to establish banks at Iquique, and abandon to strangers the exploiting of the nitrate works of Tarapacá. . . The foreigner explores these riches, and takes the profit of . . . native wealth . . . to give to other lands and unknown people the treasures of our soil, our own property and the riches we require.[62]

Such speeches excited attention, if not indeed some apprehension, in foreign business circles connected with the nitrate industry.[63] Yet, before 1889, except in the rather particular case of the Nitrate Railways Company, the *actions* of the Chilean government with regard to nitrates certainly showed little disposition to move against foreign capital.[64] In fact, they suggested the contrary. In his annual message to Congress in 1888, Balmaceda outlined a government proposal to sell by auction a number of state-owned nitrate-grounds and, on 8 June, sought congressional approval to do so over a period of three years.[65] In the extensive debate on this proposal, the Senators for Tarapacá and Talca, Luis Aldunate and Luis Pereira, expressed grave doubts on the wisdom of open auction in view of the strong competition of foreign capital, and Aldunate pleaded eloquently for the nationalization of the nitrate industry[66] For the government, however, the *Ministro de Hacienda*, Enrique Sanfuentes, lauded the merits of *laissez-faire* over state control: 'to us', he said on 1 August 1888, 'falls the honour of defending commercial liberty with all its inestimable benefits', and, he said later, 'let us stimulate private interests so that they make their logical contribution to the development of the nitrate industry'.[67] This speech was strongly reminiscent of those made during 1882 in defence of the government's decision

[62] Consul-General Newman to Lord Salisbury, Valparaiso, 19 January 1889. Report on the Nitrate Industry of Chile, loc. cit.

[63] W. H. Russell, *A Visit to Chile and the Nitrate Fields of Tarapacá*, pp. 42–3. See also *The Financial News*, 11 February 1889, and *The South American Journal*, 2 February, 1889.

[64] Cf., however, Ramírez, *Balmaceda*, pp. 86–8, where the contrary argument is put forward.

[65] See Yrarrázaval, 'La Administración de Balmaceda y el Salitre', pp. 51–3.

[66] *Boletín de las Sesiones de la Cámara de Senadores de 1888* (Santiago, 1888), pp. 190–1, 219–26, 241–5.

[67] Ibid., pp. 239–40.

at that time to return the nitrate industry to private enterprise, a decision for which, as Aldunate recalled and Sanfuentes acknowledged, Balmaceda as Minister of the Interior was partly responsible. And the proposal under debate was passed unanimously by the Senate on 1 August 1888, after Aldunate had left the Chamber.[68] But it then remained in abeyance, to be resurrected later.

Balmaceda's hints about the nitrate industry in 1888 may not have been translated into action, but it is unlikely that he was not clearly aware of the growing power of British capital and control over this ultimate source of finance for his own internal programme. And he must certainly have known something of the industry's situation, in which over-production might lead to a saturated world market, producing, in turn, a combination agreement to limit output until supply and demand again moved into equilibrium. The effect of such an agreement on government revenues and on the employment of Chileans in Tarapacá was not a matter to which Balmaceda could remain indifferent, and he well knew that the fewer the hands that controlled output, the easier the combination might be formed. It was well appreciated in Santiago that Colonel North was building up an impressive, if not monopolistic, position in Tarapacá.[69] Hence, if a combination was in the offing, North would have a big hand in it. From Balmaceda's point of view, therefore, a visit to the nitrate regions, where he could see what was happening for himself, had attractions on the economic, as well as on the political side.

On 4 March 1889 Balmaceda, accompanied by a large entourage, including several ministers, embarked at Valparaiso on the Chilean warship, *Amazonas*.[70] On the voyage to Iquique, the President gave further proof of his patriotic sentiments by

[68] Ibid., pp. 242, 246.

[69] During the latter part of 1888, various attacks were made on North's growing power, but he did not lack defenders in Chile itself. See *El Ferrocarril*, 2 January 1889, for a long letter, signed by 'Various Chileans', defending North as a benefactor to Chile, and pointing out that he could hardly be blamed for the indolence of others with regard to the exploitation of Tarapacá.

[70] Accounts of this visit may be found in all the books on Balmaceda cited in note 15, p. 69 above. My interpretation is based on these and on Chilean press reports taken from *La Tribuna*, *El Ferrocarril*, *El Heraldo*, *El Mercurio* and *The Chilean Times*.

ordering the ship's commander to steam directly over the spot where, in 1879, the Chilean wooden vessel, the *Esmeralda*, captained by the national hero, Arturo Prat, had fought a hopeless battle against Peruvian ironclads.[71] When the *Amazonas* arrived at Iquique on 8 March, 15,000 people lined the shore to give the presidential party an extraordinary reception. That day and the next were taken up with official visits to schools, the hospital, the army barracks and so on, and on 9 March, at a grand dinner in his honour, Balmaceda made his most significant public speech on his government's attitude towards the nitrate industry.[72]

The industry's problems, Balmaceda said, arose from two sources: first, the foreign monopoly which attempted to raise the price of nitrate by limiting production and, secondly, the prohibitive freight-charge of the Nitrate Railways Company, which also tended to hold back exports of nitrates. The industry's importance demanded the attention of the legislator, he continued:

private property is owned almost exclusively by foreigners, and is being rapidly concentrated in the hands of persons of one sole nationality. It would be preferable that the property should belong to Chileans also; but if Chilean capital is indolent . . . we ought not to be surprised if foreign capital fills . . . the void which . . . is caused by the negligence of our countrymen.

Chilean investors would have their chance in the forthcoming sale of state nitrate-grounds, and such a development would counter the dangers of a possible foreign monopoly. Finally, he declared, the time had come to make a statement before the entire republic that

an industrial monopoly of nitrate is not an undertaking for the State, whose fundamental mission is to guarantee the rights of property and liberty. Neither ought it to be the work of . . . individuals . . . natives or foreigners, because we will never accept the

[71] *La Tribuna*, 9 March 1889. This newspaper, a strong supporter of Balmaceda, had a special reporter on the visit whose reports were telegraphed to Santiago, and reproduced by other journals as well as his own.

[72] All commentators, contemporary and later, agree on this point, but there is wide disagreement on what Balmaceda actually meant by what he said. Cf., for example, Ramírez, *Balmaceda*, pp. 92–6, and Yrarrázaval, 'La Administración Balmaceda y el Salitre', pp. 54 ff.

tyranny of the many or of the few. . . . The State must forever retain sufficient production and sale, and to frustrate, in any case, an industrial dictatorship in Tarapacá.

As to the Nitrate Railways question, this, the President said,

ought to be equitably settled, without injuring lawful private interests or harming the convenience and rights of the State. I hope [he added] that at an early date all the railways in Tarapacá will become national property; my aspiration is . . . that Chile may become the owner of all the railways that traverse her territory . . .[73]

Much has been read into this particular speech of Balmaceda's. One historian has interpreted it as a proposition to solve the nitrate problem by the nationalization of the industry, the prohibition of any monopoly which might attempt to limit production in order to raise prices, and the expropriation of the Tarapacá railways.[74] Another has seen in it 'a veritable declaration of war against monopolistic British capital which was exercising a real economic dictatorship over the nitrate region',[75] and the same writer cites two contemporary newspapers, suggesting that they expressed a similar view.[76] Such interpretations were certainly made at the time, and not least by foreign observers, one of whom thought the speech a warning to foreigners that the President

intended, if he could, to close the course to any but native competitors, to handicap those who had been the winners, to refuse industrial concessions . . . to non-Chilean residents, and to reserve the State-lands still unappropriated, exclusively and inalienably, to citizens of the Republic.[77]

A number of other opinions, however, put the emphasis elsewhere. *The Chilean Times*, for example, felt reassured by Balmaceda's clear indication that 'the Government, contrary to the wishes of a certain circle, will not enter the lists as a producer of nitrate', and, for those who had hoped it might, 'the

[73] This translation, which is accurate, is taken from *The South American Journal*, 4 May 1889. The full Spanish text is given in *La Tribuna*, 11 March 1889.

[74] O. Hardy, 'British Nitrates and the Balmaceda Revolution', p. 178.

[75] Ramírez, *Balmaceda*, p. 94.

[76] Ibid. The papers cited are *El Ferrocarril* and *El Mercurio*.

[77] Russell, *A Visit to Chile and the Nitrate Fields*, p. 315. Cf. *The South American Journal*, 1 June 1889; *The Economist*, 14 September 1889, and *The Financial News*, 11 February 1889.

presidential discourse has completely blasted their hopes'.[78] To *La Tribuna*, one of Balmaceda's most consistent supporters, the President had shown himself to be

a frank and open supporter of the widest industrial freedom . . . rejecting not only a state monopoly . . . but also the possibility of a coalition of great capital resources setting up a monopoly to overwhelm industrialists of modest means.[79]

For *El Heraldo*, one of Balmaceda's most persistent critics, a significant feature of the speech was its vagueness, and clarification was required on many points, but *El Heraldo* also expressed the strong opinion that what was needed above all in Tarapacá was for the nitrate industry, and the railways, to be left in the liberty they then enjoyed, 'which has been and is the real cause of the astonishing progress His Excellency has admired'.[80]

The Chilean press as a whole was certainly not disposed to see in Balmaceda's speech anything remotely resembling a proposal for nationalization of the nitrate industry, and their comments on his alleged attacks on foreign capital were, like Balmaceda's speech itself, so hedged about by qualifications and muted in tone that it is difficult to believe that they took them seriously.[81] Balmaceda certainly referred to the dangers of a foreign monopoly in nitrate, but he also emphasized that within Chile's free enterprise economy foreign capital and enterprise undoubtedly had a place.[82] Close analysis of the

[78] *The Chilean Times*, 16 March 1889.

[79] *La Tribuna*, 15 March 1889. The paper added that the speech might also be seen as a warning against those contemplating a new combination of producers.

[80] *El Heraldo*, 18 March 1889. In its issue of 25 March, *El Heraldo* attacked Balmaceda violently, saying that he was quite ignorant of nitrate problems but that 'the superficial [knowledge] he has acquired on this ostentatious trip . . . will merely allow his petulant arrogance to assume that he alone is capable of coping with these delicate questions'.

[81] E.g., *El Mercurio*, 25 March 1889, said that Balmaceda's speech was, perhaps, somewhat contrary to North's ideas for Tarapacá. Cited by Ramírez, *Balmaceda*, p. 94. The paper added, however, that 'even so it would still leave him [North] a vast field to exercise amongst us that honest activity which foreign or Chilean capitalists and industrialists ought to show'.

[82] In his opening remarks, Balmaceda expressed his delight at being at the scene of great developments 'of a spirited cosmopolitanism, which breathes life into hundreds and hundreds of industries, thousands and thousands of enterprises, all of them producing in complete freedom, without anxieties for the rights of

speech as a whole, however, indicates that Balmaceda was, ✓
perhaps deliberately, avoiding specific suggestions, and the
entire discourse was an exercise in studied vagueness.[83] His
attack, if attack it was, was levelled against monopolies of whatever kind, coupled with the hint that if native capital were
willing to enter into competition with foreign capital in the
nitrate industry, the government would see what it could do to
help. But he made no suggestion that if that did not happen, the
government would do anything about foreign capital, and he
reiterated several times his belief in private enterprise as the
basic motor of development. Some contemporaries, indeed,
were disappointed that Balmaceda had not taken the opportunity to go further. *La Epoca*, for example, in two editorials,
urged the government to enlarge its role beyond that of a mere
tax-collector in Tarapacá, and argued that the remaining state
nitrate-fields in the province could be the means to build up a
native nitrate industry to compete with foreigners.[84] Somewhat
later, another newspaper published a long article by a very
knowledgeable correspondent, attacking Balmaceda's government, no less than its predecessor, for its failure to stop Tarapacá being converted into an 'English hacienda . . . a small
part of British India, exploited by a multitude of joint-stock
companies organized outside Chile . . . leaving to the nation a
sovereignty more nominal than real'. The writer regretted that
Balmaceda had committed a 'dreadful error' in not realizing that
the retirement of paper money was far more crucial for the sound
economic development of Chile than his programme of public
works: nevertheless, the President could now do something
significant for the nitrate industry by creating the conditions
for the formation of viable national companies

under Chilean laws, companies whose management, accountability
and majority share-holding would be Chilean, with a prohibition
against shares being transferred to foreigners resident outside Chile,

a development in which the government would play the key
nationals or foreigners, for in this district, as well as outside it, we are all equal
under the sovereignty of our institutions'. *La Tribuna*, 11 March 1889.

[83] Even with regard to the Nitrate Railways question, where the government
had a clear-cut policy already in operation, Balmaceda tempered his remarks with
qualifications.

[84] *La Epoca*, 17 and 19 March 1889.

role, and could, indeed, become a shareholder itself. Finally, the writer urged Balmaceda to think again about his public works programme, and look at what had happened in Peru, where past dissipation of windfall wealth had led to present misery.[85] And in yet another journal, a well-known Chilean politician, Agustín Ross, pointed out, in the light of Balmaceda's speech at Iquique, that it was precisely the government's negligence in failing to support native capital in the nitrate industry which accounted for foreign dominance:

the truth is [he said] that foreign capital, precisely because it is foreign, has more guarantees in Chile. It is regarded with greater respect and even with a certain unjustified fear.

Ross spelled out the facts: the southern nitrate-fields of Taltal and Aguas Blancas, in which much Chilean capital had been invested, not least on the strength of promises of official protection, had been allowed to stagnate simply because production costs in Tarapacá were much lower, and, at the very time that Balmaceda was preparing for his northern journey in February and making his speech in Iquique, the German firm of Vorwerk was acquiring, cheaply, eight *oficinas* in Taltal, and other sales were being negotiated. For Balmaceda to speak of the indolence of Chilean capital in these circumstances was really too much, when the high export tax levied on nitrate shipments from Taltal and Aguas Blancas was ruining the Chilean owners of these deposits.[86]

These comments and criticisms make it abundantly clear that Balmaceda had a very limited understanding of the nitrate industry's problems and that at this stage of his thinking, at any rate, his sole preoccupation was the intimate relationship between nitrate exports and government revenue. The hallmark of his administration was his programme of public works, and his personal prestige was tied up with it. That programme depended on continuing large revenues from export taxes on nitrate, and, if there were any threat to government income, it must lie in the possibility of a producers' combination to restrict output. The producers were few, and they were largely

[85] *El Ferrocarril*, 26 May 1889. The article was signed by Julius y Mayo.
[86] *El Mercurio*, 4 April 1889.

foreign: hence Balmaceda's expressed aversion to monopolies and his hints of support to native capitalists served the same end. Both parts of the speech at Iquique suggested that the government had reserve powers which it might call into play if they were necessary, to create a national buffer against a foreign monopoly of nitrate production, and against a foreign combination to limit output. It could be argued that Balmaceda's vagueness might have been deliberate, since it would encourage speculation—as it did—about his real intentions, and thus induce hesitation among the foreign producers. On the other hand, it is equally possible that Balmaceda was vague simply because, at this point, he himself was not really sure what to do.[87]

Meanwhile, the speech at Iquique served other useful purposes. It showed the province of Tarapacá and its capital, so recently incorporated into the republic, that their President from far-off Santiago was interested in their affairs.[88] It focused national attention on the tour itself, and Balmaceda had undertaken the journey, at least in part, to strengthen his political position.[89] And, lastly, the speech at Iquique set the tone for the rest of the tour of the northern provinces, during which Balmaceda displayed his oratorical gifts in a series of addresses, superbly tailored to particular local audiences, to make the maximum personal and political impact.[90] Throughout, the emphasis was on the great labour of his government in promoting public works, and on many occasions he made specific promises to local audiences that amenities which were lacking would be provided.[91]

During the visit to Tarapacá, Balmaceda and his large entourage travelled into the nitrate *pampa* by means of the

[87] Cf., however, Ramírez, *Balmaceda*, pp. 93–4, which includes the statement that on this visit to the north, Balmaceda's 'central idea was to seek . . . to put a stop to future and greater English expansion in the nitrate region'.

[88] As late as 1887, Iquique had a population one-third non-Chilean. Castle, *Sketch of the City of Iquique*, p. 6.

[89] *El Heraldo* saw the visit almost entirely in this light. See the issue of 25 March 1889.

[90] Cf. Balmaceda's speech at Iquique with speeches he made later at Copiapó and La Serena, in the provinces of Atacama and Coquimbo respectively, reported in *La Tribuna*, 25 March 1889.

[91] *La Tribuna*, 28 March 1889. See also *El Heraldo*, 18 March 1889.

Nitrate Railway, and they were lavishly entertained at two of North's *oficinas*, Primitiva and Jazpampa, and at North's house in the port of Pisagua.[92] Balmaceda's impressions have gone unrecorded, but one reporter expressed the view that he must have been impressed by the modernity of the establishments which could accommodate in comfort a party more than thirty strong.[93] While it would be natural, however, for foreign interests to vie with native Chileans in the reception they offered the head of the nation, Balmaceda was clearly under no obligation to accept their hospitality, and the fact that he did so is, perhaps, further negative evidence that at this time his relations with North were somewhat more cordial than some commentators have suggested.[94]

Balmaceda returned to Santiago, via Valparaiso, on 25 March. He was reported to have been much impressed by what he had seen in his three weeks' tour of the northern regions.[95] But he returned to the capital to the same political situation he had left behind, and to mounting hostility to his public works programme, which became an increasingly easy target for the opposition parties to attack. The strictures on economic and political grounds which had been made against Balmaceda's predecessor for his much smaller programme of public expenditure were now enlarged, and they were fed further by the deepening political crisis and by Balmaceda's own personality. Identifying himself so thoroughly with the progress of Chile, and confident of his own capacity to achieve his objectives, no matter how formidable the obstacles, Balmaceda was a man in a hurry who tended to neglect details in pursuing his grand, and sometimes grandiose, designs. He tended also to override the finer points of law and administrative practice, which seemed to him as mere hindrances to his great plans. And he was most impatient of criticism. Yet criticism there was. The day after he reached Iquique, and appropriately in *El Ferro-carril*, the state railway system was attacked on grounds of

[92] *La Tribuna*, 16 March 1889.

[93] *El Heraldo*, 18 March 1889. Russell, *A Visit to Chile and the Nitrate Fields*, pp. 175 ff., gives an interesting picture of Primitiva and other *oficinas* belonging to North.

[94] E.g., Ramírez, *Balmaceda*, p. 97; Salas Edwards, *Balmaceda y el Parlamentarismo*, i, 154; Hernández, *El salitre*, pp. 128–37.   [95] *The Chilean Times*, 30 March 1889.

faulty construction and the inadequacy of personnel.[96] Another newspaper noted that in his journeys in Tarapacá Balmaceda had used the privately-owned railway lines, and there had been no reports of 'derailments, crashes, breakdowns of engines, etc., weaknesses which only afflict the State railways'.[97] But far worse was to come. In 1888, Balmaceda's government had made a contract with a railway construction company in the United States for it to build over 1,000 kilometres of line in Chile.[98] Apparently, however, the government had accepted the company's tender without due attention, and by early 1889 the company was virtually bankrupt:

The levity and easy manner of His Excellency [complained *El Heraldo*] in weighing the republic down with millions of debt is [now] producing its fruits. The celebrated railway contract, which had neither a solid base nor effective scrutiny, is now seen to be completely disorganised, and the only glimmering light we can see is the damage to Chile.[99]

When the company collapsed, the country was involved in serious loss, and the government was bitterly attacked in Congress.[100] This particular case had considerable repercussions:

in view of the miserable result of the American Syndicate [wrote the manager of Antony Gibbs & Sons in Valparaiso] Congress may throw all sorts of obstacles in the way of any fresh contractors.[101]

And it was largely because of this egregious failure, the British Minister reported later, that 'there exists a strong opinion in Congress and in the country that the State Expenditure is too great and that no new works should be undertaken'.[102]

---

[96] *El Ferrocarril*, 7 March 1889.

[97] *El Mercurio*, 25 March 1889. See also *La Epoca*, 22 March 1889 and *El Ferrocarril*, 23 March 1889 for other examples of concern expressed about the inadequacy of the state railways.

[98] For details, see *Ministro de Industria y Obras Públicas. Antecedentes Relativos al Contrato para la Construcción de los Ferrocarriles en Proyecto* (Santiago, 1888).

[99] *El Heraldo*, 10 March 1889.

[100] See *Boletín de las Sesiones Estraordinarias de la Cámara de Diputados de 1889* (Santiago, 1889), pp. 891–4, 917–33, 939–59, 961–2, 984–1000.

[101] Antony Gibbs, Valparaiso to London, 15 July 1889. Private. AAG, MS. 11,470. Vol. 12.

[102] Kennedy to Lord Salisbury, Santiago, 25 October 1889. F.O. 16/256. No. 3. Commercial.

As time went by, indeed, the Chilean Congress became increasingly critical of the vast public expenditure involved in Balmaceda's programme, and of the lack of care devoted both to estimates and planning. Thus, in 1889, in the Extraordinary Sessions of both chambers, Ministers were subjected to very vigorous questioning, not only on the heads of estimated expenditure, but also on the ways in which congressional approval for them was sought, since members felt that they conformed neither to the laws governing the presentation of estimates nor to the practice the chambers understood.[103] Apart, moreover, from the apparent profligacy of the Balmaceda administration, there were other serious consequences of ill-planned initiatives, on which important sections of the press had much to say.

A considerable part of the public works [programme] [said one newspaper] currently being undertaken by the government is in the hands of unscrupulous men, of contractors and inspectors of work who, far from thinking of carrying out their obligations . . . have no other objective than that of exploiting the Treasury, and enriching themselves with the filthy lucre they get from their disgraceful conduct.[104]

Commenting on the discovery and dismissal of one such person in April 1889, *La Epoca* pointed out that to argue in favour of the Minister of Public Works simply because he was not an accomplice of the man concerned showed just how far standards of public morality had declined.[105]

Yet another cause of concern was the government's system of decision-making

by means of decrees and administrative regulations, arrangements of a permanent kind which really can only have validity by means of laws; and this system . . . is one of the most effective means of putting an end to the republican institutions our forbears gave us.[106]

---

[103] See the *Boletín de las Sesiones Estraordinarias de . . . Diputados, passim,* and the *Boletín . . . de Senadores* (Santiago, 1889), *passim.*

[104] *El Independiente,* 6 April 1889.

[105] *La Epoca,* 5 April 1889. The defence of the Minister had been made by *La Tribuna,* which also asserted that Balmaceda had certain discretionary powers, for example, in promising public works on his visit to the north, which other newspapers had criticized. See the issue of 28 March 1889.

[106] *La Epoca,* 12 April 1889.

This particular comment was made shortly after Balmaceda had returned from his visit to the north, and it was in connection with the establishment by government decree of 1 April of a new department of the *Ministro de Hacienda*—the *Delegación Fiscal de Salitreras*.[107] That this department was a direct consequence of Balmaceda's visit to Tarapacá seems very likely, and its establishment might well have been necessary. But what perturbed *La Epoca*, apart from the fact that the new department had been given a budget of some $100,000, for which no estimates had been approved, was the simple fact that the Chilean Constitution specifically prohibited the creation of public offices, the definition of their functions, and the determination of appropriate salaries, except by means of a law, and in the making of laws Congress was a necessary partner of government.[108]

Many other examples could be cited to indicate a rapidly-growing concern by the organs of Chilean public opinion not only about the enormous cost of Balmaceda's programme, but also about the constitutional implications of much that he did to implement it.[109] And the opposition parties were to grow even more suspicious in the weeks and months which followed Balmaceda's visit to the northern provinces. On the day he returned to Valparaiso, however, Balmaceda had something else to think about, for arrangements had been made for him to receive a visitor immediately on his return. John Thomas North, 'the Nitrate King', was already in Chile, and he had asked for an audience.

The 'Nitrate King' on Progress[110]

North actually announced his intention of visiting Chile early

---

[107] Ramírez, *Balmaceda*, p. 89, summarizes the new department's functions which were largely concerned with the state-owned nitrate and guano fields.

[108] *La Epoca*, 12 April 1889.   [109] Cf. Ramírez, *Balmaceda, passim*.

[110] There are a number of accounts in print of this celebrated visit by North to Chile, often inaccurate in detail and dubious in interpretation. But see particularly, Hernández, *El salitre*, pp. 128–37; Ramírez, *Balmaceda*, pp. 53–9, and Bunster, *Bombardeo de Valparaiso*, pp. 162–75. I have not been able to see one contemporary source used, apparently, by these writers: J. Abel Rosales, *El coronel don Juan Tomás North* (Santiago, 1889), but their citations suggest that it mostly consists of translated extracts from the European press, which I have surveyed.

in December 1888.[111] Between that date and his departure, on
6 February 1889, he took care to see that his preparations were
carried out in a characteristic blaze of publicity. The Bank of
Tarapacá and London was shortly to be launched,[112] and North
had also recently chaired meetings of the Colorado and Primitiva Companies in typically ebullient fashion.[113] It was also
in December that he was introduced to the Prince of Wales by
Lord Randolph Churchill at a dinner given by Baron Alfred
de Rothschild, and it was rumoured that he was soon to be
sponsored for membership of the Carlton Club by the Marquis
of Abergavenny, Lord Randolph Churchill and the Earl of
Kintore, Governor-designate of South Australia.[114] 'No man
in these days', said *The South American Journal*, 'is more talked
about in and out of City circles.'[115] Encouraging news from
Chile, too, came in with the New Year: on 3 January, the
Intendant of Iquique granted some 200 claims of North and his
local partners, including John Dawson, to grounds on the *pampa*
of Pintados for mineral exploitation; North purchased at the
same time the property of a minor nitrate producer near his
own grounds of Buena Ventura, and perhaps best of all, on
5 January, the municipality of Iquique accepted the offer of
the Tarapacá Waterworks Company to supply the town with
drinking water, and referred the competing tender of Carlos
Wüth to the consideration of a committee.[116] That week, however, North was less preoccupied with business than with the
biggest social coup he ever attempted.

On 4 January 1889, over 800 guests, representing, in the
words of one journal, 'the aristocracy, the plutocracy and the
histrionocracy of the kingdom', attended a fancy dress ball
given by Colonel North and his wife at the Hotel Metropole in
Whitehall Place.[117] This glittering occasion attracted a large
number of distinguished people—thirteen peers, including Lord
Randolph Churchill, Lord Dorchester and the Marquis of

---

[111] *The Sidcup and District Times*, 14 December 1888.
[112] See above, pp. 60–62.
[113] *The South American Journal*, 15 December 1888.
[114] *The European Mail*, 27 December 1888.
[115] *The South American Journal*, 22 December 1888.
[116] *The Chilean Times*, 19 January 1889.
[117] *The South American Journal*, 12 January 1889.

Stackpole; fifteen knights, one of the Sheriffs of London, a number of high-ranking officers of the armed forces, and some of the best-known representatives of the City, such as the Barons A. and E. de Rothschild.[118] Apart from the family of North himself, the nitrate interests were much in evidence in the persons of the Harveys, Locketts, Evans, and Graces, as well as many others whose names were associated with the industry.[119] Appropriately, for the dispenser of regal hospitality, North was dressed as Henry VIII, a character well-suited to his portly figure, mutton-chop whiskers and ruddy complexion, while his wife appeared as the Duchesse de Maine. The ballroom and dining-rooms were lavishly decorated with flowers and plants, the principal columns carrying bouquets of white chrysanthemums and lilies bearing a large red 'N' in the centre, while the Volunteer Regiment of Tower Hamlets, resplendent in the uniforms North provided, served as a Guard of Honour and sounded fanfares of trumpets as occasion required.[120] The ball was reckoned to have cost North £10,000, but he probably thought the money well spent: apart from the fact that he simply liked spending money, the occasion showed him in his element—the rich entrepreneur of humble origin playing host to the cream of London society. And the publicity he derived from it was worth a good deal.[121]

There were other things to do besides giving farewell parties. One was to make up the group which was to travel with North to Chile, and here, again, North produced a master-stroke. Quite by chance, on 28 January, he met the celebrated former correspondent of *The Times*, William Howard Russell, at a luncheon party, and promptly invited him and his wife to accompany the Norths and their friends to Chile instead of going to Egypt for the winter, as Russell had intended.[122] Russell's account is worth quoting in full, in view of the

[118] List of Guests with Characters Represented for Col. J. T. & Mrs. North's Fancy Dress Ball at the Hotel Metropole, London, on Friday, 4 January 1889, in the possession of Mrs V. Proctor, to whom I am indebted for this material.

[119] List of Guests, passim. No representatives of the families of Gibbs or Williamson were present, apparently.

[120] The Sunday Times, 6 January 1889.

[121] Cf., however, Ramírez, Balmaceda, p. 54, where press comment is regarded as sarcasm.

[122] Russell, A Visit to Chile and the Nitrate Fields, p. 1.

significance which was attached to his concurrence, both at the time and later:

I was invited to go out that I might see and report what had been done and what was being done, and to examine the works which had transformed the desert of Tarapacá . . . into a centre of commercial enterprise, and which had covered it with animated industry and prosperous life. It had been asserted in certain journals that commercial enterprises in that region were shams—'swindles', indeed, would be the word to use if they were what those organs described them to be—and that a railway, in which the public had invested largely, was 'a tramway ending in a marsh'.[123]

Russell had never been to South America and he was very interested in the proposal, which he accepted, provided that he could rearrange his plans and that his wife, who was prone to sea-sickness, proved, in fact, in the first few days after joining North's vessel at Lisbon, a sufficiently good sailor to continue the voyage.[124] These obstacles were overcome, and the Russells then accompanied North to Chile.

One historian has asserted that Russell 'was persuaded to cancel his plans for a cruise in the Mediterranean by an honorarium of £15,000', and implies that the ex-correspondent went out purely as a propagandist.[125] This view appears to have been accepted also by two other writers, both of whom cite a contemporary Belgian newspaper, which alleged that Russell was to receive 75,000 francs from North for his services as official chronicler of the visit.[126] It is true that some of Russell's friends raised their eyebrows at the news that he was to go out with North, and one of them wrote, amusingly quoting Molière: 'Que diable allait-il faire?'[127] Russell himself,

[123] Russell, ibid., p. 2.

[124] Ibid., pp. 2–4. Arrangements were made, of course, to take the Russells off if necessary.

[125] Hardy, 'British Nitrates and the Balmaceda Revolution', p. 176, note 52. No source is given for this interesting piece of information.

[126] Hernández, El salitre, p. 129; Ramírez, Balmaceda, p. 54. The paper was L'Independence Belge of Brussels, 14 February 1889, which Ramírez certainly and Hernández probably got from Abel Rosales, El Coronel Juan Tomás North. This is a good illustration of the acceptance of unproved assertion, repeated so often that it eventually passes for truth.

[127] J. B. Atkins, The Life of Sir William Howard Russell (2 vols., London, 1911), ii, 326. The original letter may be found among Russell's papers. London, Printing House Square, Archives of The Times.

however, only agreed to go on the express condition that anything he subsequently wrote would be his own opinion,[128] and
he made this quite clear in a prefatory note to his book.[129] As to
the sums he was alleged to have received, there is no source
known which could verify them, any more than the figure of
£3,000 quoted by another contemporary journal can be veri-
fied.[130] But, of course, in common with the rest of the party, the
expenses of Russell and his wife were met by their host on the
voyage.[131]

Two other journalists accompanied North to Chile. One, a
fellow-director of the Nitrate Railways Company, was Melton
R. Pryor, staff-artist of the *Illustrated News*.[132] The other
was Montague Vizetelly of *The Financial Times*.[133] The rest of
the party consisted of North's daughter, Emma, and her
friend, Miss Wentworth Smith; North's secretary, Arthur de
Courcy Brewer; a certain Captain Brough, a Mr J. M. Power,
an engineer, and a Mr Beauclerk.[134] In addition, Ernest
Spencer, M.P., chairman of the Tarapacá Nitrate Company,
and his wife, who were also visiting Chile at the same time,
were introduced to North at Liverpool by Henry Pirbright,
later Baron de Worms, Under-Secretary of State for the
Colonies, and promptly invited to accompany the party.[135]

North's other preparations concerned his public relations in
Chile, where he wished to show that the 'Nitrate King' was
just as capable of generosity abroad as he was at home. The

[128] Atkins, loc. cit.

[129] Russell, op. cit., p. iv.

[130] *The South American Journal*, 9 February 1889.

[131] North subsequently said at a meeting of the Liverpool Nitrate Company that
'He had taken Dr. Russell [to Chile] at his own cost. It had cost him £20,000 to
take people with him.' *The South American Journal*, 21 December 1889. If this
figure may be taken at face value, and given the size of North's party, Russell's
honorarium was probably much nearer £3,000 than £15,000.

[132] Pryor was responsible for the fine engravings which adorn Russell's book, *A
Visit to Chile and the Nitrate Fields*. The pictures, however, were not drawn from life
but were based on a collection of photographs taken during the visit, and now in
the possession of Mrs V. Proctor.

[133] Vizetelly's name occurs in a number of English and Chilean press reports but,
curiously enough, is not included in Russell's list of the party. Russell, op. cit., p. 5.

[134] Ibid. Russell also omitted Brewer from his list, but included four people
picked up at Lisbon, a Mr and Miss Gilling and Messrs Cook and Blain, 'two
young gentlemen who were travelling for pleasure and improvement'.

[135] *The South American Journal*, 16 February 1889. Russell, loc. cit.

gifts he intended to present in Chile were very well-chosen. First, there was the capstan of the Chilean warship *Esmeralda*, which had been salvaged from the wreck off Iquique after the War of the Pacific: North had it mounted as a shield, with plaques in silver relief-work depicting scenes of the heroic combat against the Peruvian ironclads. Around the brass top of the capstan ran a silver border with raised stars, bearing the names of those who died in the battle, the national heroes' names—Prat, Uribe, Serrano, Sánchez, Wilson, Fernández, Zegers, Riquelme and Hurtado—being inscribed on another shield below the capstan, supported by two figures—'Peace' and 'Prosperity'.[136] He also bought two fine Cleveland horses from a well-known English stud for presentation to the Chilean state.[137] Finally, for the municipality of Iquique, he had bought a new fire-engine, a replacement for one he had provided at the end of 1887, but which had been lost in a shipwreck.[138] The new machine was named 'Balmaceda', and bore, in addition to that inscription, a bronze plaque with the words: 'Presented to the town of Iquique by Col. J. T. North on the coming of age of his son Harry North, Dec. 26th 1887'.[139]

One or two other matters had to be attended to before North's departure. On 25 January 1889, he was presented with the Honorary Freedom of the City of Leeds, and this must have been an event of great pleasure and pride, the local boy who had made good returning to receive his native's city highest honour.[140] The other matters were less agreeable, however, for they touched directly on North's interests. In mid-January, the prospectuses of two new nitrate companies, the Lautaro and the

[136] Russell, op. cit., pp. 83-4.

[137] Another myth surrounds these horses. It has been alleged that they were intended as a *personal* present for Balmaceda, but that he refused them, and asked that they be given to the Quinta Normal, the Agricultural Institution. Hernández, *El salitre*, p. 135; Hardy, 'British Nitrates . . .', p. 178; Ramírez, *Balmaceda*, p. 55. This is, however, complete fabrication. On the day after North arrived in Santiago, and six days before Balmaceda returned from the north, there was a report in a Chilean newspaper on the horses with North had brought 'to present to the Quinta de Agricultura'. *El Ferrocarril*, 20 March 1889. Cf. Russell, op. cit., p. 84.

[138] *El Ferrocarril*, 20 March 1889.

[139] Ibid., 20 April 1889. Cited also by Ramírez, *Balmaceda*, p. 56.

[140] See *The South American Journal*, 26 January 1889. The illuminated address presented to North on this occasion is preserved with the Records of Leeds Corporation at Leeds Town Hall.

Julia, were presented to the public.[141] The Lautaro Nitrate Company was launched by a group headed by F. H. Evans, M.P., and W. MacAndrew, to work the nitrate-grounds of Lautaro, Santa Catalina and Bella Vista in the Taltal region, south of the Tarapacá deposits, at a capitalization figure of £300,000 in 30,000 shares of £10 each.[142] The Julia Nitrate Company was formed by a group of entrepreneurs whose names had not hitherto figured in the formation of nitrate companies, with the solitary exception of the Taltal Nitrate Company, formed in 1888.[143] The Julia called for a capital of £150,000 in 30,000 shares of £5 each, to work nitrate-grounds in Taltal also.[144] The Tarapacá Nitrate Company, so adversely discussed by *The Economist*,[145] was formed at the same time.

From North's point of view, the development of the Taltal grounds was a serious matter since, if brought to full productive capacity, they might well compete with Tarapacá, over which he exercised, particularly through the Nitrate Railway, a fairly dominant control. He had, therefore, to warn the public off investing in these new concerns, and the occasion he chose was a banquet given in his honour by his Liverpool friends at the Adelphi Hotel on the very eve of his departure. His tactics were the ones he had employed before over the Tarapacá water-supply question:[146] they consisted in lauding his own concerns, founded by a professional in nitrate matters, and running down those of others who were clearly amateurs in the business. He was going to Chile, he said, to look after his own, and his audience's, interests; he would not be satisfied with his Primitiva Company unless it paid dividends in 1889 'cent by cent', and he intended to make the Bank of Tarapacá and London the chief bank on the west coast of South America. As for the

---

[141] *The Economist*, 12 January 1889. *The South American Journal*, same date.

[142] Data from *Burdetts Official Intelligence*, viii (1890), pp. 826–7. For Evans and MacAndrew, see above, p. 35.

[143] *Burdetts Official Intelligence*, loc. cit., p. 823, lists the directors of the Julia Nitrate Company. Cf. vol. vii (1889), p. 823, also for the directors of the Taltal Company. The two names which occur in both lists are those of H. W. Carter and J. W. Anderson. One of the directors of the Taltal Company was J. H. Thomas, British Vice-Consul in Santiago.

[144] *Burdetts Official Intelligence*, viii, pp. 822–3.

[145] See above, p. 67, n. 5.

[146] See above, pp. 57–8.

new companies, he added, 'if you put money in Taltal, you will not see a single cent'.[147] Robert Harvey, who was also present, endorsed this opinion, and *The South American Journal* got the point:

Taltal has not yet shown that it can do anything in the earning of dividends, and until it does it will be wise for investors to heed the warning of experienced men such as Colonel North, as a nitrate maker, and Mr. Harvey, who was formerly a Government inspector of nitrate works.[148]

On the following day, North's party embarked on the S.S. *Galicia*, bound for Chile, and thus missed by a week the comments of another contemporary which were in a very different vein:

By this time [said *The Financial News*] Colonel North will be on the bosom of the broad Atlantic, thinking out his beneficent plans for the benefit of the bankers, brokers and ballet girls who worship him as their 'Nitrate King'... In his farewell speech at Liverpool... by a single wave of his magic wand over the province of Tarapacá, he was to bring forth a new galaxy of Primitivas, Liverpools and Colorados. With a frown from his Jove-like countenance, Taltal was to be cast into Egyptian darkness, and the 'pessimists' of the Financial News were to be extinguished for ever...

While ... we wish the Colonel every success ... we cannot pretend to be quite so sanguine as his beefeaters are about ... results... The Chilians may not be so utterly overwhelmed ... as they are expected to be when the Nitrate Jupiter lands among them. The flash of his Olympian eye and the phosphoric gleam of his sandy whiskers may not blast them before they have had time to bid him welcome ...

In fact, our recent study of the Chilian press hardly leads us to suppose that the maudlin enthusiasm displayed at Liverpool will be very warmly reciprocated at the other end ... Chilian editors, both English and Spanish, have yet a great deal to learn in North worship ... from their narrow, bigoted point of view he is only a bloated monopolist, a lucky speculator, a foreign interloper revelling in the wealth of Chili![149]

[147] *The South American Journal*, 9 February 1889.

[148] The *Journal*'s editorial of the same date, however, suggested that with regard to Taltal 'with the best intentions, his opinions may be affected by his interests', and North had, perhaps, been somewhat indiscreet.

[149] *The Financial News*, 11 February 1889.

This was certainly hyperbole: while there had been comments in Chilean newspapers on the possible dangers of the
growth of British interests in Tarapacá in general, and sometimes of North's in particular, most of them were remarkably
muted, and it was widely recognized that Chilean failure to
invest there was partly responsible for the dominance of British
enterprise.[150] Visitors to Chile also commented on the fact
that Chileans did not seem anxious to exploit the country's
natural resources, preferring to leave that task to foreigners.[151]
And, so far as nitrates were concerned, the ease with which
foreign capital acquired Chilean-owned *salitreras* after the War
of the Pacific is further evidence of this fact.[152] Vague Chilean
criticisms of foreign control over nitrates in the late 1880s
turned less on the actual fact of ownership than on the dawning
realization that over half the state revenue might be subject to
foreign manipulation, especially of a monopolistic kind. But
this was still a minor fear of what could happen rather than the
consciousness of a positive threat when North made his visit,
which was reported in terms of genuine interest, not critical
rancour.[153]

Before his departure, North obtained from the Commercial
Department of the Foreign Office a letter of introduction to
Consul-General Newman at Valparaiso: this informed Newman that North would be in Chile 'on business connected with
the Nitrate Mines in which he is interested' and requested such
assistance as could properly be given.[154] But North also had

[150] See above, p. 81, n. 69.
[151] E.g. Russell, *A Visit to Chile and the Nitrate Fields*, p. 313, and F. Gautier,
Chili et Bolivie: Etude Economique et Minère (Paris, 1906), p. 99.
[152] See above, p. 86.
[153] *La Epoca*, 24 March 1889, said of North: 'Men of his stature honour not only
the country to which they belong, but also any other in which their powerful
genius unfolds.' This paper, it should be noted, was a keen supporter of Balmaceda's alleged ideas to support native capital in nitrates. See also *The Chilean Times*,
16 and 23 February 1889, for similar eulogies of North's contribution to Chilean
development.
[154] Commercial Department of the Foreign Office to Newman at Valparaiso,
26 January 1889. F.O. 16/256. Drafts. No. 1. Commercial. The back of this draft
bears a note in the hand of the Permanent Under-Secretary of State, Sir Thomas
Sanderson: 'Colonel North being engaged in various speculations, this does not
seem a case for the ordinary social letter of introduction but should be dealt with
by the Commercial Dept.' Ramírez, *Balmaceda*, p. 55, sees this letter as clear
evidence of North's importance in England, but it was, of course, quite normal

other interests in Chile he was anxious to inspect, and, consequently, the *Galicia* made its landfall in Chile at Coronel in the
south, on 16 March, to enable the party to investigate progress on the Arauco railway and to see the adjacent coalfields.[155]
In the three days which were spent here, North established the
pattern of activity he was to follow throughout his visit to
Chile, a masterly exercise in public relations in which his
reputation for philanthropy, bonhomie and sound business
sense would be shown to be perfectly true. He gave £100 to the
crew of the *Galicia* on taking leave of them, and performed
other newsworthy acts of benevolence in the towns of Coronel,
Lota and Concepción; he invited the local press to lunch, and
flattered both their local pride and national sentiment; and he
wined and dined many English friends who were working in
the region and who had been his old colleagues in the north a
quarter of a century before.[156] Then, on 19 March, he and
his party left Talcahuano by train for Santiago, to be met at
the station by many Chilean friends and escorted to the Hotel
Oddo, which was to be his residence in the capital.[157]

During his stay in Santiago, North constantly figured in the
national press. Much of his time was taken up by entertaining
and being entertained. A constant stream of visitors called at
his hotel, to be given champagne and his opinions; dinner-
parties were arranged in his honour, visits made to local
attractions such as the Quinta Normal and the celebrated *fundo*
of Macul, owned by the millionaire Cousiño family; and
numerous press conferences gave North ample opportunity to
display both his generous hospitality and his ideas on Chilean
development.[158] At the first of these in a talk he gave after lunch
at his hotel on the day after his arrival, North said that he was
visiting Chile to make the country better known in Europe, and

practice to provide such letters for any British visitor to a foreign country, and
Ernest Spencer also received one. Commercial Department to Newman, 31
January 1889. Loc. cit., No. 3. Commercial.

[155] Russell, *A Visit to Chile and the Nitrate Fields*, pp. 46–66.

[156] *El Ferrocarril*, 20 March 1889, gives a detailed account, much of it taken from
El Heraldo of Concepción, 16 March 1889.

[157] *El Ferrocarril*, loc. cit. Russell, however, went by boat to Valparaiso. Op. cit.,
p. 59.

[158] Data from *El Ferrocarril*, *El Mercurio*, *El Heraldo* and *The Chilean Times*.

to look at his interests in both nitrates and coal.[159] He also expressed the view that a railway line to link Tarapacá with central Chile—a project mooted by Balmaceda on his current visit to the north—would not really benefit the province: what was needed was the extension of the existing line in Tarapacá to the *oficinas* further south. Moreover, he had it in mind, if the nitrate industry continued to develop, to promote a steamship line, under the Chilean flag, between Chile and Europe: the capital would be £1,500,000, half to be raised in Chile and half in England, and he was already working with Rothschilds on the scheme.[160]

On 21 March, North interrupted his programme in Santiago to spend a few days in Valparaiso. Balmaceda was due to return there from the north on 25 March, and would then be going to the presidential vacation residence at the nearby resort of Viña del Mar: North would, therefore, be conveniently at hand if an interview could be arranged and, meanwhile, he could be just as well occupied in Valparaiso as in Santiago with the same kind of activities as before. On the 22nd he gave a lunch for the Fourth Estate and other friends at the Hotel de France in Valparaiso, at which he made a well-received speech on Anglo-Chilean friendship. Russell and Pryor also spoke, emphasizing that anything they might write for their respective British newspapers on the visit would be the result of personal observation and judgment alone.[161] The following day, North gave an interview to the editors of the local newspaper, *El Heraldo*, during which he recounted his early history in Chile and his services to the country in the War of the Pacific.[162] Asked about his steamship project, he repeated his previous remarks, adding, however, that the project had the more significance for Chile in that it could aid cheap immigration to the country. On nitrates, he thought that the world market was still in its infancy, and he had himself spent £20,000 in recent years on advertising the fertilizer in Europe. He did not believe that a monopoly of production was now possible: that could have happened when only eight or nine people controlled the industry and the Nitrate Railway, but now there

[159] *El Ferrocarril*, 21 March 1889.   [160] Ibid.
[161] Ibid., 23 March 1889.   [162] *El Heraldo*, 25 March 1889.

were thousands of stockholders and hundreds of directors of companies, operating in complete freedom.[163] He answered further questions about rumours of his intention to start a bank in Santiago—which he denied—and stressed throughout his great friendship for Chile, his absolute unwillingness to do anything which might harm her interests, and his constant readiness to put his personal fortune behind any worthwhile national enterprise for which his aid might be sought. That same weekend North captained his own cricket team against a local side, losing the match but gaining further favourable publicity.[164]

'Public attention', it was reported on 23 March, 'is divided just now between the progress of the President and his party, and the arrival of Colonel North and his party.'[165] That the two should meet was regarded as inevitable, and it was well known that North wished to see Balmaceda for more than reasons of courtesy. Russell later put the matter succinctly:

It was known that Colonel North had come from Europe to solidify and extend interests, in respect of any increase of which President Balmaceda's programme, as reported, might be taken as adverse. It was not known how far the reports of the President's discourses were correct, but it might be inferred that they were not all accurate, because he had already found it necessary to make a formal correction of, and to explain away, one important passage which had caused serious uneasiness.[166]

North, no doubt, wished to find out for himself, if he could, what the President had meant by his recent speeches, but there were also more specific matters on his mind at that time. *The Chilean Times* understood that North's main objective in coming to Chile was 'to obtain a concession for a railway from Lagunas to connect the Patillos district with Iquique', though the paper thought he was unlikely to get it.[167] More important, however,

---

[163] This, of course, was disingenuous, at least so far as the Boards of North's own companies were concerned. There, his dominance was complete. Cf. above, p. 42, and below, pp. 108–9.

[164] *La Tribuna*, 26 March 1889; *El Ferrocarril*, 27 March 1889.

[165] *The Chilean Times*, 23 March 1889.

[166] Russell, *A Visit to Chile and the Nitrate Fields*, p. 81. What the 'formal correction' was I have not been able to discover.

[167] *The Chilean Times*, loc. cit.

was the unresolved question of North's recent purchase from the Delano group of the grounds of Lagunas themselves, a transaction to which the Chilean government had not yet given its agreement.[168] The issue of Lagunas, indeed, had recently come up again: when North purchased the grounds in September 1888, the agreement stipulated a payment of £30,000 on account and the balance of £90,000 to be paid by 11 March 1889, but between these two dates the government had contested Delano's title to the *salitreras* which it claimed for itself.[169] North, therefore, had instructed his Chilean lawyers to desist from completing the transaction and to appeal to the Chilean courts to declare that this was in order, in view of the uncertainty of his position, but the Delano group insisted that if the balance of the purchase price was not paid by the due date the entire contract should be nullified.[170] The case was still before the courts when the first meeting between Balmaceda and North took place on 25 March 1889.

On this visit to Balmaceda, at the house at which he was then staying at Viña del Mar, North was accompanied by Ernest Spencer, John Dawson, William Howard Russell, George Hicks—the manager of the Arauco Company—Captain Brewer, and Consul-General Newman.[171] They were escorted from Valparaiso by a senior aide-de-camp of the President, General Valdivieso, and Dawson acted as interpreter during the hour-long interview with Balmaceda. According to Russell,

the President declared that he was desirous of giving every facility to the introduction of foreign capital in developing the resources of the country, and the gist of the interview was that he had not the smallest intention of making war on vested interests. He was especially full of praise for the Nitrate Railway . . . and he said 'he considered it a complete model of good management and organization'.[172]

---

[168] See above, pp. 52-4.   [169] *El Ferrocarril*, loc. cit.
[170] *El Ferrocarril*, 27 March 1889.
[171] Ibid. Although Newman probably accompanied the party as an official duty, he may well have had mixed feelings about it, since, in a recent commercial transaction with Dawson, he felt that he had been cheated. F. H. James to Dawson at Iquique, Valparaiso, 19 January 1889. Dawson File, BOLSA Archive.
[172] Russell, *A Visit to Chile*, p. 82. North, apparently, never learned to speak Spanish.

Since some historians have taken the view that North's meetings
with Balamaceda in 1889 were very far from cordial, and that
North, indeed, was most disappointed with them,[173] it is interesting to note contemporary press opinions of this first meeting,
which mostly agree with Russell. *El Ferrocarril* reported that
Balmaceda's reception of North and his party was very cordial
indeed, and that the President referred to his recent visit to the
north where he had himself seen something of the very important interests represented by the distinguished British industrialist, adding that Chile would welcome foreign capital and the
support of enterprising men like Colonel North.[174] Other newspapers, including *La Tribuna*, noted for its Balmacedist views,
carried similar reports of the great cordiality with which the
meeting was conducted, and of North's satisfaction at his
reception by the President.[175]

In the absence of other evidence, it must remain a moot
point whether Balmaceda's affability on this occasion con-
cealed thoughts he was not disposed to reveal. This was, after
all, a social occasion, and the President was a man of great
charm. North, at any rate, continued to enjoy himself: on the
evening of 26 March, he was the guest of honour at a mag-
nificent ball given by the British community in Valparaiso,[176]
and three days later it was reported that a Chilean composer
had written a waltz for the piano entitled, and dedicated to,
'the Nitrate King'.[177] Back in Santiago towards the end of the
month, North continued to give the Chilean press plenty of
copy, as he and his entourage continued the round of social
visits, press conferences, excursions to local places of interest,
and banquets offered by prominent Chileans.[178] During this
time, at the President's invitation, he met Balmaceda again, on
29 March, probably at the Moneda, the presidential palace,

[173] E.g., Hernández, *El salitre*, p. 135; Hardy, 'British Nitrates', p. 178; Ramírez,
Balmaceda, p. 55.

[174] *El Ferrocarril*, 27 March 1889.

[175] *La Tribuna*, 27 March 1889. *El Heraldo*, 26 March 1889. Cf. Russell, op. cit.,
p. 82. 'Colonel North was very much gratified by the assurances of President
Balmaceda, and in view of the interpretation which had been placed on the
speeches [of Balmaceda] to which I have alluded, the interview was, in fact, most
satisfactory to him.'   [176] *El Ferrocarril*, 27 March 1889.

[177] Ibid., 29 March 1889.

[178] Russell, *A Visit to Chile*, pp. 90-127, *passim*, gives a good account.

but on this occasion the conversation was not confined to mere generalities.

Senor Balmaceda [Russell noted in his diary] thinks that the property which Colonel North has bought from a Chilian gentleman—whose right to sell it is disputed by the government—is worth very much more than it has been arranged to pay for it. At the same time he is very anxious to encourage foreign capitalists to push forward Chilian railways.[179]

Curiously enough, this meeting went unrecorded by the Chilean press, and Russell was tantalizingly brief, but it seems clear that the property to which he was referring was the Lagunas nitrate-field.[180] And his apparent *non sequitur* relating to railways suggests that Balmaceda, while saying that North was getting too much of a bargain in Lagunas, was anxious to avoid giving any impression of being generally anti-foreign in economic matters.[181]

North and Balmaceda had one more meeting before North proceeded on his travels to the north of Chile on 1 May. Again, Russell is the only witness, but by his account this meeting, probably in mid-April, was a formal occasion to mark the presentation by North of the shield made from the capstan of the *Esmeralda* and of the two pedigree horses he had brought for the State Agricultural Institution.[182] North divided his time between Santiago and Valparaiso during the month of April, offering and receiving still more lavish hospitality, before leaving for Iquique on 1 May.[183] He probably left Santiago in quite good humour, for if the affair of the Lagunas nitrate-field and the related issue of the Patillos railway remained unsettled, at least one important matter had recently come to a satisfactory conclusion. On 30 April, the Chilean government had finally recognized the legal existence of the Bank of

[179] Ibid., pp. 90–1.

[180] Reference has already been made to allegations that Russell was a mere propagandist for North. Above, pp. 93–5. His report of this particular incident, however, and, indeed, his writing on North's interests in Chile in general suggest that, if he *was* a propagandist, he was very badly briefed.

[181] For further discussion of Balmaceda's attitude to foreign capital and interests, including North's, see below, pp. 147ff.

[182] Russell, op. cit., p. 120. There is some confusion in Russell's dates. Twice he refers to 20 March when he clearly means 20 April. Loc. cit. and p. 114.

[183] Russell, *A Visit to Chile*, p. 138.

Tarapacá and London, by accepting its manager, John Dawson, as the agent in Chile of this English enterprise.[184] The other affairs could wait, though North also left his chief legal adviser in Chile, Julio Zegers, with instructions to make a financial offer to the Chilean government for its claim on the Patillos railway line.[185]

The ship carrying North and his party from Valparaiso reached Iquique on 7 May, to be met by most of the sizeable English colony and a large number of Chileans 'who intended to give a great reception to the man who had done so much for Iquique . . .'[186] The next month was spent in precisely similar activities to those which had occupied North in Santiago and Valparaiso, though trips on the Nitrate Railway into the Atacama desert to visit the various *oficinas* now took the place of visits to rich *fundos* in the fertile Central Valley. But dinners and dances formed no less a part of North's programme in these barren regions than they had in the cities further south.[187] The chief ceremony performed by North in what many regarded as *his* capital was the presentation to the municipal fire-brigade of the new engine he had brought from England but finally, on 7 June 1889, North took leave of his kingdom for the last time, returning to London by way of Panama and New York. What his grand tour had accomplished, few could then say:[188] but in his long absence abroad, things had been happening at home which boded no good for the realms of 'the Nitrate King'.

---

[184] *El Mercurio*, Valparaiso, 9 May 1889. Citing *La Libertad Electoral*. Cf. Joslin, *A Century of Banking*, p. 180.

[185] *El Ferrocarril*, 2 October 1898. The paper printed a long letter from Julio Zegers giving this information. For the occasion of the correspondence, see below, pp. 246-9.

[186] Russell, op. cit., p. 138.

[187] Ibid., pp. 138-257, gives an exhaustive account. Russell (p. 140) says: 'I have not thought it necessary to give particular accounts of the hospitalities and festivities which were inaugurated at Coronel, continued at Valparaiso, at Viña del Mar, at Santiago and at Iquique, and which did not come to an end till the party left Callao for Panama on their way home . . . I think my readers will not care to read of the gaieties of people they do not know, or to study the menus of dinners at which they did not assist.' Here, I follow Russell's example.

[188] Even before North left Santiago, however, two newspapers, *La Epoca* and *La Tribuna*, both on 29 April 1889, published the same paragraph to the effect that North's negotiations had not turned out well for him, and that, with regard to the Chilean government, North had found 'the door closed'.

IV

1890, THE YEAR OF CRISIS

Nitrates and North in 1890

One of North's reasons for visiting Chile in the spring of 1889 had been to bolster confidence among investors in his own promotions at a time when nitrate prices were beginning to fall in an overstocked world market. As it happened, however, his absence from England had quite the opposite effect since it was primarily his own personality which sustained the expectations of investors. 'During the past few weeks', reported *The Economist* towards the end of March, 'there has been a very heavy fall in the prices of nearly all nitrate shares, especially of those carrying on business in Tarapacá, with which Colonel North is identified.'[1] A few weeks later, the journal published a long letter from 'a Nitrate Merchant' which was even more to the point, declaring that when shareholders realized how

prices were forced up last autumn in order to facilitate the floating of the companies, and that a much larger quantity of nitrate has been shipped than can be consumed this season, causing prices to drop enormously, they will gladly realise their shares at the comparatively high quotations ruling, before the inevitable and complete collapse overtakes nitrates, as it came in . . . every other artificially inspired speculation.[2]

Uncertainty continued to grow as other newspapers expressed similar views, *The Financial News* in particular taking gleeful advantage of events to pursue its personal vendetta against North:

If nitrate shares [the paper said] have made any progress during the five weeks in which he has been cut off from all communication with them, it has been crab-like backwards. . . Colonel North, when he learns how the market has gone in his absence, will very probably cable over . . . some of the most volcanic English that the Chilean telegraphic operators can be induced to accept.[3]

[1] *The Economist*, 23 March 1889. [2] Ibid., 4 May 1889.
[3] *The Financial News*, 14 March 1889.

Private opinions echoed public pronouncements on the state of the nitrate market in the spring and summer of 1889. 'I look', wrote Stephen Williamson to his manager at Valparaiso in February, 'with great disquiet and apprehension *for the share-holders* on what is being done',[4] and a few weeks later he indicated what his own firm, at any rate, should do in the deteriorating situation:

My fear [he wrote] is that supply is to overpass demand and that stocks will accumulate. Directly that happens farewell to profit! In the meantime, we must act cautiously and not allow cargoes to accumulate in our hands. So far as I can forecast it may be dangerous to be holding back cargoes this autumn . . .[5]

Informed observers, such as Stephen Williamson, well knew that the basic problems of the nitrate industry lay outside North's control, though the alarming fluctuations of share prices in North's own companies—by far the largest number quoted on the Stock Exchange—were clearly affected by North's own movements.

It is seldom [wrote *The Economist* in August 1889] that the movements of one individual have such important consequences as the goings and comings of Colonel North have with regard to the stocks which form what it is the fashion to call the nitrate group. . . When the 'Nitrate King' went to Chili, in the early part of the year, the market lost its buoyancy at once; prices fell away rapidly, and despite reassuring statements . . . they continued to decline, until it was announced that the leader of the market was on the point of returning. . . Then there was a slight recovery, but it was not until Colonel North actually reached our shores that anything like strength was restored to the market . . .[6]

And it is indicative of North's dominance of the nitrate interests that his supporters in the commercial press, while recognizing the underlying market forces which depressed prices, and therefore profits, continually urged investors not to panic while he was away but to have confidence both in his judgement of the

[4] Stephen Williamson to W. R. Henderson, Liverpool, 21 February 1889. Balfour Williamson Papers. Letter Book No. 3. Copy. Letter No. 118. His underlining reproduced as italic.

[5] Same to same, Liverpool, 18 April 1889, in ibid., Letter No. 134.

[6] *The Economist*, 3 August 1889.

situation and his ability to control it.[7] Control it, in fact, he could not, but manipulate it he did: from the date of his return to England in July, North worked very hard to revive the waning confidence of investors, and he enjoyed a measure of success, since share prices in his own companies, though fluctuating like the rest, did not fall so far as others in the months that followed.[8] His favourite device was to offer stock-holders a fixed percentage return 'if he were allowed to take the balance of the profit accruing upon their shares', a gesture of such confidence that share values generally rose whenever he made it.[9] But it was a constant battle, in that summer of 1889, and it required his unwavering attention. When he made a short business trip to Paris and Brussels in September, prices declined immediately and only recovered on his return.[10] A sudden illness in October depressed the stock of his Primitiva Company so drastically that it was feared the company might collapse altogether, but North's recovery enabled Primitiva to survive.[11] Its prospects were helped by an inspired rumour of a forthcoming dividend of 100 per cent, though this, in fact, was false.[12] There were, however, limits even to North's ingenuity, and by the autumn of 1889 the fundamental weakness of the world market in nitrates could no longer be disguised.

During 1889, many of the *oficinas* in Tarapacá which belonged to the new companies floated by North and others in the previous two years reached their full productive capacity. But, while the market expanded, it did not do so sufficiently to absorb the increased production, and stockpiling ensued: by September 1889 it was estimated that stocks of nitrate held in Europe—the major market—for use in the spring of 1890 were already 200,000 tons more than the total amount available in the corresponding period for the previous year.[13] Moreover, by the beginning of November the total quantity afloat from Chile to Europe stood at 410,000 tons, compared with 267,000

[7] See, for example, *The South American Journal*, 29 June, 27 July, 7 September 1889.
[8] *The South American Journal*, 14 September 1889.
[9] *The Economist*, 3 August 1889.
[10] *The South American Journal*, 5 October 1889.   [11] Ibid., 19 October 1889.
[12] Ibid.
[13] Letter in *The Economist* from 'A Nitrate Broker', 14 September 1889.

tons for the same period in 1888. The spot price of nitrate at
Liverpool, the major import point, had been over ten shillings
a hundredweight in October 1888 but had fallen to eight
shillings and fourpence by October 1889.[14] The wide fluctuations in share values of the nitrate companies in the summer and
autumn of 1889 were the natural response to a state of affairs
which was undeniably bad on statistical evidence, and likely to
get worse unless extraordinary measures could be taken to
bring nitrate production more realistically in line with consumption. What had been done before was mooted once again
—the formation of a producers' combination to restrict the
output of nitrate until equilibrium of supply and demand was
restored.[15]

But the times had changed, as a correspondent of *The
Economist* pointed out. The Chilean government, he said, could
not force any producer to work at a loss, 'but, on the other
hand, it will assuredly checkmate any move (whether combined diminution of output or temporary stoppage of works)
calculated to reduce the revenue from export duty'.[16] In 1888,
that revenue had amounted to over 40 per cent of Chilean
government income,[17] and was, in effect, a large part of the
means whereby President Balmaceda hoped to pursue his
domestic policy of expanding public works.[18] It was very unlikely that he would stand idly by while foreigners took the lead
in promoting policies which would have the effect of jeopardizing his own domestic programme.

There was a further complication. While the British-owned
companies operating in the nitrate regions accounted for well
over half of total nitrate production, and while North himself
was the most significant personality concerned, there were
other British companies involved whose directors might not
necessarily see eye-to-eye with the 'Nitrate King', and there
were foreign companies, too, to be taken into account. Production costs of the new British companies with their up-to-date
machinery were somewhat lower than those of many others,

[14] *The Economist*, 9 November 1889.
[15] See above, pp. 30–31, and also J. R. Brown, 'Nitrate Crises', op. cit., p. 234.
[16] *The Economist*, 23 November 1889. The correspondent was a Mr A. Nicholson.
[17] Hernández, *El salitre*, p. 177.
[18] See above, pp. 43–5, 71.

and the combination which lasted from 1884 to 1886, in similar world market conditions, had collapsed in part because low-cost producers insisted on preferential rights in the allocation of production quotas.[19] Similar difficulties might well arise in the attempt to form a new combination.[20] Meanwhile, however, something had to be done while negotiations for a new combination got under way, and late in November 1889, after a meeting of representatives of the leading London companies at North's offices, it was resolved to suspend the working of all their *oficinas* in Tarapacá for a period of one month, after which, on the resumption of production, the monthly output was not to exceed the output for November 1889 and no producer was to sell nitrate at a lower price than £9 a ton.[21] By the year's end, however, this agreement had not been implemented, and nitrate shares moved deeper into the doldrums with the news that dividends in North's companies would henceforth be paid half-yearly and not quarterly as hitherto.[22] And it was not only the nitrate industry itself which gave serious cause for concern: North's prize possession in Tarapacá, the Nitrate Railway, was also seriously threatened by events in Chile in the autumn of 1889.

It will be recalled that the Chilean government's cancellation of the monopoly privileges of the Nitrate Railways Company in Tarapacá had been challenged by the Company in the courts, and that, early in 1888, the government had referred its dispute on the matter with the judiciary to the Council of State.[23] Throughout the period of North's visit to Chile in 1889, the issue lay with the Council, and it was not, indeed, until September that the Council finally gave its opinion. On 13 September, with the dissentient opinion of Judge Eulogio Altamirano, the Council decided that an ordinary court of law had no jurisdiction over the Company's petition.[24] Altamirano,

---

[19] See above, p. 34, and also Brown, 'Nitrate Crises', op. cit., pp. 232–4.
[20] As was suggested by a correspondent of *The Economist*, 23 November 1889.
[21] *The South American Journal*, 30 November 1889.
[22] Ibid., 21 December 1889.
[23] See above, pp. 50–55.
[24] *Translation of the Decision of the Council of State dated 13 September 1889* (Canterbury, 1889), *passim*. Pamphlet printed for the Nitrate Railways Company encl. in F.O. 16/286.

for his part, claimed that, though the government might annul a contract, any objection on the part of the concessionaire automatically made the matter contentious and, therefore, a question for the judiciary.[25]

This development added to the complications of the Nitrate Railways question which, though basically economic in character, was now invested with a constitutional significance. Whereas the aim of North's company was to reassert the validity of its concessions in order to continue the great economic benefits it derived from them, the interests of the Chilean government, with Balmaceda as president, were both economic and constitutional. It was seeking to destroy a transport monopoly which it believed charged excessive tariffs on nitrate shipments, thus affecting exports which brought it so much of its revenue, but it also sought to assert the powers of the president in the Chilean constitutional system in a question of competency between the executive and the judiciary. The Nitrate Railways case thus became an additional contentious issue between government and opposition in Chilean domestic politics, providing the opposition to Balmaceda with further ammunition for its charge that the president's obsession with his grandiose plans for development led him to act unconstitutionally.[26] For North, on the other hand, the decision of the Council of State threatened to destroy once and for all the principal prop of his fortunes in Tarapacá, and the threat soon became a real one.

On 30 September 1889 the firm of Campbell Outram and Company, clearly heartened by the Council's decision, solicited a concession from the Chilean government to construct a narrow-gauge railway from the *oficina* of Agua Santa to the port of Caleta Buena. Two memoranda, supporting this petition, argued cogently on both economic and legal grounds the case for granting this request.[27] The petition itself was couched in

[25] Altamirano added that perhaps the President's interest in the case was such that he was induced to 'sacrifice private interests ... to ... the glory of his government'. *Translation of the Decision* ..., pp. 9–19.

[26] See above, pp. 88–91, and below, pp. 120, 137–8.

[27] Terms of the Concession solicited by Campbell Outram and Company, 30 September 1889. Trans. from Spanish in longhand in F.O. 16/286. The memoranda were dated 10 October 1889.

terms very favourable to the Chilean government: the company undertook to construct branch lines to all *oficinas* requiring them in the Negreiros district, a region rich in nitrate, and, while requesting a lower tariff for freights than that of the Nitrate Railways Company, it agreed that the government, in consultation with the concessionaires, should reserve the right to lower this. The government might also buy up the line whenever it wished and, in any event, the line would revert to the state after twenty-five years. The government's reply took the form of an open invitation for tenders from constructors to build the Agua Santa line, such offers to be received by 26 December 1889.[28] Contrary to appearances, however, this was not intended to promote competitive bids, but simply to ensure that Campbell Outram's tender would secure the contract: only twenty days were given for submission of proposals, and the condition was laid down that the railway must be constructed within four months of signing the contract, provisos with which only the Agua Santa Company could comply, since it had done all the necessary preparatory work on surveys and estimates in framing its previous solicitation.[29]

Events were moving fast to undermine the Nitrate Railways Company and it clearly had to take action. It did so both in Santiago and in London. Shortly after tenders had been invited to build the Agua Santa Railway, the company's legal representatives in Chile addressed a long memorandum to the Chilean Senate: after calling attention to the economic benefits the company had brought to Tarapacá, the memorandum put greater emphasis on the constitutional question, looking to the Senate to safeguard not only its property, but also the Chilean constitution by refusing to allow the executive power to appropriate the functions of the judiciary.[30] And it went further than this.

The sentence of the Council of State [it said] is not susceptible or modification, but it is a subject for meditation whether anyone should attempt to make it a basis for the exercise of those

[28] Notes, undated and unsigned, in F.O. 16/286.
[29] Antony Gibbs & Sons, Valparaiso, to London, 6 December 1889. AAG, MS. 11,470. Vol. 12. Letter No. 25.
[30] Yrarrázaval, *El Presidente Balmaceda*, i, 464–5.

discretional powers which the Constitution has conferred upon Congress.[31]

This was a reference to constitutional provisions giving Congress power to prefer accusations against ministers for infraction of the constitution, a possible way in which Congress could attack the president through his cabinet.[32]

This remonstrance well illustrated the company's tactics in Chile in its fight against the cancellation of its railway monopoly: it sought to exploit the political situation in Santiago by stressing the constitutional aspects of the case to Balmaceda's detriment. In London, meanwhile, the company's lawyer looked for assistance from the Foreign Office by emphasizing the importance of protecting British interests abroad where there seemed to be inadequate machinery for the redress of wrongful action by a foreign government.

On 17 December 1889, a deputation from the company called at the Foreign Office to ask that the British Minister in Santiago be instructed to support the company's representatives in Chile in their protest against the government's action.[33] The deputation left with the Foreign Office the opinion of Sir Horace Davey, a former Solicitor-General, who had said:

If, according to the law of Chile, the declaration of forfeiture is an administrative act which the Company has no right to challenge in the Courts . . . it is a very singular state of things . . .[34]

The Law Officers of the Crown agreed with this view and, accordingly, the British Minister in Santiago was instructed to give his good offices to the company's agents there.[35] He

---

[31] Remonstrance of Señor Molina. Copy in English enclosed in Mr Budd to Sir Thomas Sanderson, 10 February 1890. F.O. 16/287. Molina was one of the Company's lawyers in Chile; Budd, of the firm of Budd, Johnson and Jecks, acted for the Company in London. Sanderson was Assistant Under-Secretary of State at the Foreign Office. Cf. this remonstrance with *Boletín de las Sesiones Estraordinarias de la Cámara de Senadores, 1888–9*, pp. 320–2.

[32] *Constitución de la República de Chile con las reformas . . . hasta 1888*, Articles 83–92, pp. 40–3.

[33] Notes, undated and unsigned, in F.O. 16/286.

[34] Opinion of Sir H. Davey, 20 November 1889. Copy in long-hand in F.O. 16/286.

[35] Salisbury to Kennedy, 18 December 1889. F.O. 16/286. No. 7. Telegraphic. See also Salisbury to Kennedy, 18 December 1889. F.O. 16/286. No. 39. Diplomatic.

brought the subject before the Chilean Foreign Minister at the end of December 1889, but opposition to the government's action was also manifested in both chambers of the Chilean Congress where it was hotly criticized and extensively discussed until 18 January 1890, when President Balmaceda suddenly closed the session.[36]

That the Nitrate Railways question would continue to exercise the Chilean government, the British Foreign Office and the various interested parties in both Chile and England was clear at the beginning of 1890. It had begun as a purely economic controversy and had developed into a constitutional issue of some importance in Chile, while the intervention of the Foreign Office had introduced a diplomatic factor. From Balmaceda's point of view, the railway monopoly had been breached but at the price of exacerbated political conflict, the end of which could not clearly be seen. From that of North, the case represented the most serious challenge he had yet faced to his interests in Tarapacá, and it had come at the worst possible moment, with his other companies in serious straits. The year which had begun with his historic ball and banquet was drawing to its close in despondency and gloom.

The Chilean Political Crisis

If 1889 was a year of increasing uncertainty for North in England, it was no less a time of troubles for Balmaceda in Chile. The political crisis in Santiago, already acute when Balmaceda made his celebrated visit to Iquique in March,[37] deepened in the course of the year and was, in fact, partly connected with that event. The large entourage which had accompanied the president on his voyage to the north included the Minister of Industry and Public Works, Enrique Sanfuentes. Sanfuentes was a wealthy landowner who had earned Balmaceda's undying gratitude in the 1870s for his timely assistance to the future president who was then experiencing some difficulty in the administration of the family estates.[38] But

[36] Kennedy to Salisbury, Viña del Mar, 15 February 1890. F.O. 16/287. No. 15. Diplomatic.   [37] See above, pp. 78–9.
[38] See Figueroa, *Diccionario Histórico*, iv and v, 766–8.

Sanfuentes' rise to favour in 1888 and 1889 aroused the fear of some Liberal groups in Congress that he was destined to be Balmaceda's choice as government candidate in the presidential election of 1891.[39] Though the idol of some sections of the Government Liberal party, Sanfuentes was 'cordially detested' by the other Liberal groups,[40] which were, in any case, already at loggerheads with Balmaceda because of his apparent neglect of their political interests and his predilection for personal adherents.[41] Though Balmaceda denied the existence of any 'official' candidate for the presidency in 1891, and Sanfuentes went so far as to resign from office in April 1889, the critical Liberal groups—the Nationals, the Radicals and the *Sueltos*—did not trust either Balmaceda's word or Sanfuentes' gesture. After the resignation of Sanfuentes, the ministry was reorganized on 1 May 1889, but only after considerable delay, since the President 'was not sure . . . of a sufficient majority in the Senate . . . with the Cabinet constituted as it was'.[42] A *Suelto* was brought in, to the further annoyance of the more powerful National and Radical parties who, supported by the permanent opposition party, the Conservatives, and, indeed, also by some Government Liberals who themselves objected to the new minister, defeated the government on a measure in the Senate, whereupon the new ministry immediately resigned.

Balmaceda then approached the prestigious National party, but they required him to give an assurance that he would not bring pressure to bear on any joint Convention of the Liberal groups called to elect the next presidential candidate, and this he declined to give. The Nationals, accordingly, refused Balmaceda's invitation to join the ministry. Increasingly frustrated by his failure to reach accommodation with the politicians, Balmaceda regarded the Nationals' action as a deliberate affront, and formed his next ministry from those members of the other Liberal groups who were noted for their antipathy to the Nationals. This, however, released the National party from

[39] Encina, *Historia de Chile*, xix, 148 ff. I have largely followed Encina in the account which follows.

[40] Maurice H. Hervey, *Dark Days in Chile*, p. 97.

[41] See above, pp. 78, 90–91.

[42] Consul-General Newman to Salisbury, Valparaiso, 3 May 1889. F.O. 16/256. No. 1. Political.

its tradition of supporting the Head of the State and it marked the definite rupture of the old Liberal–National alliance. As a result, the government lost its majority in the Senate while, in the Chamber of Deputies, its majority fell to an unstable ten.

The consequence of these events was the resignation of the ministry on 7 October 1889: the ministry had begged the President to form a ministry of the three principal Liberal groups—Nationals, Radicals and *Sueltos*—in order to secure a majority in Congress and it had resigned because it could not command such a majority.[43] It took sixteen days for Balmaceda to form a new ministry and this was only achieved after he had published in the *Diario Oficial* 'a species of Declaration of his political sentiments', in which he pledged the absolute neutrality of the government 'in all that concerns the designation by political parties of the future candidate for the Presidency of the nation'.[44] The parties themselves were now proclaiming their aims to be freedom of elections, the independence of the parties from the President, and the subordination of the President to the will of Congress. Of these, only the first had been a major and professed aim of opposition parties before Balmaceda's administration.

The ministry of 24 October was composed of representatives of all the Liberal groups, though on the government side a further complication had been produced by the events of 1889: yet another distinctive political group, the *Convencionalistas*, had emerged, as those Government Liberals who opposed the presidential succession of Sanfuentes and who sought a solution to this difficult problem in the calling of a Liberal Convention to elect the Liberal candidate. For the moment, however, a brief political armistice followed the formation of the new ministry. Balmaceda's promise to abstain from interference in the presidential succession improved the atmosphere, and Congress approved the estimates for 1890 and other essential laws. But once again hopes were dashed. On 5 November 1889, the Minister of Industry and Public Works resigned on a minor pretext, and in his place Balmaceda

---

[43] Minister Kennedy to Salisbury, Santiago, 11 October 1889. F.O. 16/256. No. 14. Diplomatic.

[44] Same to same, Santiago, 24 October 1889. F.O. 16/256. No. 15. Diplomatic.

appointed the recognized leader of those who supported Sanfuentes, José Miguel Valdés Carrera.[45] As a result, the *Convencionalistas* broke with the government and joined the opposition: in so doing, they deprived the President of his Congressional majority for the first time in Chilean history.

It was precisely while this political crisis was going on that
the Chilean government invited tenders for the construction of
the Agua Santa railway, and sought thereby to make absolutely
clear that the monopoly of railway transport in Tarapacá held
by the Nitrate Railways Company was completely at an end.
This action, as already noted above, was the occasion for a long
debate in the Chilean Congress in December 1889 and January
1890. One of the Chilean advisers of the company, Luís
Martiano Rodríguez, laid great stress on the constitutional
aspects of the Nitrate Railways question, asserting that the
government had 'trampled underfoot the rights of Congress'
when it cancelled the company's monopoly by administrative
decree.[46] For the government, Deputies Juan N. Parga and
Manuel A. Cristi argued that not only was the government's
action legally justified, but also that there were grounds for
believing that Colonel North had used his money to interfere
in Chilean politics in order to preserve the company's monopoly.[47] Replying to these assertions, which were couched in
parliamentary language and without specific references to
actual persons, Rodríguez pointed out that the charge of an
enterprise using its resources to defend its position was just as
applicable to the Agua Santa Company as to the Nitrate Railways Company, and he continued to attack the government on
constitutional grounds:

I censure [he declared] a decree that tramples on our administrative
legislation, that upsets the rights and reciprocal interests of the
nitrate business in general, and that creates difficulties for the
tribunals in settling the rights of both the established railway company and the new ones to be formed . . .[48]

[45] A staunch supporter of Balmaceda, Valdés Carrera had not been prominent
in public life until Balmaceda became president. He was an enthusiastic advocate
of Balmaceda's programme of public works. See Figueroa, *Diccionario Histórico*,
iv and v, 965–6, and also below, pp. 124, 128, 135–6, 240.

[46] *Boletín de las Sesiones Estraordinarias de la Cámara de Diputados de 1889–1890*,
p. 467.   [47] Ibid., pp. 697–705, 731–8.   [48] Ibid., p. 739.

In the long and involved debate, a prominent part was played by the new Minister of Industry and Public Works, Valdés Carrera, who was, in effect, the government's spokesman in the matter. He not only defended the government's legal position with regard to the Nitrate Railways Company, but also presented an impressive amount of documentation to show how the company's transport monopoly bore very heavily on the nitrate interests in general.[49]

Meanwhile, the *Convencionalistas* had been urging Balmaceda to call a Liberal Convention to elect a Liberal candidate for the presidential election of 1891, but although this proposal had originally been made by the President himself, his chief supporters, the Government Liberals, now turned it down.[50] On 18 January 1890, Valdés Carrera resigned from the Ministry of Public Works since, as a result of the breakdown of discussions on the issue of a Convention, the opposition Liberal groups had elected one of their number as Vice-President of the Chamber of Deputies instead of a Government Liberal, and he regarded this as an indirect vote of censure. The rest of the ministry followed his example on the same day, but this was not all. With the debate on the Nitrate Railways still in progress, Balmaceda closed the Extraordinary Sessions of Congress and proceeded to choose a new ministry.

The Liberal Party [reported Kennedy] are furious; they denounce the President's action as a coup d'état and they will, on the reassembling of Congress, offer a more violent opposition than ever to the dictatorial attitude which has been assumed by the President.[51]

The dissolution of Congress deprived the opposition of its main platform against the President, and Balmaceda had secured complete freedom of action to choose a new ministry, though at the cost of exacerbating the political crisis. But the closure of Congress also obeyed another objective: in the debate

[49] Ibid., pp. 381-8, 415-16, 466-72, 474, 672-84, 697-705, 731-44. See also Yrarrázaval, 'La administración Balmaceda y el salitre', *Boletín de la Academia Chilena de la Historia*, pp. 68-9.

[50] For the *Convencionalista* interpretation of these events, see Athos (pseud. for José Joaquín Larraín Zañartu), *La Convención Independiente* (Santiago, 1890), and for the Balmacedist view, Bañados, *Balmaceda*, i, 389.

[51] Kennedy to Salisbury, Santiago, 19 January 1890. F.O. 16/259. No. 10. Diplomatic. By 'Liberal Party', Kennedy obviously meant the Liberal opposition.

on the Nitrate Railways Company, Deputy Rodríguez had
proposed that the state itself should undertake the building of
a new railway in Tarapacá, rather than leaving it to the Agua
Santa Company.[52] This was, however, quite contrary to Balmaceda's policy: he was already committed to supporting the
Agua Santa Company, though its tender was not received until
March 1890.[53] In that month, the British Minister reported
that:

The real history of this episode [the Agua Santa concession] is that
the Government have decided in favour of the Agua Santa Company purely on political grounds. Some five or six members of the
Chamber of Deputies, so far supporters of the President, are interested in the success of the above Company: had the Government
decided in favour of the Nitrate Railways Company, the above
Deputies would have joined the Opposition Liberal Alliance.[54]

One explicit connection between the Chilean political situation and the affair of the Nitrate Railways had thus been made
clear. But there was yet another, more important, aspect for
the opposition in the Chilean Congress, namely the cancellation of the Nitrate Railways monopoly by administrative decree
and the invitation of tenders to build a competing line. In the
eyes of the opposition, this constituted yet further evidence that
in pursuit of his grandiose objectives, Balmaceda was prepared
to override existing laws and traditional practices. In the course
of 1890, much more was to be heard of this argument.

These complicated political manœuvres taking place in Chile
in 1889 set the stage for the most profound constitutional crisis
in the country's history. It was a crisis compounded of many
elements, some of which had been maturing over a long period
of time. Throughout the nineteenth century, the overwhelming
preponderance of executive power, enshrined in the constitution of 1833, had been somewhat weakened, first by constitutional amendments transferring more power to the

---

[52] *Boletín de las Sesiones . . . de 1889–90*, pp. 740–4. See also Yrarrázaval, loc.
cit., p. 69.

[53] The original closing date for tenders (26 December 1889) had been postponed to 1 March 1890. Undated notes in F.O. 16/286, referring to a telegram
containing this information sent to London by Mr F. Rowland, manager of the
Nitrate Railways Company at Iquique.

[54] Kennedy to Salisbury, Viña, 25 March 1890. F.O. 16/287. No. 24. Diplomatic.

legislature, and, secondly, by a rising tide of political opinion in favour of further reform of the existing balance of prerogatives. In addition, certain precedents had been established which remained unwritten in law, notably the convention that a ministry appointed by the President should resign if defeated in Congress by a majority vote. The President still retained the dominant position in the constitutional system through his near-personal control of administration, and his power thereby to influence the electoral process was generally sufficient to ensure a co-operative Congress. Nevertheless, by the time of Balmaceda's presidency, all Chilean liberals, however they might be defined, tended to idealize electoral liberty and further reform of the written constitution to give the legislature a much greater say in government, both *de jure* and *de facto*, and such aspirations were often deeply felt. But the translation of aspiration into reality depended on the particular political system which had by then evolved in Chile. That system was already a multi-party system: while members of all political groups, from the clerical Conservatives on the right wing of the spectrum, to the anti-clerical Radicals on the left, believed in the need to diminish the role of the executive and enhance that of the legislature, only these two parties possessed the binding cement of an ideology which was easily comprehended, namely their respective attitudes towards religious issues.[55]

Between these two parties, however, lay the amorphous groups of liberals—Government Liberals, Nationals, *Sueltos* and *Convencionalistas*—sharing some parts of a common creed which was very ill-defined. Formerly, these liberals had been sufficiently united, together with the Radicals, to pursue a common historical objective—the diminution of the power of the Church. But once this objective had been achieved, with the clerical reforms of Santa María in the 1880s, Chilean liberalism had begun to lose its cohesion, fractionalization ensued, personalities assumed new significance and group loyalties took the place of common ideologies and objectives. Government thus

---

[55] This, of course, was much more than a matter of faith. The issue of education —whether it was the province of Church or of State—was a basic question for Conservatives and Radicals alike, since the nature of the educational system determined the kind of society it was designed to produce.

depended on the President's ability to command wide support across new party lines and on his capacity to manage men. He still had considerable freedom of manœuvre in the absence of a catalyst to create a united opposition around clearly-defined objectives. For, although the constitution of 1833, as subsequently amended, prescribed certain limits to presidential power, the restraints imposed both by the political system and by public opinion were far from being a similar visible line within which the President was bound to work. The office itself was largely what its holder made it. Provided he retained control of Congress and pursued policies sufficiently acceptable to ensure that vague opposition aspirations were not transformed into quite concrete demands, the President of Chile had ample scope to promote his own programme. The test of statesmanship, however, would lie not only in what he might do, but also in the manner in which he did it; and here personality could well be a crucial factor. The reason for this lay to a very considerable extent in the fact that Congress was undoubtedly the preserve of the Chilean upper classes, and its members, many of whom had had long careers in public life, had acquired a strong sense of their own significance in the system. Although previously, under the government of fairly conciliatory presidents, such as José Joaquín Pérez, 1861–71, Federico Errázuriz Errázuriz, 1871–76, and Aníbal Pinto Garmendia, 1876–81, the constitutional powers of the executive had been somewhat reduced, it was less this visible shift of power, from President to Congress and to the parties, which counted than the unwillingness of these executives to make the most use of the power they had. Domingo Santa María, 1881–86, was a very different President: an authoritarian by nature, with very definite views of his own prerogatives, he had, in effect, sought to recover that power which constitutionally belonged to the presidency, but which had fallen somewhat into desuetude. The consequences, however, were to strengthen the belief of politicians that Santa María was seeking not so much to recover presidential prerogatives as to *extend* his power; and the Santa María presidency saw a marked exacerbation of relations between executive and legislature.

A key question in this relationship was the President's

ministry. Under the constitution, the President undoubtedly had a completely unfettered freedom to appoint his own ministers and to dismiss them at will. But prudence demanded that, in choosing his ministries, he should have an eye to the particular political interests which individual ministers represented, carefully weighing the strength of parties in Congress so as not to lose majority support there. The more fragmented the party structure, the more difficult did this manœuvre become, and it was particularly hard for a President who had very positive policies to secure a delicate balance of forces to implement his policies and, at the same time, maintain his own prerogatives. The choice of ministers was thus the crucial issue, and congressional votes of censure on ministries became the legislature's basic weapon to attack the executive.[56]

Such was the political and constitutional situation inherited by Balmaceda in 1886. At that time, the executive had overwhelming support in Congress, and could count on 23 senators against 6 for the opposition in the upper house, and 94 deputies against 29 in the lower chamber.[57] But the failure of his initial attempt to unite the various Liberal factions by conciliatory policies on such issues as electoral intervention led Balmaceda to abandon this policy abruptly in 1888, though this did not affect his Congressional majority.[58] In fact, as a result of massive intervention, government support in Congress actually increased: of 123 deputies, 76 could be classified as Government Liberals, 18 as Nationals, 7 as Radicals, 8 as *Sueltos* and dissident Liberals and 14 as Conservatives, while the composition of the 29-member Senate was 16 Liberals, 7 Nationals, 1 Radical, 4 *Sueltos* and dissident Liberals and 1 Conservative.[59] But Balmaceda then made his fundamental error in appearing to favour Enrique Salvador Sanfuentes as presidential candidate for the election of 1891, and failing to satisfy the anti-Sanfuentes Liberals.[60] Indeed, at this juncture, in 1889, his

[56] 'Except in the heat of electioneering and party contests, personal attacks on the President are not common—he is smitten through the body of the minister.' Russell, *A Visit to Chile*, p. 83.

[57] Crisóstomo Pizarro, *La revolución de 1891* (Valparaiso, 1971), p. 27.

[58] See above, p. 78.

[59] Encina, *Historia de Chile*, xix, 117–18.

[60] See above, pp. 115–18.

whole political conduct lacked judgement, and he gradually dissipated the majority support in Congress he had once had.[61] The situation deteriorated further as a result of the confluence of other factors. In the first place, Balmaceda's complex personality, visionary nationalism and complete identification of himself with the material progress of Chile led him to oversimplify the motives of opposition figures: confident of his own capacity to achieve his objectives, no matter how formidable the obstacles, he tended to see himself as always in the right and to conclude that all who opposed him did so from motives of self-interest and lack of patriotism.[62] Secondly, the vast expansion of public works which was taking place under his administration was not only increasing rapidly the number of public employees directly dependent on the central government: it was also creating in the camp of the Government Liberal party strong personal adherents and new political figures, such as Valdés Carrera, whose fortunes depended on their personal attachment to Balmaceda and his policies. That many of them shared Balmaceda's own views on national development, of which opposition figures were becoming increasingly critical, did nothing to diminish the suspicion that a new kind of party was in the making, a Balmacedist party, a mere tool of the government.[63] And, as the political crisis grew, a third important factor emerged in Balmaceda's increasing

[61] In this opinion, I follow Encina, loc. cit., *passim*; Rodríguez Bravo, *Balmaceda y el conflicto entre el Congreso y el Ejecutivo*, i, pp. 134 ff.; Yrarrázaval, *El Presidente Balmaceda*, i, 383 ff. For the contrary view, putting the responsibility on the political factions, see Bañados, *Balmaceda*, i, 222 ff., and Joaquín Villarino, *José Manuel Balmaceda* (Mendoza, 1892), pp. 30 ff.

[62] See below, pp. 169–73, for further evidence of this view. Some years later, the British Minister in Santiago said of Balmaceda that his better qualities were outweighed by 'his extraordinary vanity, obstinacy and duplicity. His chief object seemed to be to place himself and his opinions above all other men . . .' Memorandum on the Chilean Revolution of 1891, encl. in Kennedy to Sanderson, Burton, 24 September 1892. Private. F.O. 16/280. Diplomatic. Various.

[63] There is, in fact, some evidence that the suspicion was not unfounded. In July 1888, Balmaceda wrote to a correspondent: 'Today no one thinks of *caudillos*; everyone is dedicated to labour, and we have established the cabinet and all the authorities of the Republic resolved to fight against *caudillismo*, and to oblige the political fractions [*sic*] to co-operate with or subordinate themselves to the permanently predominant action of the Liberal party.' Cited in Encina, *Historia de Chile*, xix, p. 120. By 'Liberal party', Balmaceda obviously meant the Government Liberal party.

disdain for the politicians: with the dignity of his office and his own self-esteem committed to a conflict he believed he had sought to avoid, all opposition became sordid factionalism, if not, indeed, something worse.[64]

As for the opposition, it had found surprising unity in mistrust of Balmaceda by the beginning of 1890. Many of the political leaders were prominent public figures, long accustomed to having a say in national issues. Balmaceda's conduct and policies seemed to them a denial of rights they expected to exercise and a gross affront to the public opinion they believed they represented.[65] In these circumstances, the long-standing disputes between executive and legislature assumed much sharper focus. Congressional desires for an end to executive interference in elections and for the appointment of ministries accountable to the Congressional majority hardened into demands, and these demands were less and less negotiable.[66] Everything was now grist to the opposition mill, and not least Balmaceda's programme of public works. But, as criticism of this programme developed in Congress, so the government looked for counter-arguments, and, among them, it placed in the forefront the bogy of the interference by foreign capital in Chilean politics.

British Nitrates and Chilean Politics

Given the extensive participation of British capital in the Chilean nitrate industry, it is hardly surprising that many companies employed Chilean lawyers to advise them. Expatriate managers could run the *oficinas* in Tarapacá, often administering their own kind of justice, but they were not versed in Chilean law, nor, it may safely be said, were any

[64] As Balmaceda himself said later to Maurice Hervey: 'This theory of Parliamentary Government is a new idea, a mere pretext of discontented factions to work out their own ends.' Hervey, *Dark Days in Chile*, p. 91.

[65] See, for example, Athos, *La Convención Independiente*, pp. 129–69, for an admirable expression of this view in the form of a series of biographies of prominent members of the opposition.

[66] The two demands were, of course, connected, since the best guarantee of non-intervention by government in elections was for the ministry to be responsible to Congress.

members of the British legal profession.[67] Yet a knowledge of
Chilean law was clearly necessary for any company operating
in the country, and the employment of local experts seems to
have been a long-standing, common and accepted practice.[68]
The nitrate companies, in particular, needed access to persons
with competence in property law and the law of contracts,
since they were, in effect, the inheritors of rights deriving from
arrangements made previously with Peru and subsequently
assumed by Chile when she annexed the nitrate regions, and
the confirmation of titles to *salitreras* was often a protracted
process of litigation. But, among the foreign companies operating in Chile, the Nitrate Railways Company needed more
advice than most: operating under a concession originally made
to others by the government of Peru, a concession, moreover,
hedged about with all kinds of qualifications, the company
found itself, after 1886, in the difficult situation of having the
legal basis of its concession challenged by the Chilean government itself.[69]

The company's chief lawyer in Santiago, Julio Zegers, was
also a prominent Liberal politician.[70] He was, in a sense,
inherited by North and the Nitrate Railways Company, having
acted as legal adviser to the previous concessionaires.[71] But as
North's interests in Tarapacá grew in the 1880s, the legal work
expanded, and Zegers became, in addition to chief legal
adviser, a recruiting officer for other Chilean lawyers, most of
whom were also public figures, with seats in the national
Congress.[72]

[67] It may be noted here that in the Foreign Office archives relating to the
Nitrate Railways Company (F.O. 16/286–8, 298, 317) many documents are replies
by the Law Officers of the Crown to questions of law raised by the Foreign Office,
and that their opinions often reveal complete ignorance of Chilean law and of the
Chilean Constitution.

[68] Antony Gibbs & Sons, for example, employed as legal adviser in Chile for
many years Don Jorge Huneeus, a distinguished jurist, Congressman and Rector
of the University of Chile. Antony Gibbs, at Valparaiso, to London, 5 July 1889.
Letter No. 14. AAG, MS. 11,470. Vol. 12. Balfour Williamson employed an
equally well-known figure, Marcial Martínez. Stephen Williamson at Liverpool to
W. R. Henderson at Valparaiso, 21 February 1889. Balfour Williamson Papers,
Letter Book No. 3. Copy. Letter No. 118.   [69] See above, pp. 45–55.

[70] For biographical details, see Figueroa, *Diccionario Histórico*, iv and v, 1126–8.
[71] Letter from Zegers in *El Ferrocarril*, 10 February 1898. See also Silva Vargas,
'Los ferrocarriles salitreros . . .', loc. cit., *passim*.
[72] A full list is given in J. M. Valdés Carrera, *La condenación del ministerio Vicuña:*

A large number of Chilean Congressmen had been trained in the law, the most natural avenue to politics in nineteenth-century Chile, and, since members of Congress were unpaid, most of them carried on other occupations, though some, of course, were sufficiently wealthy not to need to do so.[73] It was, therefore, perfectly natural for lawyers in Congress to accept particular briefs from foreign companies or to be retained by them as legal advisers and, so far as can be judged on present evidence, the relationships between foreign companies and Chilean lawyers—certainly well known at the time—excited little public attention. Simply because the relationship existed is no ground for supposing that it was nefarious, and if, in specific circumstances, a question of incompatibility arose between the public duty and the private employment of a Chilean member of Congress, he could, of course, either decline to act for his employer or resign his office. A case which occurred in 1889 illustrates the point. The death of Don Jorge Huneeus, their Chilean legal adviser, made it necessary for Antony Gibbs and Sons to approach another well-known lawyer and public figure, Don Vicente Reyes. He 'expressed his willingness' to serve, but, on being informed that one of his duties would be to act for the company in a particular matter which would probably go to Congress, he declined, as the Valparaiso house reported:

on the grounds that as a Senator (he is President of the Senate) he could not undertake any questions that had to be decided either by the Executive or by Congress, for it was impossible for him to appear as advocate of measures over the discussion of which he would afterwards have to preside, as he would find himself in the embarrassing position of having to temporarily cede his office as an implicated party.

el Ministro de Hacienda y sus detractores (Paris, 1893), p. 108. Also cited by Ramírez, *Balmaceda*, p. 75, who adds biographical details, pp. 75–85.

[73] Chilean historiography would greatly benefit from a series of studies on Congress in the nineteenth century designed to reveal the social origins and affiliations of its members, on the lines of L. B. Namier's researches on the British legislature in the eighteenth century. Little of this kind has been done for Chile, though Pizarro, *La revolución de 1891*, p. 47, gives a table of occupations of members of the Chamber of Deputies in 1876. At that time, 27 per cent were in public administration, 15 per cent in commerce, mining and finance, and 23 per cent

Reyes was, however, perfectly willing to act for Gibbs in other cases, if they wished him to do so.[74]

Exactly the same situation occurred with Julio Zegers over the case of the Nitrate Railways Company: he had been appointed a member of the Council of State by President Balmaceda, but when the Council was asked to adjudicate the conflict between the executive and judicial branches of government arising from the cancellation of the company's concession by administrative decree,[75] Zegers resigned from the Council of State, since he was the company's lawyer.[76] But the position of Zegers was far more complicated than that of Reyes, and it has been the subject of much controversy. In the first place, Zegers was himself the leader of the Liberal faction known as the *Convencionalistas*, whose continuing support was vital to President Balmaceda in the deteriorating political situation of late 1889.[77] Secondly, his resignation from the Council of State was insisted upon—if we are to believe him—by J. M. Valdés Carrera, who was also a member, and it was Valdés Carrera who later, as Minister of Industry and Public Works, was most closely associated with Balmaceda in the policy of terminating the monopoly of the Nitrate Railways Company.[78] Consequently, it has been alleged that Zegers took the *Convencionalistas* into the opposition camp, and thus deprived Balmaceda of majority support in Congress, precisely because of these events.[79] Yet, in fact, Zegers continued to support the government long after he resigned from the Council,[80] and he himself claimed subsequently that Balmaceda offered him a ministerial post in October 1889.[81] Only a month later did the

were lawyers. Only 4 per cent were in agriculture, but the percentage of unknown occupations is as high as 27.

[74] Antony Gibbs & Sons at Valparaiso to London, 5 July 1889. AAG, MS. 11,470. Vol. 12. Letter No. 14. Private.   [75] See above, pp. 55, 111–112.

[76] These facts are noted in all the authorities cited in note 15, p. 69.

[77] See above, pp. 117–118.

[78] Valdés Carrera, *La condenación del Ministerio Vicuña*, p. 23. Valdés here refers to 'the odious Zegers–North monopoly which caused such harm to the nitrate industry'.

[79] By, e.g., Figueroa, *Diccionario Histórico*, iv and v, p. 1127; Bañados, *Balmaceda*, i, 364 ff.

[80] See Salas Edwards, *Balmaceda y el Parlamentarismo en Chile*, i, 186–90, and also Yrarrázaval, *El Presidente Balmaceda*, ii, 373–5.

[81] Letter in *El Ferrocarril*, Santiago, 25 February 1898.

Convencionalistas definitely join the Congressional opposition.

Nevertheless, it has been strongly argued by several writers that a number of Chilean lawyers, and notably Zegers, put their private interests before their duty to Chile, and that, in effect, they were bought by foreign gold; further, that Balmaceda's government, pursuing a policy of economic nationalism, inimical to foreign interests, and particularly in nitrates, found itself opposed within Chile mainly for economic reasons, and that within a complicated mosaic of motives and actions, a very significant role was played by the Chilean lawyers employed by foreign business.[82] To these writers, the alleged political and constitutional differences between Balmaceda and his Congress were no more than a convenient pretext for opposition to the President.

In this interpretation, Colonel North is the natural villain of the piece, the veritable incarnation of British imperialism, a man who spared no effort to preserve and, indeed, extend his kingdom in Tarapacá, through a network of collaborating Chileans led by Zegers.[83] And, since other British companies, some of which had been operating in Chile before North was born, also employed Chilean lawyers and public men to defend their interests, these fall under the same condemnation, and no distinction is drawn between their activities and those of the *parvenus* nitrate capitalists.[84] President Balmaceda himself was far more subtle. Not only did he draw a clear distinction between North's interests and those of other British entrepreneurs, but he sought to use the very real differences between them for his own ends. Secondly, even so far as North was concerned, Balmaceda's objectives were clearly limited. For certain purposes, however, the relationship between North's interests and Chilean opposition figures could be turned to useful account, as the continuing story of the Nitrate Railways case reveals.

During January and February 1890, the British Foreign Office sought to obtain the fullest information from the Nitrate

---

[82] See Blakemore, 'The Chilean Revolution . . .', loc. cit., *passim*. The most detailed presentation of this thesis is Ramírez, *Balmaceda, passim*.

[83] Ramírez, *Balmaceda, passim*. See also Valdés Carrera, *La condenación del Ministerio Vicuña*, pp. 23–4, 108, and Villarino, *J. M. Balmaceda*, p. 130.

[84] Ramírez, loc. cit., and Pizarro, *La revolución de 1891*, pp. 62–4.

Railways Company to put before the Law Officers of the Crown, and the Company was only too pleased to do anything which might induce the British government to assist its cause in Chile.[85] North himself wrote personally to the Foreign Secretary, Lord Salisbury, from Nice on 11 February that 'clear statements on the part of Her Majesty's Government will have the greatest weight in protecting these very important interests',[86] and this view was also emphasized by representatives of the company in London in meetings with the Permanent Under-Secretary of State, Sir Philip Currie.[87]

Consulted on 4 February, the Law Officers gave their opinion a week later, supporting the British government in protesting to Chile against the infraction of the Nitrate Railways Company's monopoly. The British minister in Santiago was instructed accordingly; he was to urge on the Chilean government also that, in any event, the company should have the right of appeal to the Chilean courts.[88]

These views were embodied in a memorandum drawn up by Minister Kennedy on 15 February, and left with the Ministry of Foreign Affairs in Santiago. Kennedy subsequently saw the Chilean Foreign Minister who recapitulated familiar arguments, justifying the cancellation of the Nitrate Railways Company's concession, and emphasizing the competence of the Council of State to act as the final arbiter in the matter, as it had done. In a second despatch, which followed his first report within twenty-four hours, Kennedy reported that he had had conversations not only with the Foreign Minister but also with the German Minister to Chile, 'who', he said, 'takes an especial interest in the industries of Tarapacá'.[89] As a result of these talks, Kennedy was far from optimistic in view of

the strong feeling which exists in official circles in Chile in favour of

---

[85] See the extensive correspondence and notes in F.O. 16/287.

[86] North to Salisbury, Nice, 11 February 1890. F.O. 16/287.

[87] Two Directors of the Company, one of whom was Robert Harvey, the Company Secretary, and one of its London lawyers, Mr Budd, went to the Foreign Office on 4 February. Notes in F.O. 16/287.

[88] Law Officers of the Crown to Salisbury, 10 February 1890. F.O. 16/287; Foreign Office to Kennedy, 12 February 1890. F.O. 16/287. No. 2. Telegraphic.

[89] Kennedy to Salisbury, Viña, 16 February 1890. F.O. 16/287. No. 15. Diplomatic; 16 February 1890. F.O. 16/287. No. 16. Diplomatic. Confidential.

the infractions of the Monopoly enjoyed by the Nitrate Railways Company . . . due partly to a jealous dislike of all enterprises promoted and directed by Colonel North, and partly to the political influences working in favour of the Agua Santa Company (which has constituted itself a Chilean Company)—under the management of deputies interested in its success.

He added that in the political climate of extreme antagonism between the opponents and supporters of the President, 'everything is subordinated to party politics', and this state of affairs was

unfavourable to the cause of the Nitrate Railways; many Liberals who still support the President are interested in the success of the Agua Santa Company, and the able advocate retained by the Nitrate R. Co. [sic], who is a leading Liberal, has lately placed himself in the front rank of the opposition to the President.[90]

But the Foreign Minister, Kennedy concluded,

could not give me any satisfactory reasons for the hostility shown towards Colonel North, who seems to have inspired a feeling of envy and jealousy by his successful development of the industries and resources of the province of Tarapacá which contribute nearly one half of the annual Treasury receipts.

Despite Kennedy's fears, Balmaceda appeared anxious to avoid offending the British government, and on 22 February, he complied with a suggestion made by Kennedy and telegraphed the Minister of Public Works, recommending the postponement of the date fixed for the receipt of tenders for the construction of the Agua Santa line to 1 March.[91] The intervention of the Foreign Office was probably very unwelcome to Balmaceda: the political crisis in Chile had made him critically dependent on the deputies interested in the Agua Santa line, though he himself, of course, saw in this project the actual means to destroy the Nitrate Railways Company's monopoly of rail transport in Tarapacá. British official remonstrances were

[90] Ibid. This was clearly a reference to Zegers.
[91] Kennedy to Salisbury, Viña, 22 February 1890. F.O. 16/287. No. 5. Telegraphic. Balmaceda was at Viña, at his vacation palace, since Congress was closed and it was the height of summer. Both the Minister of Public Works, Valdés Carrera, and the Foreign Minister, Juan Mackenna, were then in the south of Chile.

something he could well do without, given the political situation and the use being made of the Nitrate Railways case by
the Congressional opposition in their fight to portray the
President as overriding the law. At this point, however,
Balmaceda was suddenly and opportunely assisted in London.

In March 1890 Antony Gibbs and Sons, the most important
British business house operating in Chile, took a hand in the
Nitrate Railways question. After an interchange of correspondence, the Assistant Under-Secretary of State for Foreign
Affairs, Sir Thomas Sanderson, gave an interview to Mr
Herbert Gibbs on 4 March. Gibbs explained that 'the monopoly of the Nitrate Railways was weighing unmercifully on the
British capital invested in the Nitrate works' and emphasized
the fact that many nitrate producers supported the Chilean
government in its action to destroy that monopoly. Sanderson,
while saying that Gibbs' views would be borne in mind, pointed
out that the remonstrance addressed to the Chilean government had a purely legal basis and that nothing further could be
done until the Chilean government replied to Kennedy's
memorandum.[92]

But the Foreign Office was embarrassed. 'This question',
wrote Sanderson, 'is rather awkward', since before Gibbs' visit
'we had heard nothing of the opposite side of the question'.[93]
They were now, however, to hear a good deal, as Gibbs insisted
on pressing their case in very forthright language. The head of
the House, Henry Gibbs, wrote to Sir Philip Currie, the Permanent Under-Secretary of State, the very same day that his
son, Herbert, had called at the Foreign Office, saying that the
facts which Herbert had stated were true:

As it is [he added] the lucky speculators who bought the Railways
for a trifle, have been still further lucky in obtaining the support of
the F.O. [sic] in a monopoly which benefits them, but injures everyone else. . . I hope [he concluded] the F.O. will not forget that my
House really does know all that can be known about the West
Coast of S. America . . .[94]

[92] Notes of Sanderson to Salisbury, 6 March 1890, in F.O. 16/287.
[93] Ibid. See also Brown, 'Nitrate Railways', loc. cit., pp. 476–7.
[94] Henry Gibbs to Currie, 4 March, 1890. F.O. 16/287. It is interesting to note
that Ramírez, *Balmaceda*, pp. 119–20, cites one document in F.O. 16/287 in dealing
with the Nitrate Railways issue and also mentions the fact that the Agua Santa

A conciliatory reply did not shake Gibbs off: the House now had the bit between its teeth, and Herbert Gibbs began to ask a number of awkward questions, implying that when the Foreign Office consulted the Law Officers of the Crown inadequate documentation had been sent.[95] He also referred to alleged remarks made by Sanderson when they met:

You spoke to me [he wrote] of the Council of State having been packed; the facts giving colour to this interpretation are the following. In March last year there were at least four members of the Council of State liable to be challenged as interested parties, if the case between the President and the Supreme Court came before them for decision; they were, Mr. Zegers, the lawyer to the Railway Co., Messrs Besa and Castillo, who had already expressed an opinion, and Mr. Cousiño, who was a member of the Supreme Court. . . I have little doubt that the packing you referred to was merely the prohibition of these men from serving and the replacing them with others who were disinterested.

Gibbs again alleged that the reason why oppressive freights on nitrate were levied by the Nitrate Railways Company was in order to pay dividends on a highly-inflated capital, and he went on to express the hope that the Foreign Office would suspend further action in the case and resort to its customary neutrality where there was a conflict between British interests abroad, particularly in this issue where, despite its long connection with Chile, his firm had been given no opportunity to express its views.[96]

Piqued at the tone of such remarks, Sanderson declared that Gibbs had misapprehended statements he had made, and Lord Salisbury, the Foreign Secretary, himself expressed some annoyance.[97] Nevertheless, Gibbs' intervention does seem to have had some effect on the Foreign Office.[98] When, after much procrastination, the Chilean Foreign Minister replied

Company was an English firm, controlled by Campbell Outram & Co. He does not, however, mention this correspondence.

[95] Gibbs to Sanderson, 10 March 1890. F.O. 16/287.

[96] Same to same, 13 March 1890. F.O. 16/287.

[97] Sanderson to Gibbs, 14 March 1890. F.O. 16/297; Note in Salisbury's hand on reverse of draft of Sanderson to Gibbs.

[98] Cf., however, Brown, 'Nitrate Railways', loc. cit., p. 477, taking the opposite view.

to Kennedy's memorandum of 15 February on 21 March 1890, rejecting diplomatic intervention in the Nitrate Railways question, and Kennedy proposed to refute this officially, he was instructed to forward the full text of the Chilean reply for consideration in London, reserving the rights of the company pending the British answer.[99] Though the Foreign Office wished to consult the Law Officers of the Crown again, this new caution probably derived in part from the interference of Antony Gibbs and Sons. This was certainly the view taken by the firm's representatives in Iquique: on being informed of the interviews and correspondence in London, the agents at Iquique expressed the opinion that Gibbs' intervention would 'make them [the Foreign Office] more careful in future of interfering on *ex parte* statements . . . without thorough investigation of the facts'.[100]

In any case, the rights of the Nitrate Railways Company were already doomed. On 19 March 1890, the *Diario Oficial* announced that the Government had accepted the tender of the Agua Santa Company, received on 4 March, to build a railway from that *oficina* to the port of Caleta Buena.[101] The concession was granted to Campbell Outram and Company, but, three days later, was transferred to two Chileans, Lauro Barros and Pedro Wessel, by whom it was later to be transferred to the *Compañía de Salitres y Ferrocarril de Agua Santa*. This company was registered in Chile on 1 September 1890, the controlling interest being retained by Campbell Outram and Company, who also received a substantial cash payment. The Chilean government approved these transactions on 3 November 1890: it could hardly do otherwise, for Lauro Barros, who had played a major part in the negotiations, had become *Ministro de Hacienda* in Balmaceda's ministry of 15 October.[102]

[99] Kennedy to Salisbury, Santiago, 21 March 1890. F.O. 16/287. Telegraphic in cipher. Salisbury to Kennedy, 22 March 1890. F.O. 16/287. No. 3. Telegraphic.

[100] Antony Gibbs & Sons, Iquique, to London, 30 April 1890. Private Letter No. 218. Iquique Archive.

[101] Kennedy to Salisbury, Santiago, 21 March 1890. F.O. 16/287. Telegraphic.

[102] Yrarrázaval, 'La administración Balmaceda y el salitre', loc. cit., pp. 69–70; see also below, p. 182.

These events, the logical result of Balmaceda's political dependence on Barros and other deputies interested in the Agua Santa company, and also of his own attitude to the Nitrate Railways question, lay several months in the future when the British Minister in Santiago had an important interview in March with Valdés Carrera, the Minister of Industry and Public Works.[103] At this meeting it was made quite clear to Kennedy how the Nitrate Railways question was inextricably bound up with the Chilean political situation and how adamant Balmaceda was in his intention to destroy the company's monopoly.

At the outset, Kennedy protested both at the delay in getting a reply to his memorandum and at that reply itself.[104] Valdés Carrera, however,

began by an attack on Colonel North alleging that he had become very unpopular in Chile owing to the suspicion that he endeavoured to interfere in Chilean politics: in fact, that he was trying to play in Chile the part successfully acted in Peru a few years ago by Messrs. Dreyfus, who by corrupt means had secured the election of their own candidate, Señor Piérola, to the Presidency.

Kennedy, of course, refuted these charges: though he did not know North personally, he said that

he might safely deny on his behalf any such ambitious political designs. Colonel North [he declared] would be satisfied if he could count on the protection of the laws of Chile on behalf of his numerous enterprises in the province of Tarapacá, whence the Government of Chile drew such enormous revenues, derived almost entirely from the resources developed if not created by Colonel North.

Valdés Carrera then shifted the grounds of his attack from North to Julio Zegers who had, he said,

with funds supplied to him from the Nitrate Railways Company, corrupted Deputies, bought up newspapers, and inaugurated a system of general corruption hitherto unknown in Chile . . .

[103] The interview was reported in two separate despatches both of which were dated 25 March 1890.
[104] Kennedy to Salisbury, Viña, 25 March 1890. F.O. 16/287. No. 23. Diplomatic.

and the Minister went on to point out that Zegers had been an intimate friend of President Balmaceda's but was now one of his most violent opponents

to such a degree that the interests of the Nitrate Railways Company were sacrificed to the personal and political feelings of Señor Zegers . . .[105]

Though Valdés Carrera assured Kennedy that

no hostile feeling existed on the part of the Government of Chile against British enterprise in the province of Tarapacá: that he believed that Colonel North would soon obtain official sanction for his proposed Railway Extension to the district of Lagunas, and that he hoped Colonel North would make good his title to the district itself of Lagunas which was known to be rich in Nitrates,[106]

he also implied, said Kennedy, that the success of North with these enterprises might be secured 'provided Señor Zegers no longer represented the Company'.[107]

In the reports of this conversation Kennedy also emphasized the political aspect of the Agua Santa concession, and dilated on the 'tricks and deceptions' practised on him to thwart his efforts on behalf of the Nitrate Railways Company. Earlier in the month, indeed, before he had seen Valdés Carrera, he had stated that

at present in Chile, everything is subordinated to domestic politics. The President is grossly abused by the Press and the Liberal Opposition, and he is wildly exasperated and excited. . . The President says that the Nitrate Railways question has become 'más odiosa' by my interference . . .[108]

[105] Kennedy to Salisbury, Viña, 25 March 1890. F.O. 16/287. No. 24. Diplomatic. Confidential. For a convenient short summary of the relationship between the French banking house of Dreyfus and the Peruvian lawyer-President, Nicolás de Piérola, see F. B. Pike, *The Modern History of Peru* (London, 1967), pp. 122–5.

[106] Kennedy to Salisbury, Viña, 25 March 1890. F.O. 16/287. No. 23. Diplomatic. For the Lagunas enterprises of North, see above, pp. 52–5, and below, pp. 228–9.   [107] Kennedy to Salisbury, loc. cit. No. 24. Diplomatic.

[108] Kennedy to Sanderson, Santiago, 9 March 1890. F.O. 61/386. Private. Kennedy had a poor opinion of Balmaceda's trustworthiness. After a meeting with the President in December 1889, he had written of a strong feeling of insincerity and of Balmaceda's 'self-asserted immunity for all private statements', adding that he would never see Balmaceda alone again. Kennedy to Salisbury, Viña, 16 January 1890. F.O. 61/386. No. 6. Diplomatic. Confidential. For the similar experience of a private individual, see below, pp. 187–9.

Balmaceda, he said later, had refused to see him owing to alleged 'pressure of business', although the President had told others that Kennedy's intervention 'had caused him great annoyance and had made the question more disagreeable'; moreover, an 'inspired paragraph in a daily paper' had reported that Kennedy intended withdrawing his memorandum and he had great difficulty in persuading the Foreign Minister that he had not the slightest intention of doing so.[109] Kennedy also referred to the political situation and its bearing on the railway question. In view of the gravity of the political crisis, he thought it would be inopportune to press the company's case, unless, he added,

the ordinary session [of Congress] next June may again force on the President a Ministry representing the majority of the Chamber instead of Ministers who, like the present occupants of State Departments, represent merely the personal will of the President.

For this reason, the company ought not to dismiss Zegers as Valdés Carrera suggested, since

account must be taken of the probability of Señor Zegers finding himself before long in occupation of an important position in the Government of the country.[110]

In short, Kennedy considered that the replacement of a personal ministry by a Congressional one would be advantageous to the Nitrate Railways Company, since the opposition's main reason for supporting the company was simply that its treatment provided an admirable illustration of Balmaceda's arbitrary conduct. As a prominent Liberal Deputy told Kennedy in April,

it would be almost impossible to effect anything in favour of the Company's rights so long as the President remained uncontrolled by Congress . . . but . . . after the meeting of Congress on 1st June, the present Ministry will be turned out . . . explanation of many arbitrary acts of the President will be demanded, and amongst them will be the legality of the action of the President in deciding the

---

[109] Kennedy to Salisbury, 25 March 1890. Loc. cit. No. 24. Diplomatic.
[110] Ibid.

question of the Nitrate Railways Company by administrative action.[111]

Though much of this was clearly for Kennedy's benefit, the speaker had put his finger on the propaganda value of the Nitrate Railways case to the political opposition in Chile. And, by the same token, Valdés Carrera's strictures on Julio Zegers, as well as Balmaceda's reaction to Kennedy's intervention, showed clearly that it was primarily in the context of the political crisis in Chile that the relationships between foreign firms and Chilean public men were now being given a somewhat sinister significance. It is extremely unlikely that strictures would have been passed on Zegers by members of the government for acting as adviser to the Nitrate Railways Company if he had maintained his political support of Balmaceda in 1890.[112]

The subsequent course of events in Chile provides further evidence for this view. In the light of Chile's reply to the British protest, and of extensive correspondence with the interested parties, the Foreign Office turned again to the Law Officers of the Crown.[113] But events in Chile again intervened. On 1 April 1890 the Chilean government invited tenders for the construction of a railway line from the port of Junín to the nitrate *oficina* of Carolina, and, on 12 April, for the construction of a line from the *oficina* of San Pablo to the southern *oficinas* of Buena Ventura and Lagunas. The second of these projects was an internal line in Tarapacá in which Colonel North was interested, but the construction of the Junín line would be the second breach—following the Agua Santa railway—of the concessions of the Nitrate Railways Company. Consequently, when the news reached London, it was immediately communicated to the Law Officers.[114]

[111] Kennedy to Salisbury, Santiago, 12 April 1890. F.O. 16/287. No. 30. Diplomatic. Confidential. On the reverse of this despatch W. E. Davidson, Legal Adviser to the Foreign Office, wrote of 1 June as 'the day of reckoning'.

[112] In a private letter to Sanderson Kennedy wrote: 'The Govt. [*sic*] ie. the President wished to defer to the wishes of H.M. Govt. but H.E. was too deeply pledged to politicians interested in Agua Santa . . .' Referring to the antagonism between Balmaceda and Zegers, he added: 'If the *Compy.* could retain Zegers, but let a non-political leading lawyer . . . advocate their Cause it would help matters.' Kennedy to Sanderson, Viña. F.O. 16/287. 31 March 1890. Private.

[113] Foreign Office to Law Officers, 12 April 1890. F.O. 16/287.

[114] Same to same, 18 April 1890. F.O. 16/287. The news came from the Nitrate Railways Company.

Giving their opinion ten days later, the Law Officers considered that the grounds on which the British government had protested to Chile would not be valid if, in fact, the Chilean constitution empowered the Council of State to overrule opinions of the Supreme Court; but since there would then be no guarantee of protection for the concessionaire, they continued,

Her Majesty's Government will be justified in . . . maintaining the protest of 15th February 1890, and enforcing upon the Chilean Government the claims of the Nitrate Railways Company. The right of diplomatic intervention belongs to the Government, and not to the individual.[115]

Kennedy, accordingly, was instructed to inform the Chilean government of these decisions, but, at the same time, he was also to obtain the opinion of eminent Chilean legal figures on the question of the competency of the Council of State to take matters out of the hands of the Courts,[116] an instruction which indicated continuing uncertainty on the part of the Foreign Office about the course it should adopt. Nevertheless, in asserting the principle that the right of diplomatic intervention belonged to the government, the Foreign Office was committed even further to supporting the Nitrate Railways Company in Chile. It could only withdraw that support if the company took further action before Chilean courts of law.

This was precisely what happened. Replying to his instructions, Kennedy informed the Foreign Office that the company's agents in Chile had filed a suit in the Supreme Court against the Agua Santa Company for infringement of its concessions; since the Court might settle the question legally by a favourable decision on this suit, renewed diplomatic intervention might be inadvisable.[117] Moreover, he and the manager of the Nitrate Railways Company in Chile, Mr Rowland, had met the Minister of Industry and Public Works on the same day that Kennedy received the Foreign Office telegram: Valdés Carrera had informed them that the Nitrate Railways

[115] Law Officers to Salisbury, 28 April 1890. F.O. 16/287.
[116] Foreign Office to Kennedy, 2 May 1890. F.O. 16/287. Telegraphic.
[117] Kennedy to Salisbury, Santiago, 6 May 1890. F.O. 16/287. Telegraphic.

Company's tender to build the Lagunas extension would be accepted, though Kennedy feared that renewed diplomatic pressure on the other issue might still prejudice that project. And there was a further point:

the President [wrote Kennedy] might profit by a renewed intervention of Her Majesty's Government . . . to seek an escape from his serious political embarrassments by arousing the patriotic feelings of Chileans against what would be represented as an attempt by a foreign power to exercise pressure on the Government of Chile in a national matter.[118]

In a later despatch, Kennedy reported that the government had not challenged the Nitrate Railways Company's latest appeal to the Supreme Court because of its embarrassed position: 'all right-minded Chileans' seemed to him to concur in the view that Balmaceda had acted wrongly in deciding questions of contract by administrative decree, and, he added, 'doubts are expressed as to the possibility of the completion by the President of his term of office'.[119]

In view of Kennedy's opinions, the Foreign Office agreed that it would be impolitic to renew its protest to the Chilean government on behalf of the Nitrate Railways Company.[120] Accordingly, there the matter rested from May to August 1890: it was left to Kennedy to renew the protest when he saw fit, and since Kennedy took the view that the suit brought by the company in Chile against the Agua Santa Company was a test case on which actions against other concessionaires could be based, if necessary, no action was taken by him while that case was pending.[121]

One such possible concessionaire was the House of Antony Gibbs and Sons, whose prompt protest to the Foreign Office at British diplomatic support for the Nitrate Railways Company was motivated by the fact that they also hoped to benefit from

---

[118] Kennedy to Salisbury, Santiago, 6 May 1890. F.O. 16/287. No. 38. Diplomatic.

[119] Kennedy to Salisbury, Santiago, 7 May 1890. F.O. 16/287. No. 39. Diplomatic. This despatch amplified a telegram of the same date.

[120] Foreign Office to Kennedy, 8 May 1890. F.O. 16/287. No. 7. Telegraphic.

[121] The suit came before the Supreme Court in May 1890. Kennedy to Salisbury, Santiago, 7 May 1890. F.O. 16/287. Telegraphic.

the infringement of North's transport monopoly.[122] Gibbs wished to build a railway line themselves in the south of Tarapacá from their own nitrate-fields of Alianza and Pan de Azúcar to a suitable shipping outlet on the coast, and so long as North's monopoly remained inviolate Gibbs kept these fields unworked, since, under the terms of the Nitrate Railways' exclusive concession, only that company had the right to build lines to the coast. Any line built by North, of course, would charge excessive freights on nitrate shipments, and from Gibbs' point of view there was no point in opening the nitrate-fields merely to benefit North. Not only would that be very bad business for Gibbs: it would also represent a further triumph for North in Tarapacá, and there was no love lost between him and the most important British business house in Chile. Personal factors certainly played a part in Gibbs' attitude: they had been in nitrates from the beginning, only to see the *parvenu* North eclipse them in the business by methods of which they certainly disapproved.[123] From the time when the Nitrate Railways' concession first came under attack in the mid-1880s, the branches of Gibbs in Chile at Valparaiso and Iquique kept a very close watch on developments, and they prepared their plans in the hope that, at some stage, they could proceed with their own project.[124] That moment appeared to have arrived in the autumn of 1889, when the Chilean Council of State ruled in favour of the President on the question of competency between the executive and the judiciary, thus opening the way to the Agua Santa Company to break North's monopoly in fact, as the Council had done so in law.[125] If the Agua Santa Company succeeded, Gibbs would have an excellent precedent for soliciting permission from the Chilean government to build their Alianza line.

[122] See above, pp. 132–4. Gibbs made no secret of the fact that they had a direct interest in the matter when they intervened with the Foreign Office in March. Sir Thomas Sanderson noted at that time that the Agua Santa issue constituted a precedent for Gibbs with regard to their own interests. Notes of 6 March 1890. F.O. 16/287.

[123] See above, pp. 36, 51–2. A near-contemporary French writer spoke of North as 'the Nitrate King' and of Gibbs as 'the princes of the blood'. A. Bellesort, *La Jeune Amérique: Chili et Bolivie* (Paris, 1897), pp. 94–5.

[124] The Gibbs Papers are full of references to the question from 1886 onwards.

[125] See above, pp. 111–13.

Two months before the Council of State reached its decision, Gibbs in Valparaiso had appointed a new Chilean legal adviser, one of whose duties would be the presentation of their petition for their railway: this was Senator Eulogio Altamirano, a well-known politician and lawyer who was also a member of the Council of State.[126] He readily undertook this task, despite his official position, and despite the fact that the Council was already seized of the question of competency in the Nitrate Railways case.[127] It was clearly in the interests of Antony Gibbs and Sons, with their Alianza plans dependent upon a decision by the Council favouring the cancellation of the Nitrate Railways Company's monopoly, that Altamirano should also support that view. In fact, however, he was the only member of the Council of State to dissent from the majority opinion supporting the President's action, and thus the only member, in effect, to favour the Nitrate Railways Company.[128] This decision, however, did not affect his standing with Gibbs who retained him as legal adviser, though relieving him of the specific task of seeing through their railway petition.[129] He did, however, continue to advise Gibbs on it, and, after the Council's decision, recommended that they wait to see what happened to the Agua Santa line, an opinion which the Valparaiso House regarded as a 'sound one'.[130] When the Agua Santa Company petitioned the President for permission to build its line in Tarapacá, Altamirano advised that 'the executive could in no case grant the petition which must be

[126] Altamirano's appointment was notified to London on 19 July 1889. Antony Gibbs & Sons, Valparaiso, 19 July 1889. AAG., MS. 11,470. Vol. 12. Letter No. 15. Private. For biographical details of Altamirano, see Figueroa, *Diccionario Histórico*, i, 401–3.

[127] It was precisely because he would have to deal with Gibbs' Alianza petition that Vicente Reyes had declined to be employed as legal adviser by them. See above, pp. 127–8.

[128] See above, pp. 111–12. Ramírez, *Balmaceda*, pp. 77–9, while citing material to show that Altamirano was indeed employed by Gibbs, also quotes two contemporary sources alleging that Altamirano was employed by North and that it was in that capacity that he cast his vote in the Council of State. There is no evidence whatever that Altamirano was employed by North, while his work for Gibbs is incontestable, and Ramírez appears not to realize that Gibbs and North were in opposite camps, though Balmaceda certainly did. See below, p. 148.

[129] Antony Gibbs & Sons, Valparaiso to London, 24 October 1889. AAG, MS. 11,470. Vol. 12. Letter No. 22.

[130] Same to same, Valparaiso, 27 September 1889, in ibid., Letter No. 20.

conceded in the shape of a law authorised by Congress', and the Valparaiso House agreed that that was also the only course to follow in their case.[131] As already noted, however, Balmaceda was so far committed to the Agua Santa Company for political reasons that he did not wish to see a hostile Congress debate the matter: accordingly, the government invited tenders to construct the Agua Santa line but on such terms that no other company could possibly compete.[132] This was a clever manœuvre by Balmaceda. Although the Council of State had apparently determined the question once and for all, fierce Congressional criticism of its decision and, indeed, also of its apparent subservience to the President's will was dangerous for Balmaceda in his exposed political position. But by asking publicly for tenders to build the Agua Santa line, he could at least argue that he was giving the Nitrate Railways Company an equal chance with others of tendering itself, though in practice, of course, it was quite impossible for it to do so.[133]

With the closing date for submission of tenders finally fixed at 1 March 1890, Gibbs' plans for their Alianza railway hung in abeyance for some months. The time, however, was not wasted, owing to the presence in Chile, from December 1889 to May 1890, of a senior member of the London House, Mr B. A. Miller, who knew the country well from previous service there and who also knew Balmaceda personally. Miller devoted a good deal of his time on this visit to discussing the Agua Santa issue and its relationship to Gibbs' own project for the Alianza railway, both with the House representatives in Valparaiso and Iquique, and with their Chilean lawyers, including Altamirano.[134] At the beginning of March, however, with the only tender for the Agua Santa railway coming from Campbell Outram and Company, things began to move, particularly as the government's acceptance of that tender in the middle of the month was soon followed by government decrees in April, calling for tenders for the construction of other railway lines in Tarapacá.[135] It looked as though the time had come, at last,

[131] Same to same, Valparaiso, 8 November 1889, in ibid., Letter No. 23.
[132] See above, pp. 112–13.   [133] See above, pp. 131–2.
[134] Correspondence in AAG, MS 11,470. Vol. 12.
[135] See above, p. 138. Reporting these events, the Valparaiso House of Gibbs referred to the severe blow suffered by the Nitrate Railways Company over

for Gibbs to move on their Alianza petition, and since he would shortly be leaving for London Miller decided to seek an interview with Balmaceda himself

in order [he wrote] to find out . . . how far he is prepared to go with his newly-invented tender system—whether if we were to feed in a petition asking to have it applied to our Alianza Railway scheme we are likely to get the port of Chucumata opened.

Miller also wished to introduce to Balmaceda a comparatively new representative of Gibbs in Chile, Mr Daubeny.[136] Balmaceda replied to Miller's letter by telegram, saying that he would receive him as soon as he reached his office, and both Miller and Daubeny took the train from Valparaiso to Santiago on the night of 4 May.[137]

Before seeing Balmaceda on 5 May, Miller had conversations with both Altamirano and Kennedy: he sought the lawyer's advice on the likely outcome of the Nitrate Railways' suit in the Supreme Court to try to stop the building of the Agua Santa railway, asking if the Court could grant an injunction to stop work on the line while the suit proceeded. Altamirano thought this possible, but he seemed 'much astonished' when Miller, who had recently been in Tarapacá, told him that Campbell Outram were already hard at work on the line, and Altamirano then said he would ask Zegers and Guerrero, the Nitrate Railways Company's lawyers, what was happening. Miller then met Kennedy at the hotel and was invited by him to his room to talk about the railway question, but while they were there, Mr Rowland, the manager of the Nitrate Railways Company in Chile, who, Kennedy had complained, 'was constantly at him', interrupted them: he seemed, wrote Miller,

---

the Agua Santa issue, which was compounded by the threat of new lines in addition, and it had cabled the news to London since it believed that Gibbs held some shares in Nitrate Railways. Antony Gibbs & Sons, Valparaiso, 14 April 1890, to London. AAG, MS. 11,470. Vol. 12. Letter No. 35.

[136] Miller at Valparaiso to Gibbs in London, 6 May 1890. AAG, MS. 11,470. Vol. 12. Private. It is interesting to note, in view of Congressional criticism of Balmaceda's tendency to make his own rules and ignore customary procedures, that Miller, a person of long business experience in Chile, referred to 'his newly-invented tender system'.

[137] Ibid. Minister Kennedy joined the train at Viña and had a long talk with Miller on the way to Santiago.

'a good deal surprised and anything but pleased to see us there. He retired immediately, Mr. Kennedy promising to see him a little later on.' After a conversation with Kennedy, in which Miller sought to put the government's case for cancelling the Nitrate Railways' concession, Miller and Daubeny went to the Moneda, the presidential palace, to see Balmaceda.[138]

The President received them very cordially, 'making', reported Miller, 'a high-flown speech about transferring to Mr. Daubeny as representative of the House, his friendship and consideration for me etc. etc. [sic]'. Miller, assuming that there would no longer be any obstacle to Gibbs' Alianza proposal since the tender-system could be applied, asked Balmaceda what would happen if they arrived at the same stage as Campbell Outram had reached, facing a lawsuit to stop construction when they had started. Balmaceda

showed some amusement at my cautious line, remarking that, if the State allowed people to construct railways for their private convenience, they could not expect to be protected from the attacks of terceros [i.e. third parties], they must protect themselves.

As the conversation proceeded, Balmaceda expressed great opposition to the idea of allowing Gibbs to have a port at the end of their proposed line, in view of the difficulties of preventing smuggling, and then asked, since the Iquique branch of the Nitrate Railways was to be extended to the southern nitrate-field of Lagunas, if that proposed line would not suit Gibbs' purpose just as well as a quite separate line from Alianza to the coast at Chucumata. This, of course, was the last thing that Miller wanted, since the proposed Lagunas extension to the Nitrate Railways would belong to the Nitrate Railways Company, with its high freight rates. Thereupon, as he reported,

I touched on the extraordinary way in which everything seemed to play into North's hands, and alluded to his present attempt to establish a monopoly by contracting to buy all the nitrate for a term

---

[138] Miller to Gibbs, loc. cit. Miller evinced no surprise that Gibbs' lawyer should consult the lawyers of the rival concern about a matter which concerned them both. Adolfo Guerrero was also a member of the Chilean Congress. Ramírez, *Balmaceda*, p. 80, Note 112. In view of the importance of this meeting, the account which follows is extensive, and is based largely on Miller's report.

of years. This seemed to hit him on the raw. He said if that Monopol [*sic*] is established we will open all the ports that you build, railways wherever you like. If we let you build your railway and open Chucumata, will your London House compromise itself to enter no combination tending to limit production, and engage to ship a minimum of say, two million quintals of nitrate annually.[139]

'This turn round was very sudden', Miller continued, but Balmaceda seemed very keen on it and immediately summoned to the meeting Pedro N. Gandarillas, the *Ministro de Hacienda*, a former director of the Treasury whom Miller had not previously met but of whom he had good reports at a time when Miller had been a director of the Banco Nacional.[140] They went over the idea again, Miller trying to check Balmaceda's new-found enthusiasm by saying that more detailed discussions would be required and that undue haste might appear to be an act of hostility to the many firms and interests with which Gibbs had long been connected.[141] Balmaceda agreed, but reiterated his proposal that Gibbs should agree to ship an annual minimum quantity of nitrate from Chucumata, one and a half million quintals in the first year, and two million afterwards, and Miller replied that he did not think this would be difficult for Gibbs to accept. The conversation ended with the understanding that on Miller's return to London he would communicate to Gibbs the proposal to give a guarantee to ship a minimum amount of nitrate annually through Chucumata in return for the concession to build a railway line there from Alianza and open the port.

Miller added two other interesting comments in his report.

[139] For North's alleged attempt to create a monopoly in nitrate in 1890, see below, pp. 153–4.

[140] Miller added that he was delighted to see Gandarillas as minister 'owing to the extreme scarcity of good men for the Cabinet willing to put up with Balmaceda's escapades in the way of fixing the election of his nominee, Sanfuentes, to succeed him in the presidency'.

[141] Miller feared that the news might get out that Gibbs had bound themselves not to enter a combination to limit production, with serious consequences for their relationships with other nitrate producers. His discussion with Balmaceda had been about a possible North monopoly which was a very different thing, though the confusion between the two was to cause Gibbs a good deal of trouble subsequently. See below, pp. 155–6, 187–9.

Referring back to the discussion about North, he stated that he had pointed out that

although they, the Government people are always talking against North and the 'Northization' of the province of Tarapacá, somehow or other everything they do redounds to the benefit of North and his friends, and I instanced the fact that while they are to be allowed to extend the Iquique line to Lagunas (their tender had not been accepted but B [*sic*] had told us it would be) Govt [*sic*] refuses us our Railway and tells us to give our Alianza traffic to swell the already plethoric income of North's railway, and aggravate the already overcrowded state of the Iquique line.

He recorded no comment by Balmaceda on these remarks, and it appears that it was only when he mentioned the word 'monopoly' that Balmaceda reacted.

Miller's second important comment on his meeting with Balmaceda was an afterthought and he recorded it at the very end of his report. If, in fact, he reflected, the port of Chucumata could be opened 'by a mere administrative decree', why could it not just as easily be closed by the same method, leaving Gibbs at the mercy of the government?

Miller's remarks about the way in which North continually seemed to prosper with his affairs in Chile, despite government propaganda against him, appeared to be borne out by other events in Chile in that same summer of 1890. Leaving aside the question of the Nitrate Railways Company's concession, which Balmaceda was quite determined to annul, in pursuance of Chilean government policy which had been framed even before Balmaceda assumed the presidency, it should be noted that Balmaceda told Miller that the company's tender to extend its Iquique line to Lagunas would be accepted. Miller probably suspected this already, since Gibbs at Valparaiso had been told in April by one of the Railways Company's advisers, Mr Linnick, that their tender was the only one submitted, and it had been put in with the rider that the submission did not endorse the legality of the government's action in asking for tenders, in effect the government's method of breaking the railway monopoly.[142] But a more important matter for North

[142] Antony Gibbs & Sons, Valparaiso to London, 26 April 1890. AAG, MS. 11,470. Vol. 12. Letter No. 36.

than the Lagunas extension was also settled in the same month: the rich nitrate-field of Lagunas itself, which North had sought to buy in 1889 from the Delano group, a transaction the government had challenged in the courts, was finally adjudicated in North's favour.[143] Miller might well complain that the government's words about North were not always backed up with actions.

On one issue, however, apart from the railway, Balmaceda's attitude to North's interests was quite clear, as he indicated to Miller. He would do all that lay in his power to prevent the formation of another combination of nitrate producers to restrict production when government revenues and his own domestic programme demanded continued high shipments of the fertilizer. And he had quickly seen that Gibbs' desire for the Alianza railway and the opening of the port of Chucumata was an excellent weapon to turn against North, as he had already used the Agua Santa Company and Campbell Outram to break the Nitrate Railways Company monopoly. Clearly, in the formation of a new combination, North would be the key figure:[144] if Balmaceda could so arrange matters that Gibbs, the most distinguished British business house in Chile, declined to join the proposed combination, the combination was doomed.[145] At that time, the combination was still in embryo, though the world market in nitrates during 1890 was no stronger than it had been in 1889, and throughout the first six months of the year nitrates was in the doldrums.[146] It was continually rumoured in both London and Chile that a combination was on the verge of being formed, but, for one reason or another, it failed to materialize.[147] Share prices followed the rumours, rising when it was believed a combination was in the

---

[143] Ibid. See also above, p. 136.

[144] See Brown, 'Nitrate Crises', p. 235. In 1888, the companies controlled by North and his associates produced approximately 8 million quintals of nitrate exported, out of a total of 16,682,000 quintals. Calculated from data in Billinghurst, *Los capitales salitreros, passim.*

[145] Referring to the proposed deal with Gibbs which was discussed with Balmaceda and Gandarillas, Miller reported that the Chileans were 'looking on any stick as good enough' to beat North with. Miller to Gibbs, loc. cit.

[146] See, e.g., *The Economist,* 4 January, 11 January, 8 February, 22 March; *The South American Journal,* 8 March, 24 May, 14 June, 21 June 1890.

[147] E.g. *The South American Journal,* 8 February, 22 March, 19 April 1890.

offing, and falling quite as quickly when the rumours proved false.[148] When the previous combination had been formed in 1884, its organizers had paid scant attention to the Chilean government's interest in the matter.[149] Now, however, as everyone knew, it seemed very likely that 'the Chilean Government' would 'have a word to say about the suggested combination'.[150]

Balmaceda himself, however, did not have quite the freedom of manœuvre that observers believed him to have. The interest of the Chilean government, like that of nitrate producers, was basically to increase the size of the world market, and the government appeared to recognize this fact in December 1889, when it sought Congressional approval—which it received—to spend $150,000 on advertising nitrate abroad.[151] Balmaceda might make speeches, as he had in 1889, including vague threats against foreign owners of Chilean nitrate-fields, but he could take no action which would, in itself, transform the world market situation. There were, after all, Chilean owners of nitrate-fields, as well as foreigners, who were all in the same position. He had tried, in 1889, to put forward proposals designed to increase the proportion of Chilean ownership of the nitrate industry. In his annual message to Congress on 1 June 1889, three months after his celebrated visit to Iquique, he had suggested that state-owned nitrate properties which might subsequently be auctioned should be divided into cantons, each containing a mixture of good, fair and inferior nitrate deposits, and that 4,000 lots of the best grounds should be placed on the market gradually but only for sale to Chileans, to be transferable to third parties only after a certain period and then only to Chileans, and, finally, that one-half of the total properties for sale thereafter should be open to foreigners and one-half to Chileans, but no properties could be transferred to foreigners.[152]

[148] See particularly *The Economist*, 11 January 1890; *The South American Journal*, 24 May, 14 June, 5 and 26 July 1890.

[149] See Brown, loc. cit., p. 234, where it is pointed out that, in fact, the Chilean government approved of the combination.

[150] *The Economist*, 11 January 1890.

[151] See Yrarrázaval, 'Balmaceda y el salitre', pp. 55–6, and also *The Economist*, 22 February 1890.

[152] *Discurso de su Excellencia el Presidente de la República al Apertura del Congreso Nacional de 1889* (Santiago, 1889). See also *The Economist*, 27 July 1889.

Although, he declared,

> ... we ought not to close the door to the freedom of competition and production of nitrate ... at the same time, we ought not to allow this rich and extensive region [Tarapacá] to be converted simply into a foreign factory.[153]

Balmaceda submitted no concrete project on these lines to the Chilean Congress, though political preoccupations may well have prevented him from doing so. Nevertheless, it is clear that these proposals, if such they may be called, had a limited objective with regard to nitrates. Secondly, even if they had been carried forward, it is a moot point whether they would have succeeded. The purpose was to encourage Chileans to invest in nitrates, thus increasing the national share in the industry and creating, Balmaceda hoped, some sort of barrier against the possibility of a foreign monopoly of the fertilizer. Yet that possibility arose from the simple fact that during the 1880s many Chileans who owned *salitreras* had been only too anxious to sell them to foreigners, and North had consolidated the interests he had acquired through the War of the Pacific precisely by this means.[154] Balmaceda, in fact, was pursuing a chimera in expecting that the very limited assistance government itself was prepared to provide to Chileans would be adequate encouragement to them to invest heavily in the nitrate industry.[155]

So far as a monopoly was concerned, however, Balmaceda's firmest allies against it were foreigners, and not least British entrepreneurs who were not linked with the North group. The case of the Nitrate Railways was the clearest example of this, and there is ample evidence, apart from that already cited, to show that not only were Houses such as Gibbs determined to prevent North from monopolizing the nitrate industry, but also that, unlike Balmaceda, they had clear ideas how to do it. For example, late in 1888, Gibbs had concrete plans for under-

---

[153] *Discurso ... de 1889*, p. 10.

[154] See above, pp. 36–7, and also Billinghurst, *Los capitales salitreros*, *passim*.

[155] See above, pp. 85–6, for some Chilean criticisms of the apparent unwillingness of Balmaceda's government to assist Chilean interests in nitrates, and p. 99 for foreign comment on the apparent lack of interest by Chilean investors in the exploitation of the country's natural resources.

mining the high tariff rates of the Nitrate Railways Company, as Herbert Gibbs explained to the company's manager in Valparaiso:

... Of the 12,000,000 quintals of nitrate carried down by the railway [he wrote] Gibbs and Co provide 1,750,000 and I suppose that including up and down traffic, G & Cos [sic] traffic is worth £80,000 a year gross to the Con. [sic]. We have therefore already considerable power as against the railway, and I want to make this influence overwhelming by increasing our stake in the Northern province and by alliance with other northern Salitreros: and then there should be no difficulty in reducing the freight to 6d and transferring from the pockets of the railway comp. to those of the Salitreros 3d on an up and down traffic of say 15,000,000 or £187,500. The first thing for us to do would be to endeavour to purchase any going oficinas that are using the railway, and could be had at a resonable price: and in doing this it would be better for our immediate plan to buy oficinas with short lives, rather than those with long ones, provided of course that the prices were proportionately lower. When this was done we could then set about forming a combination against the railway . . .[156]

Gibbs' later Alianza scheme had exactly the same purpose, and it was completely in line with Balmaceda's own thinking on the destruction of the monopoly of rail transport enjoyed by North's Nitrate Railways Company in Tarapacá.

But a monopoly was one thing, a combination another, at least to the nitrate producers in Tarapacá. Those who were not associated with North, but who were obliged to use his railway for carriage of their nitrate to the coast, could agree with Herbert Gibbs when he told Sir Thomas Sanderson at the Foreign Office that 'the monopoly of the Nitrate Railways was weighing unmercifully on the British capital invested in the Nitrate works'.[157] Of course, North's own nitrate companies paid the same tariff as did others to the railway company. But although all these were public companies, including the Nitrate Railways Company itself, North's personal holding in Nitrate Railways was approximately half of the total number of shares, and he stood, therefore, to gain enormously from the railway's high

[156] Herbert Gibbs to Mr Smail, London, 28 November 1888. AAG, MS. 11,042. Private Letters to Partners, vol. 2.
[157] Notes of Sir Thomas Sanderson, 6 March 1890. F.O. 16/287.

profits, produced essentially by charging high tariffs.[158] What
he lost on the roundabouts, he gained on the swings and, as
chairman of so many companies, he could manipulate their
separate affairs to his own advantage. Thus, next to the capital
gains North had obtained from the sale of nitrate-grounds to
the public companies he founded, his fortune owed more to the
Nitrate Railways Company than to any other single factor, and
this was precisely because it was a monopoly.

For everyone in the nitrate business, however, a combination
was very different. All were affected by falling world prices
resulting from high output and slack demand, and a combination was no more than a temporary measure to change that
situation. It was a voluntary agreement among producers to
reduce their output, according to accepted quotas, until they
agreed that world market conditions had again improved
sufficiently for them to dispense with the combination. Consequently, when the circumstances suggested that a combination should be formed, it concerned all producers alike, though,
naturally, in the bargaining process to fix quotas, some voices
spoke louder than others.

To the Chilean government, now so critically dependent on
revenues derived from export taxes on nitrate shipments, a
monopoly was dangerous in that it would concentrate in a few
hands the power to decide how much nitrate should be shipped
and when. It represented a threat not only to the government's
specific programme but also, indeed, to its freedom of action as
a whole. But so, at least in its immediate effects, would a combination. The paradoxical situation resulted that those nitrate
interests which were opposed to North and in agreement with
Balmaceda's views on monopoly, would, nevertheless, be
likely to support a combination, and in this respect be opposed
to Balmaceda. This was the position of Gibbs.

When Miller of Antony Gibbs and Sons had seen Balmaceda
on 5 May 1890, the President had appeared very anxious to
come to an agreement with the company whereby Gibbs would

[158] According to *The Financial News*, 30 May 1888, North held 15,830 shares in
the Nitrate Railways Company. Rippy, *British Investments*, p. 63, estimates that
between 1888 and 1896, dividends on ordinary shares in the Company totalled
174 per cent, an annual nominal average of nearly 22 per cent.

receive permission to build the necessary railway line and open the port of Chucumata, provided they undertook to export an agreed minimum quantity of nitrate annually through that port.[159] Through this deal, Balmaceda clearly hoped to sabotage any possibility North might entertain of establishing a monopoly of nitrate production and export, and since Gibbs were fully in agreement with that purpose, Miller saw no difficulty in agreeing to the terms in principle. At least, this is what Miller believed Balmaceda to have in mind, though his natural business caution had led him to insist on more detailed discussions before any agreement was reached, and he was particularly concerned that nothing should come out about Gibbs being bound not to enter a combination to restrict production.[160] Unknown to Miller, however, was the fact that while he was discussing in Santiago an arrangement with Balmaceda which the latter clearly believed would make the formation of a combination difficult, if not impossible, Gibbs in London had been discussing with the various nitrate interests the possibility of *establishing* such a combination or something like one. As already noted, the proposed combination hung fire throughout the first half of 1890.[161] It was a complicated business indeed, and it had been made more complex by North himself pushing an idea of forming 'a trust or syndicate' whose 'object would be to buy up the whole nitrate production, thus facilitating an increase in selling prices'.[162] Such a proposal, however, was extremely difficult to put into effect, since it required not only the agreement of all major producers in Chile to sell to the trust, but also very large bank and agency loans to the trust to enable it to buy the nitrate.[163] Among those

[159] See above, pp. 145–7. This proposal of Balmaceda's, made to the most important British business house in Chile, shows how very limited Balmaceda's alleged economic nationalism was.

[160] If it did, he reported home, 'you and we would inevitably get to loggerheads with all our present surroundings, the Rosario . . . the Tamarugal . . . etc.' Miller to Gibbs, 6 May 1890, loc. cit. The Rosario Company had on its directorate a leading member of another well-known British House, Balfour Williamson, which was also strongly antagonistic to North, but Tamarugal had been founded by a group of North's associates, including F. H. Evans, M.P. Data from *Burdetts Official Intelligence*, viii (1890), pp. 882–3, 906–7.   [161] See above, pp. 109–11.

[162] *The Economist*, 11 January 1890.

[163] Ibid. See also *The Economist*, 1 February, 22 February, 22 March 1890, and *The South American Journal*, 22 March 1890.

solicited for financial backing was the House of Gibbs in London who were informed in April that arrangements for

an intermediary company between a financial house & the producers were far advanced, that the members of the Board were to be Evans, Inglis, North, Grace and Balfour, capital half a million or a million and the Companys [*sic*] duties to consist simply of guaranteeing or acting as a buffer for the financiers . . .

Gibbs' informant, F. H. Evans, also said that North was 'undoubtedly hostile' to the approach to Gibbs 'but that he would try and talk him round'.[164]

This scheme was what Miller had referred to in his conversation with Balmaceda as North's 'present attempt to establish a monopoly by contracting to buy all the nitrate for a term of years', and it was this reference which had caused Balmaceda's sudden volte-face over the Alianza project.[165] But when Miller telegraphed to London the gist of his talk with Balmaceda, pointing out that three days after it took place the government had accepted the tender of the Nitrate Railways Company to build the Lagunas extension, and that Gibbs could only secure the Alianza line if it kept out of the syndicate, he received a reply that was very far from his liking. Gibbs in London informed him that they were under increasing pressure to join the syndicate which, in any event, was only possible if Gibbs did so; that since the government had declined to co-operate over the Alianza line, the House thought it desirable to join North's scheme, linking their Alianza interests to North's Lagunas interests and the Nitrate Railways, though they would make the proposed arrangement with Balmaceda provided he called for tenders for the Alianza line. Miller was both furious and embarrassed: he telegraphed to London immediately, saying that he wished to keep the matter open until he could explain it fully in London. On 10 May, London replied that

[164] H. L. Gibbs to Herbert Gibbs, London, 9 April 1890. AAG, MS. 11,040. Private Letters to Partners, vol. 1. The names mentioned were all prominent directors of nitrate companies in London, Inglis, Grace and Balfour being connected with family firms with longstanding connections with Chile.

[165] See above, pp. 145–7. At the same time, Miller noted that both Balmaceda and his *Ministro de Hacienda*, Gandarillas, were highly sceptical and somewhat amused at North's proposals which Gandarillas saw as a stock-jobbing move 'to get up the value of the shares of their Nitrate companies'.

they did not understand his answer, to which Miller responded that he had asked Balmaceda for a further interview, and that if the President agreed to ask for tenders, it would be best to leave everything else for discussion in London. If, however, there was some delay on the issue of tenders, or the London House declined to act and preferred to join the syndicate,

the effect will probably be imputation we have used his offer as a lever to obtain consignment of Nitrate. Do not think it possible [Miller concluded] carry out details Nitrate Consignment with the West Coast producers.

The London House then agreed that Miller should discuss the whole matter with Balmaceda again, and they would defer further decisions until he returned.[166]

Miller's second meeting with Balmaceda took place on 14 May, but before seeing the President Miller thought it advisable to consult Gandarillas.[167] Miller read Gandarillas the telegrams from London and expressed the fear that Balmaceda might be offended by them: Gandarillas, however, not only demurred at this suggestion, but added his own view that he thought Balmaceda's suggestion of a Gibbs' guarantee to ship a minimum quantity of nitrate was not realistic. He also agreed when Miller said that 'the Government *oficinas* certainly couldn't be expected to be of much use against a "monopolio" ', since they were 'only the leavings after the good ones had been picked out by the people who knew most about them'.[168] The subsequent discussion with Balmaceda went on a long time, Balmaceda making flattering allusions to the high business standards of Gibbs. When Miller said he wished to cable London some message which would persuade them to defer discussing the proposed syndicate until he returned, Balmaceda said that he might

telegraph assuring them that there would almost certainly *be no objection made to opening Chucumata* in connection with the railway

---

[166] Miller's notes on this flurry of telegrams are in AAG, MS. 11,470. Vol. 12.

[167] Memorandum of a Conversation with the President [Balmaceda] and the Finance Minister [Gandarillas] at the Moneda, Wednesday, 14 May 1890, in Miller's hand, in AAG, MS. 11,470. Vol. 12.

[168] Ibid. Said Miller, 'he nodded and winked . . . as much as to say "right, but I can't say so"'.

scheme *provided* they would undertake to enter no Combination and he added [said Miller] Dígalles también que el Gobierno de Chile está determinado a romper cualquier Monopolio del Salitre que se haga.[169]

A long argument followed on the question of what kind of combination it was that Gibbs would be binding themselves not to join, and Miller tried to differentiate between a monopoly and a combination, pointing out that Gibbs might well agree not to be a party to a monopoly, but that if it were known that they were committed in advance not to join a combination their good relations with other nitrate producers might suffer. Although Miller was quite explicit on this point, still, he reported,

B persisted, saying that all Combinations are monopolies (I suppose he meant, tend that way) to which I demurred, reminding him that under the last combination each producer sold his own nitrate on the open market.

In fact, Miller felt constrained to repeat his argument again, saying that there was a very big difference between Gibbs declining to join a specific scheme such as a combination after examining it, and announcing in advance that they had already bound themselves not to join it. Balmaceda then said that Gibbs '*need not put anything about it* in their petition . . . or in fact in any formal document but could just pass a note or give a mere verbal undertaking', but this, Miller 'absolutely declined', adding that in his view verbal or informal undertakings often led to disputes later about both what was said and what was meant.[170] Gandarillas then intervened, according to Miller, to say that

it would meet the case if an important producer like we [i.e. Gibbs] should be, once our railway is made, *undertook to export a certain minimum quantity in the first two years after its completion,* say two million quintals p/a . . .

---

[169] Memorandum, loc. cit. Miller's italics. The last sentence is the only part of the memorandum in Spanish, and would appear to be Balmaceda's precise words.

[170] As it turned out, Miller's caution on this point was fully justified. See below, pp. 187–9. In the passages cited, the italicized words are Miller's.

But the actual 'minimum quantity' was, in fact, left for further discussion, since Miller feared that the mere public mention of so large a quantity as two million quintals coming from Gibbs' Alianza grounds would provide a strong incentive to others, including the Nitrate Railways Company, to put in competing bids to build the line. The meeting ended cordially, with the discussion suspended until Miller could report personally to Gibbs in London.

In the event, it was the autumn of 1890 before Daubeny in Santiago could reopen talks on behalf of Gibbs, owing mainly to the deepening political crisis in Chile which preoccupied Balmaceda from the opening of Congress on 1 June.[171] A secondary reason for the long delay was the necessity for Gibbs to sort things out, since their discussions in London on the consignment scheme and Miller's initiative in Santiago were somewhat at cross-purposes. Nevertheless, it is clear that the conversations in Santiago, initiated by Miller, did persuade Gibbs not to go ahead with North's consignment scheme, at least for the time being. The House held off because it hoped to get its railway, and because, according to Daubeny in June, the consignment scheme was 'certain to meet with the strongest possible opposition from this Govt. [sic] . . . so long as Balmaceda is President'. If Gibbs were to join it and 'figure as mono-polistas [sic], goodbye', he added, 'to our chances of getting leave for our Chucumata Railway for a long time to come'.[172] Also, of course, the consignment scheme was fraught with difficulties, particularly financial ones, coupled with the problem of persuading all the nitrate producers to join it, though Gibbs were quite attracted to the idea in principle. But they did hold back, and it was undoubtedly for the reasons adduced by Daubeny that they did so. Whether the caution of Gibbs was the key factor in preventing North from carrying through the scheme is not known, though it seems to have been an important one. Later in the year Daubeny had a meeting with Gandarillas, then no longer Minister of Finance, and informed him that Gibbs had been induced to reject the consignment

[171] See below, pp. 187-9.
[172] Antony Gibbs & Sons, Valparaiso, 23 June 1890, to London. AAG, MS. 11,470. Vol. 12.

scheme and try for their railway in view of the conversations
Miller had had with Balmaceda, and, while admitting that
the scheme was 'hung up for want of funds to start with', he
also added that the London House could certainly provide the
funds to revive it.[173]

From Balmaceda's point of view, the hesitancy of Gibbs to
put their considerable weight behind the scheme during the
summer of 1890 was a great help in ensuring that Chilean
government revenues from export taxes on nitrate shipments
did not fall drastically, as they would have done if the scheme
had come into operation. And this, in turn, raises the interesting
question whether Balmaceda, in his talks with Miller, was
merely playing for time, and had no serious intention of granting them their Chucumata line. If this is so, it was an astute
move on the President's part, though it should be noted that,
on their side, Gibbs moved with extreme caution on the
Chucumata railway, partly because the case brought by the
Nitrate Railways Company against the Agua Santa Company
was before the courts throughout 1890, and a favourable
decision for the Nitrate Railways Company in that matter
would have rendered nugatory all the tenders solicited as a
result of Government invitations to build other lines in Tarapacá. Secondly, hesitancy was no doubt in part the result of the
acute political crisis which affected Chile after the opening of
Congress on 1 June. The sharp increase in tension created
great uncertainty for Gibbs and, indeed, for everyone concerned. Early in June, the Valparaiso House reported that 'we
even heard today that in Santiago the possibilities of a revolution, in the event of the President continuing his present policy,
are being freely and openly discussed',[174] though Daubeny
himself did not believe a revolution was likely. Nevertheless,
serious the situation was, with both Balmaceda and Congress
moving into positions of irreconcilable opposition.

Prelude to Revolution

Balmaceda's sudden closure of the Extraordinary Sessions of

[173] Antony Gibbs & Sons, Valparaiso, 16 September 1890, to London. AAG
MS. 11,470. Vol. 12.
[174] Same to same, Valparaiso, 6 June 1890, in ibid., Letter No. 39. Private.

Congress on 18 January 1890, ushered in a year of political crisis in Chile. The new ministry which he formed that day was appointed without reference to the political parties, though Valdés Carrera was the only close supporter of the President to retain office and two other appointees, indeed, had opposed Balmaceda's candidature for the presidency in 1886.[175] But, if Balmaceda hoped that the formation of a quasi-independent ministry would be seen by the opposition as a conciliatory move, he was doomed to disappointment. Deprived of its platform in Congress, the opposition argued its case in the press and at a series of banquets held in the chief towns of the republic.[176] On 20 January, at a banquet in Valparaiso, a galaxy of orators spoke against 'the personal policy of the President' and demanded 'real Parliamentary institutions'.[177] Balmaceda replied with a manifesto in the *Diario Oficial*, repudiating the theory of Congressional sovereignty espoused by the opposition and at a public banquet at Valparaiso on 12 February, in honour of the new ministry led by Adolfo Ibáñez,

the New Minister of the Interior . . . [reported the British Minister] announced the Ministerial programme to be a radical reform of the Constitution, a law to protect electoral rights and another to organize local Government. The Prime Minister added the important declaration that the President believed that the moment had come for divesting himself of a great part of his Constitutional attributions.[178]

The opposition remained unmoved, however, and continued its campaign against Balmaceda, particularly through the press which it mostly controlled. To counteract these attacks, Government supporters founded *La Nación* and *El Comercio*, the former the creation of Julio Bañados Espinosa, deputy for Ovalle, a leading orator, jurist, publicist and politician.[179] Well versed in the study of constitutional law, Bañados was to play

[175] Encina, *Historia de Chile*, xix, 186 ff. and see *ante* pp. 119–20.

[176] See Athos, *La convención independiente, passim*, for a full account.

[177] Kennedy to Salisbury, Viña, 28 February 1890. F.O. 16/259. No. 20.

[178] Ibid. Kennedy's use of the words 'the Prime Minister' when speaking of the Minister of the Interior should be noted: false analogies of this kind were quite significant in the misinterpretation of the Chilean constitutional crisis abroad.

[179] See Figueroa, *Diccionario Histórico*, ii, 98–101, for biographical details.

a prominent part in the subsequent history of the Balmaceda administration.[180]

The deadlock between government and opposition persisted throughout the first half of 1890, since Balmaceda, quite contrary to custom, called no Extraordinary Session of Congress in March or April, and it was noteworthy that during this period the government press refrained from attacking the Conservative party in opposition, and seemed, indeed, to be adopting a favourable line towards one plank of that party's programme—municipal autonomy—which it had hitherto opposed. It is, in fact, a measure of the gravity of Balmaceda's position that he had, apparently, come to contemplate a possible alliance with his most inveterate political opponents. Manuel José Yrarrázaval, the 'elder statesman' of the Conservative party and the leading advocate of municipal reform in its ranks, was invited to chair a Congressional commission to draw up a plan of reform. But after Balmaceda had promised to call Congress to discuss these matters in extraordinary session, he suddenly turned a complete volte-face, decided not to call Congress together, and thus terminated his brief, and quite unconvincing, romance with the Conservatives. He did so on the advice of Bañados, who had suggested that the political crisis might be solved if the government implemented reform on its own initiative and if, simultaneously, Enrique Sanfuentes, still regarded universally as Balmaceda's choice to succeed him, announced his unequivocal withdrawal from the forthcoming presidential election.[181]

The opposition, however, still had one card to play to bring constitutional pressure on Balmaceda, that of calling on the Comisión Conservadora to urge the President to convoke Congress for discussions on municipal and electoral reform.[182] By the Constitution, the Comisión had power 'to request the Presi-

[180] See his *Gobierno Parlamentario y Sistema Representativo* (Santiago, 1888), and his *Letras y Política* (Valparaiso, 1888) for Bañados's views. Figueroa, loc. cit., ii, 100, calls Bañados 'the inspiration and alter ego' of Balmaceda.

[181] Encina, *Historia de Chile*, xix, 205–8. Cf. Bañados, *Balmaceda*, i, 429 ff. See also Abdón Cifuentes, *Memorias* (2 vols., Santiago, 1936), ii, 282–9. Cifuentes (1836–1928), a prominent Conservative with a remarkably long career in Chilean public life, accuses Balmaceda of 'a degree of levity and informality quite out of keeping with his office'.

[182] For the role of the *Comisión* in the Chilean system, see above, pp. 4, 6.

dent . . . to convoke Extraordinary Sessions of Congress, whenever, in its opinion, extraordinary or exceptional circumstances
demanded such action'.[183] And the discussion in the Comisión
turned on this provision. After an acrimonious debate, the
motion was passed to request the President to call an Extraordinary Session of Congress, but Balmaceda refused absolutely,
and on 28 April, the Comisión dissolved.[184] It had done its
constitutional duty and could do no more: the battle between
President and Congress could not be renewed, at least in the
chambers, until the Ordinary Session of Congress began on
1 June.

Meanwhile, in the press and at public meetings, both government and opposition argued their case with increasing acer-
bity and diminishing respect, and the activities of the press
were a potent factor in the deterioration of relations between
them.[185] Personal abuse, hitherto rare, was now commonplace
and Balmaceda became increasingly convinced that the
avowed constitutional objectives of the opposition were no
more than a veneer to cover selfish and destructive political
desires.[186] The opposition, for its part, waited impatiently for
the opening of Congress on 1 June.

Two days before that event Balmaceda showed that he still
hoped for an accommodation with the Congressional majority
on the basis of Sanfuentes' withdrawal as a candidate for the
next presidential election. This was announced on 30 May
and, simultaneously, Sanfuentes was appointed Minister of the
Interior in place of Adolfo Ibáñez.[187] Nevertheless, in view of
'the general expectation of hostile demonstrations towards the
Government', there was 'an unusual display of military and
police forces along the route taken by the President' when he

[183] *Constitución política . . . Chile . . .* , Article 49, iv, p. 28.
[184] For the debate, see *Boletín de las Sesiones de la Comisión Conservadora de 1890*
(Santiago, 1890), *passim*.
[185] See Salas Edwards, *Balmaceda y el Parlamentarismo*, i, 214–18.
[186] See Villarino, *J. M. Balmaceda*, p. 130.
[187] Encina, *Historia de Chile*, xix, 213–18. It was traditional for a presidential
candidate to resign office: by accepting the Ministry, Sanfuentes thus indicated
that he would not stand for the presidency. See Salas Edwards, *Balmaceda y el
Parlamentarismo*, i, 256–8. However, since the Minister of the Interior controlled
the government apparatus throughout the country and Balmaceda had broken
with precedent so often, this move did not inspire confidence.

went to open Congress on 1 June.[188] Balmaceda's address was
in strong contrast to his previous inaugural messages; it contained little reference to the progress of Chile and was devoted
primarily to proposals for reforming the Constitution of the
Republic.

> Down the years [he said] the constitutional authority of the Execu-
> tive Power has been weakened in practice by . . . the Legislature,
> and we have come to believe in a bastard parliamentary system . . .
>   The experience of states with a parliamentary regimen and of
> countries with a representative system, including our own, shows
> that we must shun the parliamentary type as one of those anarchic
> systems in which personal circles continue to divide, either to sup-
> port or overthrow ministries, or to serve interests other than those
> of the common weal. . . Representative Government with inde-
> pendent branches . . . is the only type of Government for which the
> Republic is fitted . . . to give a solid basis for political and social
> improvement.
>   The bastard parliamentary government of the Republic in-
> evitably leads to the dictatorship of Congress. . . I will not accept
> this dictatorship for my country, neither will I support the dic-
> tatorship of the Executive. I look for a system of independence
> and freedom for the public powers, a system in which each may
> exercise its authority to the full . . . without any encroachments of
> popular rights or infringement of the sphere of action of the other
> powers . . .[189]

Balmaceda then proposed to reform the constitution of 1833 by
abolishing the Council of State and the Comisión Conservadora; by the creation of a Vice-Presidency; and by the election
of the President and the Vice-President by direct vote for a
period of six years, the Vice-President to become, in addition,
President of the Senate. The immense powers of the President
under the constitution of 1833 were to be retained. For local
government, the country would be divided into eight provinces,
each with an assembly of between 15 and 30 members chosen
by direct vote, to take cognizance of everything not reserved for
the central government and the municipalities.[190]

[188] Kennedy to Salisbury, Santiago, 2 June 1890. F.O. 16/259. No. 44. Diplomatic.
[189] *Discurso de su Excellencia el Presidente de la República al Apertura del Congreso
Nacional de 1890* (Santiago, 1890), pp. 12–14.
[190] See also *The Chilean Times*, 7 June 1890.

These proposals owed much to Bañados.[191] They also looked to the Constitution of the United States. But, above all, they reflected the impression made by recent events on Balmaceda himself. The idea of setting up provincial assemblies was probably an attempt to steal a march on Congressional plans for municipal autonomy:[192] like Balmaceda's tour of 1889, it was an appeal to the country against the aristocracy of Santiago. More strikingly, the proposals about the executive power showed that the alleged reform of the constitution was, in fact, primarily a salvaging operation to preserve the old, autocratic structure while conceding a little ground to new ideas.

In the context of political events in 1890, Balmaceda's proposals were quite unrealistic.[193] As the British Minister pointed out, the programme was 'sure of fierce opposition if discussed in Congress', since the majority there had taken a firm stand on a patently parliamentary form of government in which ministers would be responsible to Congress as well as to the President.[194] And if Balmaceda's proposals were, indeed, genuine, they eloquently revealed his total lack of understanding of the political situation in Chile.

Not surprisingly, Congress met the new proposals with glacial indifference. The next day, in the Senate, Eulogio Altamirano, given leave in violation of traditional practice to speak before the Minister of the Interior, moved a motion of censure on the Sanfuentes Ministry, levelling his attack against Balmaceda who, he said, 'sought to hoodwink the people with a mirage of reforms . . . and . . . rig the coming elections for Congress, for the municipalities and for the presidency'. Sanfuentes made a dignified reply, avowing that his ministry would remain in office so long as it enjoyed Balmaceda's confidence, but the debate took on a more acrimonious tone when Valdés Carrera attacked Altamirano for supporting the Nitrate Railways Company when its case came before the Council of State in 1889. Despite the speeches and protests of ministers,

---

[191] See Bañados, *Gobierno Parlamentario*, *passim*.

[192] Cf. Encina, *Historia de Chile*, xix, 225.

[193] Cf., however, Bañados, *Balmaceda*, i, 452–81.

[194] Kennedy to Salisbury, Santiago, 2 June 1890. F.O. 16/259. No. 44. Diplomatic.

however, the censure motion was carried on 4 June by 25 votes to 8 with 3 abstentions.[195]

It was a similar story in the Chamber of Deputies. On 3 June, Enrique MacIver rose to propose a vote of censure on the Ministry, claiming that it should enjoy the confidence of the legislature and not merely that of the executive. The President of the Chamber, however, was obliged to close the session because of disturbances in the public gallery. The ministers thereupon declared that, in view of unauthorized interruptions, they would absent themselves from the debates; the discussion continued without them; and the motion of censure was passed on 7 June by 69 votes to 7 with 23 abstentions.[196]

As a result of these motions of censure, the Ministry offered its collective resignation, but Balmaceda refused to accept it, and complete deadlock obtained between President and Congress, each side taking its stand on alleged rights and precedents.[197] Worse was to come: on 12 June, in the Chamber of Deputies, Julio Zegers moved that the assembly postpone all discussion of the law authorizing the collection of taxes until the President appointed a ministry enjoying the confidence of Congress, a very grave step as Zegers pointed out when he declared that it had no precedent in the history of the Republic. His motion was carried two days later by 69 votes to 29 with 5 abstentions, a decision virtually ratified by the Senate on 18 June, when it decided to examine the taxes bill only when a Congressional ministry had been appointed.[198]

These decisions were extremely serious. By the constitution, though laws fixing the budget and the size of the armed forces were to be passed before 1 January of the year in which they became operative, the law authorizing the Executive to collect

---

[195] *Boletín de las Sesiones Ordinarias de la Cámara de Senadores de 1890* (Santiago, 1890), pp. 80–4, 96–7.

[196] *Boletín de las Sesiones Ordinarias de la Cámara de Diputados de 1890* (Santiago, 1890), pp. 8–13, 14 ff., 41–2.

[197] The situation offered scope for the suggestion of historical analogies. The British Minister reported that 'A parallel for the contest . . . is found by the public in the struggle of Parliament against James II and . . . in the opposition of Parliament to Lord Bute in the reign of George III.' Kennedy to Salisbury, Santiago, 21 June 1890. F.O. 16/259. No. 47. Diplomatic.

[198] Encina, *Historia de Chile*, xix, 237–8. See also *Boletín . . . de la Cámara de Diputados de 1890*, pp. 64 ff.

taxes had to be approved every eighteen months.[199] Otherwise, no taxes could be recovered after 1 July in any year. Hitherto, the slightest indication of an adverse Congressional vote on the tax bill had been enough to cause the Executive to yield to Congress.[200] Balmaceda, however, was adamant. He retaliated by a notice in the *Diario Oficial*, repudiating the decisions taken by Congress, and notified the banks that

the deposits of Government money held by the Banks at thirty days notice of intended withdrawal were in future to be considered as deposit accounts at call . . .

The enforcement of this decree, the British Minister said, would bring great confusion to trade 'and even ruin to persons engaged in industries towards which advances had been made by the Banks'; and since the amount of the circulating medium, already restricted because of the political situation, could be reduced to a dangerous level, Congress was forced to act quickly. A commission was set up immediately to enquire into the administration of the state finances, the investment of the surplus on the revenue, and recent government contracts for public works.[201] A motion was subsequently proposed and passed to suspend the incineration of fiscal bills as provided for in the Paper Money Retirement Law of 1887.[202]

These economic circumstances were clearly the result of the political crisis, and at the beginning of July still more serious manifestations of a deteriorating situation occurred. On 2 July strikes began in the nitrate areas, to be followed by riots in which people were killed and property was destroyed. Kennedy reported that the strikes arose from the refusal of Congress to authorize the President to collect taxes: 'the Guilds of Dock labourers being no longer restricted by the Government tariff of pay, struck for higher wages'.[203] The riots spread rapidly throughout Tarapacá and a week passed before Government

---

[199] *Constitución política de . . . Chile . . .* , Article 28, pp. 18–19.

[200] Even the authoritarian Manuel Montt had yielded in these circumstances. See Salas Edwards, *Balmaceda y el Parlamentarismo*, i, 32.

[201] Kennedy to Salisbury, 21 June, loc. cit. See also Yrarrázaval, 'El Gobierno y los Bancos', loc. cit., pp. 28–30.

[202] For the Law of 1887, see above, p. 75, n. 44.

[203] Kennedy to Salisbury, Santiago, 11 July 1890. F.O. 16/287. Telegraphic.

troops could restore order.[204] A fortnight later similar disturbances took place in Valparaiso, when longshoremen went
on strike, threatened to attack the customs-house and, by now
somewhat intoxicated, smashed windows and looted several
establishments: 'the cry of the mob', reported Gibbs' manager,
'is . . . for higher wages, and they seem to look on the Banqueros
as their more particular enemies'. But a charge by troops, who
opened fire, dispersed the crowd and order was restored.[205]

These events added to the ill-feeling between government
and Congress: the latter asserted that the government had
deliberately allowed the disturbances to continue for a while
in order to intimidate the opposition but had then been forced
to call in the military when the strikers got out of control.[206]
It was 'confidently asserted by many' in Santiago that there
was a direct connection between the riots and the political
situation,[207] and the arrival of the news in London caused a
sudden fall in Chilean government stocks, one commentator
suggesting that the withdrawal of troops from the north by
Balmaceda previously had encouraged the strikers to go on the
rampage.[208]

Such ramifications of the political crisis naturally did nothing
to bring about a solution to it, and in July, also, Balmaceda
adamantly refused to change the ministry in response to a
resolution passed by a public meeting of 8,000 persons in
Santiago. The 'fierce and unedifying conflict' continued.[209]
Balmaceda's cold reception of all Congressional proposals was
gradually turning the country against him, and the opinion
voiced by *The Chilean Times* on 12 July 1890 reflected that of
the great majority of educated Chileans:

[204] Kennedy asked for protection of British property, but not all British entre-
preneurs in Tarapacá were perturbed. 'We have some hopes', wrote H. L. Gibbs,
'Tamarugal [a rival] may be looted off the face of the earth.' H. L. Gibbs to
Vicary Gibbs, 10 July 1890. AAG, MS. 11,040. Vol. 1. Private Letters to Partners.

[205] Antony Gibbs & Sons, Valparaiso, 10 July 1890, to London, AAG, MS.
11,470. Vol. 12. Letter No. 42. On the disturbances in Tarapacá and Valparaiso
generally, see also Encina, *Historia de Chile*, xix, 241 ff.

[206] Ibid. See also Yrarrázaval, *El Presidente Balmaceda*, ii, 99 ff., and the *Boletin
de . . . la Cámara de Diputados de 1890*, pp. 290 ff.

[207] Antony Gibbs & Sons, Valparaiso, 10 July 1890, loc. cit.

[208] *The South American Journal*, 19 July 1890.

[209] Kennedy to Salisbury, Santiago, 20 July 1890. F.O. 16/259. No. 55. Diplomatic.

It seems almost incredible [the paper said] that anyone could have been found possessed of sufficient wilful obstinacy to drive the country to the very verge of revolt on such an issue as the maintenance in office of a Ministry against the spoken will of the nation . . .

A week later, the paper characterized the speeches of the Congressionalists as 'singularly conciliatory' and those of Balmaceda as 'singularly provocative', adding that the increasing tension in Chile must soon break completely, probably with disastrous results.[210] And so it seemed. After the failure of the public meeting in Santiago in July, Congress turned to more serious proposals. On 24 July, Julio Zegers made a strong speech, advocating that Congress declare Balmaceda unfit to discharge the duties of his office, and three days later it was decided to impeach the ministry, though not without the dissent of some members who thought this step too drastic.[211] These developments caused Balmaceda to decide to dissolve Congress and to ensure himself the support of the army.[212]

Yet hope still remained that a *modus vivendi* could be found. Throughout July a moderate politician, Alvaro Covarrubias, had been seeking to mediate between Balmaceda and Congress.[213] His efforts failed, since Balmaceda insisted that the price of his agreement to change his ministry must be the passage of a tax bill made retroactive to 1 July, which Covarrubias wished to have decided by the Courts or by Congress.[214] But though this failure dashed the country's hopes, and fears were expressed that Balmaceda might dissolve Congress and declare himself Dictator,[215] it was now seen that the tax issue was the only barrier to, at least, a political armistice. After an anxious week at the beginning of August, a compromise was

[210] *The Chilean Times*, 12, 19, 20 July 1890.

[211] Encina, *Historia de Chile*, xix, 257–60. See also Bañados, *Balmaceda*, i, 546–54.

[212] Encina, loc. cit., pp. 260–3.

[213] The best account is 'Las negociaciones de Don Alvaro Covarrubias en 1890', *Revista Chilena de Historia y Geografía*, No. 74 (1933), pp. 643–60, an extract from the unpublished memoirs of a contemporary politician, Blanco Viel, edited by J. M. Echenique Gandarillas.

[214] Bañados, loc. cit., i, 563–77 reprints the correspondence between Balmaceda and Covarrubias.

[215] Kennedy to Salisbury, Santiago, 5 August 1890. F.O. 16/259. No. 61. Diplomatic. See also Encina, loc. cit., xix, 269–70.

reached. Consultations between Balmaceda and the Arch-
bishop of Santiago, Mariano Casanova, resulted in the resignation of the Sanfuentes ministry and the appointment of a
new one led by Belisario Prats, a judge of the Supreme Court.[216]
Congress thereupon voted the tax bill and received the new
Ministry with enthusiasm, although the ministers themselves
were not members of the Opposition. As Kennedy pointed out,
in view of the Opposition's violent personal attacks on Balmaceda and of the necessity for 'daily and intimate intercourse'
between President and Ministers, a ministry composed of
leading politicians would have been doomed from the outset.[217]

The appointment of Prats was undoubtedly a victory for the
Opposition. 'The triumph', said *The Chilean Times*, 'has placed
the sovereignty of the Nation, as represented by Congress, on a
broader and firmer basis than ever.'[218] To the British Minister,
however, it appeared that the new situation was one of armed
neutrality between Balmaceda and the Congressional majority,
so bitter had the strife been between them. He also thought that
the change of ministry 'may prove of considerable advantage to
British interests' since 'the late Ministers were mere servants
and mouthpieces of the President, having neither knowledge
nor opinions of their own', whereas the new men might be more
open to representations on behalf of the Nitrate Railways
Company and other British interests.[219] In that connection, he
reported later, the action of the Nitrate Railways Company
against the Agua Santa Company in the courts would be
unlikely to be overturned by the new government, if it were
favourable to them, since

The leader of the New Ministry . . . is himself a Judge of the
Supreme Court, and in that character has signed an elaborate
argument dated 23 March, 1888, in defence of the Competency of
the Supreme Court to take cognisance of the Nitrate Railways
question.

---

[216] For biographical details, see Figueroa, *Diccionario histórico*, iv and v, 550–1.
[217] Kennedy to Salisbury, Santiago, 12 August 1890. F.O. 16/259. No. 62.
Diplomatic.
[218] *The Chilean Times*, 9 August 1890.
[219] Kennedy to Salisbury, 12 August, loc. cit.

If the President again appointed personal ministers, Kennedy concluded, and the attempt was made to deny the right of the courts to adjudicate the issue, that would be the time for a renewal of the official protest he had refrained from repeating earlier in the year.[220]

The Nitrate Railways question, in fact, remained before the Chilean courts throughout the rest of 1890, and Kennedy, therefore, refrained from further diplomatic action. In this, he was supported by the company's agents in Chile and by Julio Zegers. Mr Linnick, the company's representative in Valparaiso, and Mr Rowland, the general manager in Chile, both believed that renewed diplomatic pressure would be inadvisable at this time.[221] Zegers took a similar view though he had additional reasons for waiting to see what would happen in the courts. He had, of course, played a very prominent part in the Congressional pressure on Balmaceda to dismiss the Sanfuentes ministry, and, as he told Kennedy in August, he was somewhat sensitive to

the malicious calumnies circulated by the President and his late Ministers (the Sanfuentes cabinet) to the effect that Señor Zegers employed the money of the Nitrate Railways Company for political purposes.[222]

Consequently, as Kennedy reported, Zegers, 'greatly influenced by considerations connected with his own political position', would

always be averse to diplomatic intervention in the affairs of the Company, lest a handle should be given to his many political enemies to accuse him of want of patriotism.[223]

Zegers's role in the Chamber of Deputies had been paralleled in the Senate by that of Eulogio Altamirano, whose position as an adviser to a foreign company was also affected by the political situation. After Altamirano's motion of censure on the

[220] Same to same, Santiago, 12 August 1890. F.O. 16/259. No. 63. Diplomatic and Confidential. For the 'argument' mentioned, see above, p. 50.

[221] Kennedy to Salisbury, Santiago, 11 September 1890. F.O. 16/287. No. 77. Diplomatic. Confidential.

[222] Same to same, Santiago, 18 August 1890. F.O. 16/287. No. 69. Diplomatic. Confidential.

[223] Same to same. 11 September 1890, loc. cit.

Sanfuentes ministry in June, Daubeny wrote to Gibbs in London:

... less than ever will he be a persona grata with the present President, and ... it would, we should think, be unwise to allow him to figure as the champion of our Alianza scheme, at any rate for the time being. Still [he continued] we should be disinclined to break with him, as political changes are becoming so frequent in this country that by the time we are ready to push our A [sic] scheme, he may very possibly be in a position to help us should influence be required in S[antiago].[224]

On the face of it, it might seem more than a remarkable coincidence that the two principal opposition spokesmen against Balmaceda in 1890 were both also employed by foreign firms as part-time legal advisers. Yet, coincidence it certainly was. In the first place, the companies that each represented in Chile were opposed to one another, precisely in the matter for which their Chilean advisers were employed. Secondly, both Zegers and Altamirano took exactly the same stand on the cancellation of the privileges of the Nitrate Railways Company by administrative decree, namely that it was an unconstitutional act and, in any case, they believed that the company should have the right of appeal to the Chilean judiciary.[225] Altamirano was already employed by Gibbs when he cast his vote in the Council of State in support of this view, and Zegers continued to support Balmaceda politically long after the Council of State had given its decision.[226] There was nothing surprising in the fact that Altamirano and Zegers played a prominent part in the Congress of 1890; both had been members of Congress for several years, both were considerable orators, and each had served previously as Ministers of State, though not under Balmaceda. It is possible that they felt more strongly than some of their colleagues about the President's alleged infringements of the constitution and of precedent because of his actions in the Nitrate Railways case, but since

[224] Antony Gibbs & Sons, Valparaiso, 6 June 1890, to London. AAG, MS. 1,470. Vol. 12. Letter No. 39. Private.
[225] See the letters from Zegers in El Ferrocarril, 10, 16 and 25 February 1898, and a letter from Altamirano in ibid., 4 March 1898.
[226] See above, pp. 128–9, 142–3.

it was well known at the time that they represented foreign companies involved in that issue, it could hardly be *because* of that involvement that they acted as they did.[227] And, indeed, the conduct of Altamirano and Zegers, like that of most of their colleagues in Congress, must be seen essentially in the Chilean political context of 1890, in the erosion of support for Balmaceda, whose word they no longer trusted when he denied that he had a candidate for the presidency in 1891 and that the government would refrain from interference in elections. The short history of the Prats ministry seemed to justify that mistrust.

On 7 October 1890, the Prats ministry resigned. Given Balmaceda's character and the circumstances in which Prats assumed office, a quarrel between them was almost inevitable. Neither trusted the other, and the fundamental issue between them was control of the electoral machinery. Though Balmaceda proposed to renounce electoral intervention if the Liberal groups would agree on the bases for a convention to choose a presidential candidate, the opposition had no faith in the offer, and on Balmaceda's refusal to dismiss a minor official, suspected by Prats of being a government agent for electoral intervention, the ministry resigned.[228] A week later, Balmaceda closed the Congress and simultaneously announced the appointment of a personal ministry. The political situation was back to where it had been in June.

[227] The sensitivity of Zegers on this issue, mentioned above, suggests that he was well aware of the danger he ran in taking so prominent a stand against Balmaceda politically. Yet this did not deter him. Cf. Raúl Silva Castro, *Balmaceda* (Santiago, 1969), p. 52.

[228] See Encina, *Historia de Chile*, xix, 277 ff., and cf. Bañados, *Balmaceda*, i, 623–42. See also F. Velasco, *La Revolución de 1891: Memorias* (Santiago, 1914), pp. 10 ff. This valuable work, published posthumously, is a diary of events in Chile in late 1890 and during 1891 by an Under-Secretary in the Ministry of Foreign Affairs. According to Velasco (p. 13), Balmaceda refused to remove any government servant from office without specific charges being laid, and he also observed (p. 15) that none of the ministers in the Prats cabinet had accompanied the President at functions. Instead, Balmaceda was always to be seen with his former ministers such as Valdés Carrera, Bañados, Mackenna and Gandarillas. That electoral issues were responsible for Prats resignation was attested by Gibbs' representative in Chile who wrote: 'Their very sudden resignation was due to the President's maintaining in power certain governors agents on behalf of the presidential candidate for the Presidency.' Antony Gibbs & Sons, Valparaiso to London, 13, 14 October 1890. AAG, MS. 11,470. Vol. 12. Letter No. 50. Private.

Whether the Prats ministry and the Congressional opposition were justified in suspecting Balmaceda of duplicity over
both the presidential succession and electoral intervention has
been a subject of much discussion.[229] But that distrust of
Balmaceda was growing is not open to doubt. In the middle of
August, for example, the British Minister pointed out that a
marked feature of the Chilean political situation was the complete change of loyalties of many of Balmaceda's former friends:
'nearly all the Deputies', he said, 'owe their seats to the President who controls all elections', but most of them, including a
high proportion of the fifty or so persons who had held ministerial posts under Balmaceda, had subsequently been alienated
by his lack of sincerity; the 'treacherous conduct', Kennedy
wrote, 'and the somewhat visionary and very expensive projects
of His Excellency . . . have created a feeling of distrust which
will not disappear until His Excellency's term of office shall
have expired'.[230] There was, it is true, a certain bias in Kennedy's opinion since he did not get on well with Balmaceda.
But his view of the President's untrustworthiness was shared by
clearly impartial witnesses such as Velasco.[231] And it is remarkable that a number of Balmaceda's intimate friends were
alienated by his conduct during 1890, as they came to regard
his confrontation with Congress not only as a serious political
blunder but also as evidence of his aggrieved personal vanity
and obstinate pride. Pre-eminent among his disillusioned supporters was Enrique Sanfuentes, the very man whose alleged
candidature for the presidency had been the real catalyst for
Congressional discontent: Sanfuentes, in 1890, retired from
public life altogether, more in sorrow than in anger at the
President's course of action.[232] Another was José Besa, Senator
for Valparaiso, and a close friend of Balmaceda for twenty

[229] Cf. the various authorities cited in note 15, p. 69.

[230] Kennedy to Salisbury, Santiago, 12 August 1880. F.O. 16/259. No. 63.
Diplomatic. Confidential. It is interesting to note, further, that when Balmaceda
became President, Kennedy's predecessor wrote of his great qualities, but then
added: 'On the other hand, he is a very vain man, fond of pomp and display, and
not scrupulously careful of his word.' Fraser to Rosebery, Santiago, 31 July 1886.
F.O. 16/242. No. 65. Diplomatic.   [231] Velasco, *Memorias, passim.*

[232] See René León Echaiz, *Evolución histórica de los partidos políticos chilenos* (2nd
ed., Santiago, 1971), p. 77; Salas Edwards, *Balmaceda y el Parlamentarismo*, i,
351–2; Velasco, *Memorias*, note 15, p. 69.

years, who, throughout 1890, urged Balmaceda to reconcile himself with Congress and, in the end, felt obliged to join the opposition.[233] And, as a final example, though many others could be cited, there was Balmaceda's own brother, José Vicente, who in May 1890 had voted in the Senate for the censure of the ministry with these words:

I had resolved to abstain from voting for reasons which the Chamber will readily understand; but after the speech of the Honourable Minister of the Interior [defending Balmaceda's position], I deem it a patriotic duty to vote for the censure.[234]

There were many, and indeed very varied, reasons for the alienation of these people from Balmaceda in the course of 1890, though it is quite clear that such well-known public figures as Sanfuentes and Besa were not affected by 'the influence of North's gold on the politicians and the aristocracy'.[235] Like the great majority in Congress, they were swayed by Balmaceda's own behaviour, by lack of confidence in his choice of advisers and also, perhaps, by the belief that, despite his firm promises to the contrary, Balmaceda was quite determined to use the full power of the government machine to control the elections of 1891, the key issue between President and Congress.[236] How important that factor was is revealed by the passage in the summer of 1890 of a new electoral law, intended to eliminate a number of existing abuses, a law which was passed by both Houses of Congress and which received the President's assent.[237] But the law did not, and could not, affect in any way the immense power of patronage possessed by the President, which covered almost every post in the administration, and which was his most powerful electoral weapon. That power, moreover, had been greatly expanded by the recent rapid growth of programmes of public works. Whereas,

[233] Figueroa, *Diccionario histórico*, ii, 192–3.

[234] Cited by Bañados, *Balmaceda*, i, 493.

[235] The phrase is that of Encina, *Historia de Chile*, xx, 48, who did not believe it.

[236] See Velasco, *Memorias*, pp. 42–3, for Velasco's report of a conversation on 20 November with Domingo Godoy, then Balmaceda's Foreign Minister, about the presidential succession, and Velasco's comments on Balmaceda's rise to prominence as a strong critic of electoral intervention.

[237] For the debate on this law, see Yrarrázaval, *El presidente Balmaceda*, ii, 130 ff., and for its provisions, Cifuentes, *Memorias*, ii, 286–9.

according to one calculation, the total number of state employees in Chile—excluding the services—was some 2,500 in
1875, by 1891 the number supporting Balmaceda amounted to
around 5,000.[238] That Congress saw in this development a
notable accretion of presidential power and influence cannot
be denied, but that it also saw it as a serious threat to the predominant social status of its members is a much more debatable
proposition. Yet, it has been argued that the rapid expansion
of the state bureaucracy was not only a threat to the political
position of the aristocracy, but also an indication of considerable social change in Chile, challenging the oligarchy's pre-
dominance.[239]

Evidence for this view is very hard to find.[240] On the other
hand, there are a number of indications to suggest that the
relationship between public office, political power and social
position was a somewhat complicated one, and certainly not
capable, in the present state of knowledge, of bearing the
positive and straightforward interpretation which has been
placed upon it. In the first place, patronage pervaded all levels
of Chilean society, and the President, as the chief dispenser of
public patronage, was continually solicited by many people to
provide employment for their relatives and friends.[241] While
many of these requests came from people unknown to Balmaceda, others were from personal friends and acquaintances and
from well-known or well-connected figures in Chilean society[242]
Thus, for example, in October 1890, Juan E. Mackenna, a
long-time confidant of Balmaceda and one of his former
ministers, sought the President's intervention on behalf of
Alejandro Valdivieso who wanted a post in the Treasury.[243]

---

[238] Pizarro, *La revolución de 1891*, p. 67.

[239] By, for example, Pizarro, loc. cit., pp. 77–82, and by Ramírez, *Balmaceda*,
pp. 199–210.

[240] I know of no systematic investigation into the social composition of the
public administration during Balmaceda's presidency, nor, indeed, of similar
research into the social background of both Congress and Government in the same
period.

[241] This account is based upon a number of letters written to Balmaceda in
1890 in my possession, and cited hereafter as Balmaceda MSS.

[242] The form of address used in the correspondence is often a clear indication of
the writer's standing with the President.

[243] Mackenna to Balmaceda, Iquique, 14 October 1890. Balmaceda MSS. For

Manuel García, Archdeacon of the Metropolitan Diocese of Santiago, and a former member of Balmaceda's Council of State, sought a position in Valparaiso for a cousin, Manuel Concha García.[244] B. Arteaga Alemparte, a member of the distinguished Liberal family whose two most prominent members, the brothers Domingo and Justo Arteaga Alemparte, had worked closely with Balmaceda in the 1870s on the famous Liberal newspaper, *La Libertad*, sought the President's assistance on behalf of his son, Juan, holder of a temporary post in the customs-house at Arica who was, allegedly, blocked in his promotion to permanent status by the head of the office, Señor Medina.[245] Many more examples could be cited to indicate the widespread and correct belief that administrative posts were very much in the gift of the President.

But although the President possessed this tremendous instrument of political power and influence, its mere existence did not necessarily mean that through the exercise of patronage he automatically secured adherents to his cause. In the first place, the disposal of public office for political reasons must have been something of a hit-and-miss affair so far as the loyalties of appointees was concerned. Clear evidence of this lies in the fact that even before relations between Balmaceda and the Congress reached the point of armed conflict in 1891, the government felt obliged to begin to purge the public services of Congressional supporters.[246] And, indeed, there was some scope in favourable political circumstances for the opposition to make use of patronage for its own ends. Thus, in October 1890 the Administrator of the railway line under construction between Calera and Ligua protested to Balmaceda about a recent regulation of the Minister of Public Works in the Prats Ministry which, he alleged, made possible the use of state funds for political purposes rather than for building the line,

Mackenna's relationship with Balmaceda, see his *Carta Política* (Valparaiso, 1893), *passim*.

[244] García to Balmaceda, La Serena, 17 October 1890. Balmaceda MSS. For García, see Jordi Fuentes and Lía Cortes, *Diccionario Histórico de Chile* (2nd ed., Santiago, 1965), p. 183.

[245] Arteaga to Balmaceda, Arica, 8 October 1890. Balmaceda MSS. For the brothers Arteaga Alemparte and their relations with Balmaceda, see their *Los Constituyentes de 1870*, *passim*. [246] Encina *Historia de Chile*, xix, 311-12.

particularly since the chief engineer and a number of his subordinates were 'staunch monttvaristas' (i.e. supporters of the National party): the writer himself, however, was annoyed primarily because *his* political activities on behalf of the government had thus been upset.[247]

Moreover, in the disposal of public office for political reasons there were always competing claimants within the ranks of the President's supporters. At the end of October 1890, for example, in a letter which well illustrates the possible complexities of the patronage system, Manuel Goyenechea, a firm supporter of Balmaceda, wrote to the President about a local difficulty in Copiapó, at a time when political excitement was high as both President and Congress prepared for the preliminaries of the elections of 1891:

Here [he wrote] we are all working hard, though we are few; but with great hope of success. For that result, however, we have to be very careful.

I refer [he went on] to the appointment of a *Defensor de Menores*, which is a somewhat delicate matter at the moment. One of my political colleagues, Villegas Tulio, recommends through Don Ismael Pérez Montt the lawyer Señor Demetrio Gomes; and others, such as Señor Toro Marín, recommend Don Juan B. Avalos. The first of these is a Conservative, and the second is a Radical: both claim to be Liberals but they have not given the slightest proof of this. Pérez Montt has written to Villegas Tulio saying that Avalos will be appointed, and this has caused a great scandal amongst our adherents who say: 'it's not worth being a Balmacedist, since you work very hard and the jobs are given to those who fight against us'.

Goyenechea's solution, therefore, was to leave the appointment until after the elections, 'when we can see what both of them really are'.[248]

Nevertheless, control of patronage was a crucial issue in the struggle for political power, particularly at election time, and it was precisely on this issue that the Prats ministry resigned in

---

[247] Pedro A. Verduga to Balmaceda, Calera, 24 October 1890. Balmaceda MSS. The writer said: 'Your Excellency knows that much as I desire the completion of the line, I also have solemn political undertakings to fulfil. . . I need to press on with the work itself in order to arrange the personnel of the line *politically*.' His italics.

[248] M. Goyenechea to Balmaceda, Copiapó, 29 October 1890. Balmaceda MSS.

October. That Balmaceda would use his powers to the full to win the elections of 1891 was uppermost in the minds of the opposition, and their problem was how to prevent him from doing so. Throughout the country, in the autumn of 1890, the President's supporters and the opposition battled to secure the support of the electorate, and since the government controlled the local administration again, after the resignation of Prats, it seemed to be in the stronger position. Balmaceda's confidants in Santiago had no doubt that they would win,[249] but many of his adherents in the country at large were not so optimistic. In the first place, the opposition parties and their adherents worked extremely hard to secure votes for their candidates: from Valparaiso came the news that Pedro Montt, a leading member of the opposition, had secured the promise of the six hundred votes of a lay brotherhood in Casablanca, through the active co-operation of the local priest who was himself at loggerheads with the provincial governor.[250] From Illapel it was reported that

the Opposition displays much activity . . . with the Conservative and Radical parties the most powerful elements. Monttvarismo is also strongly represented in Salamanca, and . . . on the railway line under construction the director, Eduardo Barriga, the chief engineer, Emiliano Jiménez, and engineer Berroeta have made arrangements with the subordinate employees on that section of the line which belongs to this department . . .

It looks [the writer continued] as though they will not allow the workers to be registered [for voting] and if this abuse is not stopped as soon as possible . . . we are bound to lose this crucial contingent of voters for the elections . . .[251]

From Linares came a similar report of great opposition activity and the agreement between the various parties there of the candidates for the elections.[252]

A second reason for some doubt about the government's

[249] See Velasco, *Memorias*, pp. 34–5, for some revealing remarks by Valdés Carrera in November 1890.

[250] J. L. Amor to Balmaceda, Valparaiso, 6 November 1890. Balmaceda MSS.

[251] Felipe Geisse to Claudio Vicuña (Minister of the Interior), Illapel, 6 November 1890. Balmaceda MSS.

[252] Laureano González to Balmaceda, Linares, 1 November 1890. Balmaceda MSS.

strength was that, whereas the opposition seemed remarkably united for so heterogeneous a collection of political parties, in many places the Government Liberals were divided. The Intendant of Atacama, in a series of letters to Balmaceda, expounded the political problem for the Government Liberals: the Governor of Chañaral had refused to accept his proposals for ending the divisions in the local party, had sought to get the municipality of Chañaral on his side against the Intendant, and had generally acted against the interests of the Government because, the writer believed, he had gone over to the Radicals despite his former promises to continue to support the Government.[253] The same writer put forward another candidate to succeed the Governor, a nominee who had, in addition to his sterling qualities as an administrator, the advantages of being both rich and connected to a well-known local family which supported the President: 'His appointment', he continued, 'would be applauded here by all our friends, and it would strengthen their adhesion to the Government . . .'[254] In San Carlos, according to an informant sent by the President to look at the local situation, one group of government supporters favoured Don Desiderio Ponce as a candidate for the Chamber of Deputies, but another group 'of positive strength and committed friends of the administration' were opposed to his candidacy, and they, the writer was convinced, could ensure the government's triumph at the elections: he strongly recommended the withdrawal of Ponce, for if he continued his candidacy he would certainly lose the election. Although, the writer continued, 'our friends will accept whichever candidate the government proposes, and they will elect him if he is a committed friend of the government', nevertheless the personal animosity between them and Ponce himself was so bitter that the government's local supporters could not possibly support *him*.[255]

[253] D. Risopatrón Canas to Balmaceda, Copiapó, 11 and 23 October, 1 November 1890. Balmaceda MSS.

[254] Ibid., 1 November 1890, in idem. For his part, however, the Governor defended himself stoutly against Risopatrón, accusing him of having failed the government through his personalism. D. Espinosa to Balmaceda, Chañaral, 29 October 1890. Balmaceda MSS.

[255] Pedro N. Rojas to Balmaceda, San Carlos, 27 October 1890. Balmaceda MSS.

In the province of Coquimbo, a similar situation of personal rancour obtained between the Intendant and the Governor of the provincial capital, to the intense disgust of Balmaceda's personal investigator, Joaquín Villarino: despite firm instructions from the Minister of the Interior for these two government appointees to settle their differences or, at least, not air them publicly, Villarino's intervention only exacerbated the situation, and he withdrew since he did not wish, as he put it, 'to pile fresh troubles on top of those which Your Excellency [Balmaceda] already has to suffer for the good of the country'.[256] Another type of problem with possibly serious electoral consequences was raised by the Intendant of the province of Bío-Bío, when he complained to Balmaceda that various petitions for public works, such as drinking-water supply and telegraph lines, had gone unheeded, and he doubted his capacity to sustain 'the good cause' without them.[257]

To quote these examples of Balmaceda's problems in 1890 is by no means to suggest that the government's position was weak everywhere. On the contrary, again to quote at random, things looked distinctly brighter for the government in other places. Thus, the Intendant of Malleco, reporting that the registration of voters had begun, assured the President that things were going very well for the Government Liberal party.[258] Similarly, it was reported from the Department of Vicuña that 'the Liberal party has a great majority'.[259] And a correspondent who had travelled through the provinces of Arauco, Valdivia and Chiloé informed Balmaceda that, in general, the government's supporters were in good heart there, despite the activities of leading members of the opposition.[260] Nevertheless, the reports flowing in to the presidential palace in the latter part of 1890 do suggest how complex the many local situations were, and they indicate clearly how sharp was the struggle between government and opposition. In other words,

---

[256] Joaquín Villarino to Balmaceda, La Serena, 2 October 1890. Balmaceda MSS.

[257] Eujenio Vergara to Balmaceda, Los Anjeles, 1 November 1890. Balmaceda MSS.

[258] J. Vergara to Balmaceda, Angol, 5 November 1890. Balmaceda MSS.

[259] Ramon Miranda to Balmaceda, Vicuña, 25 October 1890. Balmaceda MSS.

[260] E. González to Balmaceda, Calbuco, 31 October 1890. Balmaceda MSS.

the political conflict in Santiago had been extended throughout
the country, though it was an aristocratic struggle in which the
masses did not take part.[261]

It has already been pointed out that one of the government's
problems in preparing for the elections of 1891 was the selection
of candidates for Congress acceptable to both the administration and to prominent local leaders. The policy of building up
a personal party which Balmaceda pursued in 1890 was one
reason why former supporters, such as Enrique Sanfuentes,
were alienated from him, and it was also ammunition for the
opposition in its claim that Balmaceda wished to make himself
dictator. As the case of Desiderio Ponce in San Carlos suggests,
where the local party was sufficiently strong it might try to
impose its will on the government—and succeed.[262] But, generally, the support of the government was essential to any
aspirant, in view of the power, real or imagined, possessed by
its local officials, and personal acceptability to the President
had to be obtained. Thus, for example, in October 1890 Mateo
Martel, *diputado suplente*[263] for Imperial, wrote to Balmaceda in
highly flattering terms and then went on:

I recollect that Your Excellency told me to write to you when I
thought it was time for my re-election to the Deputies, and since I
think that time has now come, I take the liberty of writing to Your
Excellency to say that I wish to continue in my post as Deputy for
the next period, with the sole aim of serving Your Excellency's
policies at all times and with the same loyalty as always and with
the unshakeable resolve of not missing a single day of the sessions.[264]

A straightforward aspirant who was not already an incumbent
had to pursue a more tortuous path of sounding out relevant
opinion before approaching the President direct: thus, Ramiro
Sánchez informed Balmaceda that he had asked Enrique

[261] All writers on the subject agree on this point, though Ramírez, *Balmaceda*,
pp. 208–9, argues that the working classes supported Balmaceda, at least passively.
Cf. also Pizarro, *La revolución de 1891*, pp. 77–80; and see note 273.

[262] Ponce was elected to Congress in 1891. Luís Valencia Avaria, *Anales de la
República* (2 vols., Santiago, 1951), ii, 333. But this was during the civil war and
all the circumstances were unusual.

[263] The *suplente* was a kind of *locum* for the deputy, but he also had to be elected.

[264] Mateo Martel to Balmaceda, Union, 23 October 1890. Balmaceda MSS.
Martel was elected to the Congress of 1891. Valencia Avaria, loc. cit., p. 334.

Sanfuentes, the local *patron*, if he was already committed to any friend for election as Deputy for Parral, and on receiving a negative reply, put forward his own case.[265] Sánchez, however, went out of his way to say that he did not wish to join the Government Liberal party, as Sanfuentes had suggested, but preferred to be an independent, working primarily for his constituency, though he was prepared to get as many votes for Sanfuentes, standing for the Senate, as he could, and he ended his letter with a request to Balmaceda to let him know whether he thought him a suitable candidate.[266]

This digression into the complexities of the political struggle in Chile in the latter part of 1890 serves to illustrate that it was precisely the struggle between Balmaceda and Congress over the control of the electoral machinery which completely dominated events, and it was, of course, on this issue that the Prats ministry, probably the last chance of a compromise between President and Congress, resigned early in October.[267] So deep by now was the mistrust between them that all other issues faded into the background, since political passions had taken control. But the question naturally arises, what part was played in creating and sustaining this situation by foreign interests, particularly in nitrates? These interests are alleged by some authors to bear a major share of the responsibility.[268] It has already been pointed out, however, that the question is far more complicated than these writers allow, and that not only were foreign nitrate interests far from united in a common front against Balmaceda in respect of his alleged economic nationalism, but also that some looked for his support against others, and, moreover, that his economic nationalism was

---

[265] Ramiro Sánchez to Balmaceda, Donihué, 29 October 1890. Balmaceda MSS.

[266] Ibid. I have found no subsequent record of Sánchez anywhere, but logic suggests that his proposal found no favour with Balmaceda. In another case, the prominent Liberal and ex-minister, Manuel A. Zañartu, refused his support to the candidate chosen by Balmaceda as deputy for Rere, since he thought the man unreliable, and he had in any case promised his influence to another. Zañartu to Balmaceda, Santiago, 4 November 1890. Balmaceda MSS.

[267] Writers with very different general interpretations are agreed on this particular point. Cf., e.g., Bañados, *Balmaceda*, i, 623 ff., and Yrarrázaval, *El Presidente Balmaceda*, ii, 147 ff.

[268] E.g., Ramírez, *Balmaceda*, *passim*; Pizarro, *La revolución de 1891*, *passim*; Villarino, *Balmaceda*, *passim*.

limited to the narrow objective of preventing a monopoly of control in the nitrate industry, a view that those nitrate interests opposed to John Thomas North fully shared.[269] Further support for this interpretation is provided by the testimony of Guillermo Billinghurst, the well-known contemporary authority in nitrate matters, indeed the first writer to reveal how 'the Nitrate King' had acquired his kingdom,[270] and himself somewhat later a reforming president of Peru.[271] In October 1890 Billinghurst, then in Tarapacá, wrote a long letter to Lauro Barros, the Chilean politician who had played a major part in the fight of the Agua Santa Company against North's Nitrate Railways, and who, in October 1890, became Minister of Finance in Balmaceda's personal ministry which followed the resignation of Prats.[272] In this letter, Billinghurst discussed the local political situation at some length, illustrating the relationship between not only the nitrate interests and Chilean politics in the very distinctive province of Tarapacá, but also between central and local government in the period.

As you will understand [he began] . . . the fact that I am a foreigner prevents me from intervening actively in the Country's politics; but this does not mean that I cannot send you information [which might be] useful for the desired objective . . .

What is happening here is quite distinctive. I do not believe that in any other province of Chile there is a greater number of government supporters than here . . . the large number of Chilean families employed here, and the great number of workers (10 to 12,000) . . . apart from their adherence to Señor Balmaceda whom they regard as the representative of the real Chilean element, see in the government the true reflection of the country itself. Here the President does not need to 'intervene' to win the election. . . All that is needed is an intendant who does not kow-tow [se plegue] to the opposition as the present incumbent does.

David MacIver, under the friendly protection of Señor Blest (though the latter has not been working personally in his favour) has gained a good deal of ground. He has even tried to get together those elements which in fact should belong to the President. The judges have helped him, and especially Martínez Romero. MacIver's

[269] See above, pp. 150–1.   [270] In Los capitales salitereros de Tarapacá.
[271] See Pike, The Modern History of Peru, pp. 199–202.
[272] See above, p. 134.

aim is that the following candidates should triumph: Senator, Don
M. A. Matta; deputy for Iquique, David MacIver; for Pisagua,
Manuel Zavala . . .

Do you imagine that MacIver has genuine supporters himself?
They are absolutely minimal. He works with the support of Dawson, and nothing else. Dawson has influence with a dozen or so
lawyers, and another dozen merchants but nothing more. The
popular electoral element is very hostile to North's circle, who have
not been able to secure the adoption of the candidacy of Don Julio
Zegers, and who believe in the likely triumph of David MacIver,
brother of the lawyer to the railway company and to North, Enrique, and of Manuel Zavala, who gets $15,000 a year salary paid
by Dawson. He [Dawson?] is trying to make himself master of the
municipality; and if the Government does not act in the matter he
will easily succeed.

The Government has here only two partisans among the better
sort [*gente respetable*]: Don José M. Pinto Agüero, and Don Manuel
Salinas. The latter is a platonic partisan. He does not want to offend
anyone. In fact, there is nothing being done in favour of the government party; absolutely nothing, and whoever tells the President the
opposite is lying.

You are now in a position to do something. . . The first step is to
change the Intendant. I believe the best Intendant here would be
Don José Manuel Pinto Agüero. This gentleman knows the situation and the men in Tarapacá better than anyone . . .

Returning to the candidacy of Don Teatino [unidentified government candidate]: I believe it would be easy for him to win. He can
count on the Agua Santa people, a sizeable group, on those of the
Banco Mobiliario, Folsch and Martin, and the nitrate-fields of
Perfetti, Vernal etc. . . .

I repeat. President Balmaceda has here many willing adherents,
and a mere nod from him would be enough to get all the popular
element on his side without resort to underhand methods. But the
present Intendant, since he is a man without character, will be an
insuperable obstacle to the triumph of the candidates of the government party.[273]

[273] Billinghurst to Barros, Iquique, 16 October 1890. Balmaceda MSS. For
biographical details of the MacIvers, see Figueroa, *Diccionario histórico*, iv and v,
148–151. Dawson is, of course, John Dawson, manager of the Bank of Tarapacá
and London in Iquique and North's chief representative there. It is worth noting
here that it was the nitrate-workers, whom Billinghurst regarded as firm adherents
of Balmaceda, who formed the Congressional army in the subsequent civil war.
Throughout 1890, Balmaceda had not the slightest intention of calling on 'the

Clearly, while this letter reveals the close relationship between certain opposition figures and North's coadjutors in Tarapacá, it also shows that, at least in Billinghurst's view, other nitrate interests would strongly support the Balmacedist candidate in the elections of 1891. And it also shows the crucial importance of the Intendant, the government's direct representative at the local level, in electoral matters. It is hardly surprising that in a province so physically isolated from the centre of power in Santiago, and one in which the foreign element was so predominant, the power and influence of the central government should be so attenuated, and that the Intendant should be regarded with suspicion by the President's supporters. Nevertheless, as Billinghurst pointed out, despite these factors, decisive action by the government might still win the day, and Billinghurst was supported in this view by Juan Mackenna who informed Balmaceda at exactly the same time that 'the provinces of Antofagasta and Tarapacá are in a most satisfactory state, and there is general approbation of the recent conduct of the Government'.[274]

But whatever may have been the feeling in the country, and no one witness could really say, there is no doubt that in the capital feeling against the government was running high. The resignation of the Prats ministry and the appointment by Balmaceda of a new cabinet consisting solely of unswerving personal adherents was the final proof of the President's insincerity, and Congress did not propose to let these events pass without making the maximum political advantage out of them. On 16 October, the Comisión Conservadora was convoked, since Congress was dissolved, and a tortuous debate took place on a motion to throw open the meetings to members of Congress, an unprecedented act.[275] To the accompaniment of vociferous applause from the public gallery whenever opposition figures spoke, the debate lasted until 31 October, when the motion was carried unanimously, in the absence of government representation. The Comisión thus became a platform for the

popular element' who were as far removed from his political calculations as they were from those of the Congressionalists.

[274] Mackenna to Balmaceda, Iquique, 14 October 1890. Balmaceda MSS.
[275] See *Boletín de las Sesiones de la Comisión Conservadora de 1890*, pp. 20 ff.

opposition to review Balmaceda's presidency in critical detail.[276]

Balmaceda remained unperturbed.[277] His new ministry, indeed, reflected his determination, for, although led by Claudio Vicuña, an able and respected politician,[278] its driving force was Domingo Godoy as Minister of Foreign Affairs, a man of autocratic temperament, and not averse from the use of force to overawe the opposition.[279] On 19 October, a great public meeting in Santiago passed a number of resolutions, praising the Comisión and condemning the government:

All honourable citizens [said one resolution] should unite their forces in order to prepare resistance, by legal means so long as the Government remains within the Constitution, but by all possible means in case the Government oversteps the Constitution.[280]

This resolution referred to the fact that Congress had not authorized the estimates and the size of the armed forces for 1891: unless it did so, Balmaceda would have to act unconstitutionally to keep government going after 1 January of that year. Yet, incredible though it may seem after the fierce recrimination which followed the resignation of Prats, Balmaceda still seemed to think that an accommodation with at least the majority in the opposition might be arranged on the basis of a Convention of the Liberal groups to choose a presidential candidate for 1891; and conversations were begun on that issue.[281] This course of action was also pressed on Balmaceda by others, including Hermogenes Pérez de Arce, a former minister with Balmaceda under Santa María, and Inspector-General of Railways in 1890. Writing to Balmaceda in October from Concepción, where he was on a tour of inspection of the southern railway lines, he devoted eight pages of a nine-page letter to political issues, urging Balmaceda to underline his historical reputation by reuniting the Liberal factions in a

[276] Ibid., pp. 121, 123–273. See also Velasco, *Memorias*, p. 24.
[277] Ibid., p. 50.
[278] See Figueroa, *Diccionario histórico*, iv and v, 1043–5.
[279] Ibid., iii, 325–6. It was Godoy's inclusion in the ministry which finally persuaded Enrique Sanfuentes to retire to his estates. See Velasco, *Memorias*, p. 46, and also Salas Edwards, *Balmaceda y el Parlamentarismo*, i, 352.
[280] Kennedy to Salisbury, Santiago, 24 October 1890. F.O. 16/259. No. 90. Diplomatic.   [281] See Bañados, *Balmaceda*, i, 644 ff.

single Convention to choose a candidate for 1891. But he
believed this could only be achieved if Balmaceda guaranteed
the neutrality of the government machine in the organization
of a Convention and in its deliberations. 'I have', he said, 'come
to the conclusion that this sacrifice . . . is inevitable . . . for the
formation of a solidly-based Ministry, founded on agreement
with the different liberal groups.'[282] Another friend of Balmaceda's, A. Vergara Albano, advised the President to delay
calling a convention until the estimates had been approved,[283]
though he did not suggest how Balmaceda could get Congress
to approve the estimates, and this, of course, was the crucial
question.

But the *modus vivendi* of a Convention was a chimera, since all
trust between Balmaceda and the opposition had quite disappeared. And, at the end of October, Balmaceda went on a
short tour of the southern provinces to inaugurate various
installations constructed under his public works programme,
taking the opportunity to attack the opposition and defend his
policies.[284] The tour was not a success, and the elaborate
precautions taken for the protection of the President did not
prevent the organization of hostile demonstrations.[285]

The complete lack of confidence between President and
Congress was well described by a foreign observer:

The feeling of distrust [wrote the manager of Gibbs in Valparaiso] in
Balmaceda is becoming very general & exchange is a pretty good
guide of people's opinion. Balmaceda seems to be determined to
have his own way in the elections for President, and the opposition
appear to be just as determined that he shall not. There is no end of
talking going on among Santiago politicians, some of whom say they

[282] Pérez de Arce to Balmaceda, Concepción, 10 October 1890. Balmaceda MSS.
[283] Vergara to Balmaceda, Santiago, n.d. Balmaceda MSS.
[284] Bañados, loc. cit., 680–6. Cf. Encina, *Historia de Chile*, xix, 308–11. It will
be recalled that it was in somewhat similar political circumstances that Balmaceda
undertook his celebrated visit to Iquique in 1889. See above, pp. 78–9.
[285] *The Chilean Times*, 20 December 1890. Gibbs' manager in Valparaiso
reported on the 'most unfavourable reception' given to Balmaceda at Talcahuano and Concepción, and on his return to Santiago. 'The alarm at the present
state of affairs', he said, 'is now very general . . .'. Antony Gibbs & Sons, Valparaiso to London, 23 December 1890. AAG, MS. 11,470. Vol. 12. Letter No. 56.
It is, perhaps, curious that these reports were not made until two months had
elapsed from the date the events took place.

would not be the least astonished if B. had a bullet put into him before long—but I don't believe it will come to more than talk & bravado. So long as he does nothing really unconstitutional, I fancy he will carry the day, but he will have to be extra careful, as the 'Comision Conservadora' is watching him like a cat watches a mouse.[286]

'The feeling of distrust' about which Daubeny wrote, was probably shared by himself, since only recently he had had a personal experience with the President which certainly did nothing to improve Balmaceda's image in his eyes.

When Mr Miller of Antony Gibbs and Sons returned to London in May 1890 to report to his superiors on his conversations with Balmaceda and Gandarillas about the Alianza Railway line and related matters, he initiated a long and detailed correspondence with the Valparaiso House about the best way of proceeding in the matter.[287] For his part, Daubeny in Valparaiso was kept very busy, sounding out informed opinion on the same business, and among those he consulted was Pedro Gandarillas who had left office when the Prats ministry was appointed in August. Gandarillas recollected the conversations with Miller and suggested that Daubeny see the President himself, while he undertook to apprise the new Ministers of Public Works and Economy of Gibbs' interests: accordingly, Daubeny went to see Balmaceda on 16 September, and offered to explain to the new ministers the scheme whereby Gibbs would undertake to ship a minimum quantity of nitrate annually, around 1,500,000 quintals, in return for permission to construct the Alianza Railway line and ship it through the port of Chucumata which was to be opened specifically for that purpose.[288] To his astonishment, however, Balmaceda asked him to

explain the basis about guaranteed export and guaranteeing to join no monopoly or combination—both the same thing in my estimation (Balmaceda's words)

when, as Daubeny reported,

[286] Antony Gibbs & Sons, Valparaiso to London, 27 October 1890. AAG, MS. 11,470. Vol. 12. Letter No. 51. Private.

[287] Correspondence in AAG, MS. 11,470. Vol. 12.

[288] Antony Gibbs & Sons, Valparaiso to London, 16 September 1890. AAG, MS. 11,470. Vol. 12. Letter No. 48.

it had been previously agreed that he gave up the no monopoly in favour of guaranteed export.[289]

It will be recalled that Miller had been very insistent on this point,[290] but when Daubeny tried to remind Balmaceda of this, the President interrupted him.

I could not help admiring [Daubeny went on] the cool way in which he coupled the export and no combination together, as both forming part of the basis [of an agreement with Gibbs] and the way he led the conversation afterwards so that without turning it abruptly or interrupting him and thus risking offending him, I could not put him right. I left him with the impression that his memory was right enough where it suited him and that he may be intending to squeeze us.

Equally surprising to Daubeny was the fact that Balmaceda alluded to the risk Gibbs ran in pressing their suit at a time when the case brought by the Nitrate Railways Company against the Agua Santa Company was still before the courts.[291] Daubeny took the precaution of seeing Gandarillas again, after his meeting with Balmaceda, and the ex-minister confirmed that he was correct in his interpretation of the previous agreement, and undertook to refresh the President's memory.[292] In his talk with Gandarillas, Daubeny pointed out that Gibbs had been induced to give up the consignment scheme for nitrate, on which North was so keen, precisely in return for the railway line on the agreed basis, and he reported to London that he

rubbed in the London House's power to help a monopoly sufficiently for him to put it very strongly to the President.[293]

This was an argument that Daubeny himself also put to the ministers concerned when he saw them at the end of September,[294] and it was one he proposed to use with the President himself at a future date. As he expressed the point to Miller,

Whether Balmaceda really intended to be slippery—or whether he

---

[289] Ibid.   [290] See above, pp. 156–7.

[291] Antony Gibbs & Sons, Valparaiso to London, 16 September 1890. AAG, MS. 11,470. Vol. 12. Letter No. 48.   [292] Ibid.   [293] Ibid.

[294] Memorandum by Daubeny, Valparaiso, 30 September 1890. AAG, MS. 11,470. Vol. 12.

simply put off coming to close quarters till his ministers had been 'primed', I don't feel quite sure. But he certainly treated the Monopoly as a *post* danger and when we (if we do have to) approach him again it will be very useful if his monopoly bugbear can be brought a little prominently forward again so that he may see that, although not an accomplished fact, the scheme is by no means dead.[295]

In fact, however, the political crisis in Chile subsequently assumed such proportions and it became so apparent to Gibbs in London that little progress could be made in the light of it that the Valparaiso House was instructed in December to postpone the whole matter.[296] Their possible lever on Balmaceda was, therefore, not used, and, in any event, although his 'bugbear of a monopoly' in nitrate was avoided, his fear of a combination to limit production—which he regarded as the same thing—was not. For, by the end of 1890, the long-anticipated combination of producers to restrict output for a period finally looked as though it would be formed, though it was not, in fact, until mid-January 1891 that the agreement was actually signed in Chile by representatives of the various companies,[297] and not until March 1891 that it came fully into operation.[298] It is interesting to note that all the companies joined except the firm of Folsch and Martin: although the negotiations for appropriate quotas were protracted, Chilean, as well as foreign, producers were quite convinced that there was no other course open to the industry in the critical condition of the world market, and, whatever the views of the Chilean government, the combination was formed.[299] It came not a moment too soon for the nitrate companies whose shares had fallen

---

[295] Daubeny to Miller, Valparaiso, 27 October 1890. AAG, MS. 11,470. Vol. 12.

[296] Antony Gibbs & Sons, Valparaiso to London, 23 December 1890. AAG, MS. 11,470, Vol. 12. Letter No. 56. Private, acknowledged the receipt of this news, and added that it was hoped the decision had been reached 'by no further causes of apprehension than those of which we are already aware, viz. the Nitrate Railways Co's case . . . and the untrustworthiness of the President.'

[297] Antony Gibbs & Sons, Valparaiso to London, 23 January 1891. AAG, MS. 11,470. Vol. 12. Letter No. 58. Private.

[298] Brown, 'Nitrate Crises', p. 236, gives details of the producers' agreement.

[299] Antony Gibbs & Sons, Valparaiso. Letter No. 58, loc. cit. 'The Agua Santa Co. came in unconditionally', the letter said, and their directors, in fact, expressed willingness to join a combination as early as September 1890. Vol. 12. Letter

dramatically by the end of 1890, and this was particularly true of the companies directed by Colonel North.

Nitrate shares [Stephen Williamson had written in November] are absolutely worthless. The Primitiva accounts are *very bad*. They show a deficiency of £60 to £100,000 against which there is the property. That is said to be now of little or no value. They owed the Bank on 30th June £158,000. Today's quotation is 5⅝ which Mr. Duncan Graham just said to me is 5⅝ *too much*. In fact, the concern is bankrupt. The Colorado [another of North's companies] lost £6,000 on the year's working. Other concerns are as bad or worse and these accounts were framed before the present bad state of affairs and prices set in . . .

The position is so serious that we telegraphed you today requesting that no payments be made for nitrate before delivery to you. . . You will require wise heads to steer a wise course, but from this point of view the prospect looks most serious and the extremest care will be essential to keep clear of large losses.[300]

That the recovery of the nitrate industry from the deep depression into which it had fallen by the end of 1890 would be a very protracted business, even with the assistance of the new combination, was obvious to those connected with it, as the year drew to its close.[301] But, for Balmaceda's government, this issue had paled into comparative insignificance in the light of the acute political crisis which now affected Chile, and which soon reached its climax.

By December, the signs of an impending catastrophe were clear. 'A false or precipitate step', said *The Chilean Times* on 13 December, 'on the part of the President or the Opposition may plunge the country into civil war.'[302] According to another contemporary observer, both sides were thinking in terms of a revolution towards the end of November.[303] The German Minister to Chile, Baron von Gutschmidt, expected an open conflict between Balmaceda and the Congress,[304] while, for his

No. 47. Private. It is, therefore, clear that the one nitrate company which, more than any other, could be regarded as a protégé of Balmaceda, certainly did not share his views on combinations.

[300] Stephen Williamson to W. B. Henderson, Liverpool (to Valparaiso), 27 November 1890. Balfour Williamson Papers. Letter Book No. 3. Letter No. 259.

[301] See *The Economist*, 11 January 1890.

[302] *The Chilean Times*, 13 December 1890.   [303] Velasco, *Memorias*, pp. 48–9.

[304] Von Gutschmidt to Chancellor Caprivi, Santiago, 23 December 1890.

part, the British Minister regarded the situation so seriously by mid-December that he wrote to Captain St Clair of H.M.S. *Champion* in Pacific waters, 'requesting him, if possible, to afford the protection of the presence in the ports of Valparaiso and Iquique of two of Her Majesty's ships'.[305] It was perfectly plain, not only that Balmaceda would be forced to act unconstitutionally, but also that he and his ministers had few qualms about doing so. Godoy began to purge the army and the Government services of opposition sympathizers at the beginning of December, while the opposition set up a small junta to prepare resistance, should Balmaceda make an unconstitutional move.[306] On 19 December, emotions were raised to a feverish level, when a meeting in Santiago of Conservative speakers was broken up by 'roughs disguised as policemen'; shots were fired, and a young aristocrat of a well-known family, Don Isidro Ossa, was killed in the mêlée. His death caused 'a profound sensation', and some 500 carriages and 15,000 people, including representatives of other cities, attended the funeral in Santiago.[307] On the same day, Balmaceda promulgated a decree prohibiting unauthorized public meetings,[308] and nine days later the congressional opposition drew up a document declaring Balmaceda unfit to continue in office: one copy, bearing the signatures of 19 senators and 70 deputies, was intended for Jorge Montt, Admiral of the Fleet and son of former President Manuel Montt, and the other, signed by 73 members of Congress, was meant for General Manuel Baquedano, the military hero of the War of the Pacific and the idol of the army.[309] Baquedano declined to join any movement against the President, but Montt pledged his support to Congress in the event of Balmaceda violating the constitution.

Die Vorgänge in Chile (Berlin, 1892), p. 4. This is the German White Book of official diplomatic correspondence on the Chilean revolution of 1891, cited hereafter as *DVC*.

[305] Kennedy to Salisbury, Santiago, 16 December 1890. F.O. 16/259. No. 90. Diplomatic.

[306] Encina, *Historia de Chile*, xix, 311–12; xx, 58–9.

[307] *The Chilean Times*, 27 December 1890.   [308] Encina, loc. cit., xix, 311.

[309] Encina, loc. cit., xx, 61 ff. See also J. M. Yrarrázaval, 'El segundo ejemplar del acta de deposición del Presidente Balmaceda', *Revista chilena de historia y geografía*, No. 82 (1937), pp. 197–200.

V

THE CHILEAN REVOLUTION OF 1891
AND ITS AFTERMATH

Armed Revolution and Civil War[1]

On 1 January 1891, the *Diario Oficial* of Chile published a manifesto from President Balmaceda to the nation.[2] It declared that, since Congress had not performed its constitutional duty by passing the laws for the estimates and the size of the armed forces in 1891, it was the President's duty to decree that the laws in force for 1890 would continue in operation. Balmaceda defended his admittedly unconstitutional act with an eloquent, though one-sided, survey of his administration, and on 5 January promulgated the decree which he had promised. He had flung down the gauntlet to the opposition, and it was immediately taken up: on 6 January, the President of the Chamber of Deputies and the Vice-President of the Senate signed a joint note to Admiral Jorge Montt, invoking the navy's assistance against Balmaceda's violation of the constitution.[3] And, on the following day, almost the entire Chilean fleet, in defiance of Balmaceda's orders, left Valparaiso harbour with a force of soldiers and many prominent politicians on board.[4]

[1] Again, the literature is enormous and partisan. Detailed accounts may be found in most of the books cited in note 15, p. 69. Velasco, *Memorias*, is indispensable, and so is the documentary collection of Carlos Rojas Arancibia, *Memorandum de la Revolución de 1891. Datos para la historia* (Santiago, 1892). A hitherto unpublished account, containing much interesting detail, is a diary kept by a member of the staff of Antony Gibbs in Valparaiso, in AAG, MS. 11,470. Vols. 12 and 13. My account is necessarily limited to the relationship of the war to the main themes of this book.

[2] Rojas Arancibia, *Memorandum*, pp. 7–25. A full English translation is in J. Sears and B. W. Wells, *The Chilean Revolution of 1891* (Washington, Office of Naval Intelligence, 1893), pp. 38–50.

[3] The President of the Senate was opposed to using force. Yrarrázaval, *El Presidente Balmaceda*, ii, 210. All the evidence suggests, however, that both sides underestimated the other's determination.

[4] Balmaceda did, however, retain the support of two torpedo-ships, the *Lynch* and the *Condell*, which were at Punta Arenas early in January. The crews disobeyed their commanders' orders to join the revolution, and declared for Balmaceda. See N. Amengual, *Episodios de la Revolución Chilena* (Buenos Aires, 1892), the account of the officer on the *Lynch* who engineered the mutiny.

These were the opening acts of one of the strangest wars in modern history.[5] For Balmaceda retained the support of the army and when, in February, the revolutionists seized the northern nitrate province of Tarapacá, a long period of stalemate ensued. While Balmaceda lacked ships to carry the war to the north, the revolutionaries lacked arms and a military force to challenge his base in the south. And between the antagonists stretched the forbidding barrier of the barren Atacama desert. The classic military metaphor of 'the whale and the elephant' obtained, and the impasse would only be resolved when one side or the other secured its military requirements to launch a decisive blow. As it happened, this issue was determined not in Chile but abroad where, from January to August, the antagonists fought a running battle to secure international sympathy, diplomatic support, funds and armaments; and it was a battle the revolutionists were to win hands down.[6]

What primarily concerns us here, however, is the part played by the British nitrate interests, and not least by North. For those writers who believe both that Balmaceda had a clear-cut policy in nitrate matters which was antagonistic to foreign interests and that these interests helped to foment revolution against him, it is only consistent to assert as a corollary to this thesis that the foreign nitrate interests gave active support and encouragement to the revolution once it had begun.[7] It has already been suggested that the first part of this thesis, however superficially attractive, is based upon a misreading, both of Balmaceda's attitudes and policies and of the comparatively minor role of nitrates, compared with the importance of the domestic political situation, as a factor in the genesis of the

[5] For the purely military history of the war, see J. Díaz Valderrama, *La Guerra Civil de 1891* (2 vols., Santiago, 1942); A. Bravo Kendrick, *La Revolución de 1891* (Santiago, 1949), pp. 93–383; Sears and Wells, loc. cit.; G. B. Aston, *Letters on Amphibious Wars* (London, 1911), pp. 4–86, and Sir William Laird Clowes, *Four Modern Naval Campaigns* (London, 1902), pp. 133–85.

[6] For this story, see my article 'Chilean Revolutionary Agents in Europe, 1891', *Pacific Historical Review*, xxxiii (1964), pp. 425–46, and the notes therein citing other sources. See also Patricio Estellé, 'Correspondencia de Don Agustín Ross sobre la Revolución de 1891', *Estudios de Historia de las Instituciones Políticas y Sociales*, No. 2 (1967), pp. 331–78.

[7] E.g. Hardy, 'British Nitrates and the Balmaceda Revolution'; Ramírez, *Balmaceda*; Pizarro, *La Revolución de 1891*.

revolution. Similarly, evidence of the complicity of nitrate interests in the revolution itself is not only sparse but partial, and close examination of the contemporary circumstances does little to support it.

Balmaceda's reaction to the movement of the fleet on 7 January was prompt and energetic: the army was mobilized and its pay increased; a state of siege, suspending the constitution, was instituted; clubs and press offices were closed, and when the Supreme Court of Justice declared on 10 January that Balmaceda had acted unconstitutionally, measures were also taken to control the judiciary. Although the leading Congressionalists had escaped from Santiago, many of their sympathizers were arrested, and domiciliary visits by the police and the violation of private correspondence soon became commonplace throughout the republic.[8] Balmaceda was ably supported by Domingo Godoy, the Foreign Minister, Julio Bañados Espinosa, the Minister of War and Marine, and Generals Orozimbo Barbosa and José Velásquez, and what, in view of Chile's past, seemed like 'a reign of terror' was established.[9] This policy was particularly the work of Godoy, 'the real dictator' who admitted to the British Minister that 'many persons are imprisoned or flogged or exiled or molested on mere suspicion'.[10] He believed that the only way to defeat the revolution was by complete repression and, indeed, by terrorism if need be, and his determination quite impressed the foreign diplomats in Santiago.[11] It also led him to seek British naval assistance in destroying the Chilean fleet in January,[12] an extraordinary idea in which he persisted for some time: in the middle of February, he again urged Kennedy to request permission from the Foreign Office to sanction the use of the British squadron in Chilean waters to put down the revolution, as well as asking that the British flag be carried on Chilean cargo-

[8] See Velasco, *Memorias, passim.* Cf. Gibbs Diary, AAG, MS. 11,470. Vol. 12, pp. 695–700.

[9] So it seemed to the British minister. Kennedy to Salisbury, Santiago, 22 January 1891. F.O. 16/264. No. 4. Diplomatic. Cf., however, Hervey, *Dark Days in Chile, passim.*

[10] Kennedy to Sanderson, Santiago, 24 January 1891. F.O. 16/264. Private.

[11] Kennedy to Salisbury, Santiago, 17 February 1891. F.O. 16/264. Nos. 13 and 14. Diplomatic. Von Gutschmidt to Caprivi, Viña, 2 March 1891. *DVC*, p. 58.

[12] Kennedy to Sanderson, loc. cit. Cf. Velasco, *Memorias*, p. 116.

steamers bringing coal from Lota to Valparaiso, that Pacific Mail Line steamers under the British flag should transport troops for the government and, most remarkable of all, that Kennedy should assist him to negotiate the purchase of the *Warspite*, the flagship of Rear-Admiral Sir Charles Hotham, the commander of the British Pacific Squadron.[13]

As [wrote Kennedy wryly to Salisbury] these wild projects were prompted by Señor Godoy's feverish desire to suppress the revolution, I simply informed His Excellency that such proposals were inadmissible and that I must decline to submit them to Your Lordship.[14]

The Chilean government was clearly anxious to secure the friendship and sympathy of foreign diplomats. Godoy's relations with Kennedy were very affable, and he assured him that British persons and property would be well protected.[15] Similarly, Balmaceda personally assured the German Minister that German interests would be well looked after,[16] while, early in February, the American Minister could report that the Chilean government took 'prompt and energetic steps' to redress American grievances arising from the war.[17] This friendly attitude towards foreign representatives was clearly determined by Balmaceda's peculiar position as a result of the revolution. On 16 January, Jorge Montt gave notice that from 18 January the ports of Iquique and Valparaiso would be blockaded by the fleet.[18] Godoy thereupon called a meeting of the diplomatic corps in Santiago and urged the foreign representatives to protest against the blockade, but while they agreed that it was illegal they also replied that they could make no official protest as the Chilean government had declared the fleet to be

---

[13] Kennedy to Salisbury, Santiago, 17 February 1891. No. 14. Diplomatic. According to Velasco, *Memorias*, p. 202, it was rumoured that Godoy was prepared to pay Kennedy £50,000 to effect the sale of the warship.

[14] Kennedy to Salisbury, loc. cit.

[15] Same to same, Santiago, 24 January 1891, F.O. 16/264. No. 8. Diplomatic.

[16] Von Gutschmidt to Caprivi, Viña, 18 January 1891. *DVC*, p. 19.

[17] Minister Patrick Egan to Secretary of State James G. Blaine, Santiago, 13 February 1891. *Papers relating to the Foreign Relations of the United States transmitted to Congress with the Annual Message of the President, December 9th, 1891* (hereafter *FRUS*) (Washington, 1891), p. 104.

[18] Kennedy to Salisbury, Santiago, 22 January 1891. F.O. 16/264. No. 4. Diplomatic.

piratical and had declined all responsibility for damage done
to neutrals.[19] All that they could do, they felt, was to instruct
their consuls at the two ports to protest to the rebel ships on the
spot. The Congressionalists' decision to blockade the two chief
ports of the republic and the government's reaction showed
clearly the former's strength and the latter's weakness: without
a fleet, Balmaceda had no hope of putting down the revolution,
and the government's impotence created a feeling of frustration
which led its members to make all sorts of charges against
foreigners, and not least against the British.

The early weeks of the revolution were a time of great
activity for Kennedy. In addition to complaints from British
ships of interference by both the Congressional fleet and by
over-zealous government officials, he was much occupied with
complaints by British nationals that they were being persecuted
for alleged complicity in the revolution.

It may seem inexplicable to you [wrote one] that I, as a British
subject, should be subject to persecution by the existing Chilean
Government, and I sincerely believe there is not a Chilean in the
country who has been so steadily pursued by the Authorities since
the breaking out of the Revolution.[20]

The writer was the manager of a Chilean sugar-refinery whose
owners had been involved in the revolt of the fleet, and it was
his opinion that the government sought to accuse him of complicity merely in order to destroy the factory by way of reprisal.
There were many other British subjects in a similar situation.
The manager of Balfour, Williamson at Valparaiso informed
Kennedy that the firm's agent was in hiding 'for holding
opinions' though, in fact, he had done nothing to excite the
suspicion of the authorities;[21] and British nationals in more
official positions were subject to similar accusations.

Shortly after the revolution broke out, Kennedy had issued
a memorandum enjoining neutrality on all British subjects, and
a copy of this was sent to Consul-General Joel at Valparaiso for
communication to senior British naval officers in Chilean

---

[19] Same to same, of same date. No. 6. Diplomatic. With enclosures.
[20] Mr Mitchell to Kennedy, Viña, 12 January 1891. F.O. 132/29.
[21] Mr Henderson to Kennedy, Valparaiso, 12 January 1891. F.O. 132/29.

waters.[22] The British warship *Champion*, under the command of Captain St Clair, had been in Chilean waters since 29 December 1890, and St Clair had on several occasions visited Admiral Montt in Valparaiso harbour to clarify Montt's notification of blockading the port, to protest against certain incidents involving British steamers, and to remove dead and wounded from Chilean ships which had suffered casualties in interchange of fire with shore-batteries.[23] St Clair's movements, however, aroused the suspicion of Godoy who protested to Kennedy that the Captain was showing 'undue friendliness towards the revolted Chilean fleet': St Clair emphatically denied this charge, pointing out that the Intendant of Valparaiso had given prior approval for all his movements, explanations which Kennedy accepted and passed to Godoy.[24] Within three weeks of this incident, however, Kennedy reported on another matter which, he said, 'shows the vindictiveness of the President towards all supporters of the Nitrate Railways Company'.[25] Towards the end of January, Montt's flagship signalled to the *Champion* that certain letters had fallen into the hands of the Chilean admiral, letters addressed to Mr Linnick, the Austrian Consul-General at Valparaiso, Dean of the Consular Corps, and also, as it happened, the agent of the Nitrate Railways Company at the port. The Intendant of Valparaiso, Villarino, insisted on the mails being opened in his office, and Linnick agreed, but when this was done Villarino opened a number of letters addressed to others, after which several arrests were made.[26] Later Godoy told Kennedy that

In consequence of the contents of those letters he had decided to arrest many persons and also to imprison or exile Mr. Linnick . . .

and when Kennedy pointed out the seriousness of these remarks, Godoy added that Linnick was

[22] Memorandum on the Chilean Revolution, 15 January 1891. Copy encl. in Kennedy to Salisbury, Santiago, 29 January 1891. F.O. 16/264. No. 10. Diplomatic.
[23] Report of the proceedings of the *Champion*. Encl. No. 2 in Admiral Hotham to the Admiralty, *Warspite* at Valparaiso, 3 February 1891. Public Record Office, Records of the Admiralty, Pacific In-Letters, 1891. Box 1/7068/Y. General Letter No. 34.
[24] Kennedy to Salisbury, Santiago, 2 February 1891. F.O. 16/264. No. 11. Diplomatic. With encls. of correspondence with St Clair and Godoy.
[25] Same to same, 23 February 1891. No. 17. Diplomatic. Confidential.
[26] Ibid.

an object of aversion to the President on account of his friendship with Señor Zegers and of his active promotion of the Nitrate Railways Company.

Any advocacy of the interests of the Nitrate Railways Company [Kennedy reported] is fiercely resented by the President as an attack on his personal policy. . . Chileans of position have entreated me to abstain from assisting the above . . . Company; Ministers have sought to blacken the character of Señor Zegers, the Company's lawyer, before me, and have also spoken ill of Mr. Linnick . . .[27]

Kennedy also added an important postscript to his account of this incident:

It is [he said] at present, the policy of the Government to ascribe the revolutionary movement to the desire of the Opposition to secure the riches of the province of Tarapacá, and the Government newspapers are full of abuse of Colonel North and of rich individual Chileans who are alleged to have corrupted Chile by having developed the resources of Tarapacá.[28]

Such assertions, made early in the revolution, were to continue in one form or another throughout its course, both in Chile and abroad. The purely political and constitutional arguments put forward by Balmaceda at the beginning of the year were soon replaced by blatant propaganda, calculated to arouse the lower classes against the aristocracy who, it was alleged, were responsible, along with foreign capitalists, for plunging the country into bloody civil war.[29] Early in January, the *Boletín del Día*, the official organ of the Government, published an attack on 'millionarios', to which a number of foreign business representatives took exception, as the manager of Balfour, Williamson informed Kennedy:

I saw both Don Claudio Vicuña (Minister of the Interior) and the Intendente Villarino regarding the paragraph in the *Boletín del Día* headed 'Millionarios'. Both told me that it was not directed against foreigners but against the Chilean families of Edwards, Matte and Subercasseaux. I told them it was a scandal . . . such a paragraph published in Europe would do immense harm to the credit of Chile.[30]

[27] Ibid.   [28] Ibid
[29] Encina, *Historia de Chile*, xx, 126 ff. My examples are necessarily selective.
[30] Mr Henderson to Kennedy, Valparaiso, 15 January 1891. F.O. 132/29.

Despite the disavowals of Chilean officials that foreign interests were not the object of attack, they were, in fact, brought under a general condemnation. On 23 February, *El Comercio* of Valparaiso accused the bankers not only of suborning revolution but also of jeopardizing national sovereignty by making a deal with foreigners:

In order [the paper said] to obtain the assistance of the English in their audacious attempt, they have promised if they triumph, a Factory in Tarapacá, that is to say a Gibraltar in America, a slice of our country upon which the British flag may wave.[31]

A day later, a more strident tone emerged in an even more personal attack:

There is no need to say anything about nitrate because the business is plain to the eye. Iquique being blockaded, no nitrate can be exported and North, who finds money for the revolution, will sell his stocks at high prices and will make great profits... The Jews, North and Dreyfus being intimately allied and mixed up in the revolution, they [the revolutionists] are disposed to share with them the advantages. If they triumph, North will have a monopoly of Tarapacá under a British protectorate, and Dreyfus will be paid the millions awarded him by Piérola.[32]

And so it went on. In March 1891 the American Minister in Santiago reported that a striking feature of the revolution was that it had 'the undivided sympathy and in many cases the active support of the English residents in Chile', and he quoted a Balmacedist general in Tarapacá who had asserted that the managers of the British-owned *oficinas* had promised their employees $2 a day to join the revolution, threatening them with the loss of all future employment if they did not. Egan also averred that North alone had contributed £100,000 to the revolutionary cause.[33] And on 8 May, a Spanish newspaper

---

Gibbs' diarist translated the paragraph in full 'as an example of what the authorities allow to be circulated'. Gibbs Diary, AAG, MS. 11,470, Vol. 12, pp. 702–3.

[31] *El Comercio*, 23 February 1891, as cited by *The Chilean Times*, 7 March.

[32] The same of 24 February, also cited. For Dreyfus and Piérola, see above, note 105, p. 136.

[33] Egan to Blaine, Santiago, 14 March 1891. *FRUS*, pp. 106–7. I have doubted Egan's credibility as a witness in 'The Chilean Revolution of 1891 and its Historiography', pp. 405–6.

repeated these rumours, though North was said to have denied
them and to have expressed the belief that Balmaceda would
succeed in crushing the revolution.[34] Similarly, in the Balmacedist Congress in the summer of 1891, speeches were made
attacking North for alleged complicity with Chilean bankers in
fomenting the revolution against Balmaceda.[35] And, finally,
this was precisely the line taken by the special correspondent of
The Times in Chile, Maurice H. Hervey.[36]

Although such rumours flew thick and fast throughout the
revolution, many attempts were made to scotch them. In Chile
itself, *The Chilean Times* contemptuously rejected 'the ridiculous
and abominable trash' put out by government newspapers, in
such a forthright fashion, indeed, that it was itself attacked by
El Comercio which pleaded that its articles had been misunder-
stood and that 'a compositor's error' had been responsible for
one of its more violent pieces.[37] Representatives of British
business houses in both Chile and England also protested at
the allegations made against North, particularly by Maurice
Hervey: none of them had business dealings with 'the Nitrate
King', and some of them such as Antony Gibbs and Balfour,
Williamson were positively antagonistic to him.[38] As for the
British Minister in Santiago, he regarded the assertions as no
more than

[34] *El Imparcial* of Madrid, 8 May 1891.   [35] Blakemore, loc. cit., pp. 401–2.
[36] Ibid., pp. 406–8.
[37] *The Chilean Times*, 7, 14, 21 and 25 March 1891.
[38] Blakemore, loc. cit., p. 407. Further research in the Archives of *The Times*,
London, Printing House Square, has confirmed the doubts about Hervey's
credibility expressed in this article. When Hervey was recalled from Chile by *The
Times* because the editor doubted his reliability, he entered into a long correspondence and a financial argument with his employer. In the course of this,
Hervey hinted at challenging the editor to a duel, said that he was going to write
a book, and reiterated his views on North. In his last letter to Hervey, the manager
of the paper said that 'anything in the book in the tone of your letter would at once
destroy all its value for it would be at once dismissed as the work of a madman
or at least of a man so devoid of judgement that his simple statement of fact could
not be accepted . . . you might as well assert [he concluded] that the revolution
of 1688 was raised by Colonel North.' Moberley Bell to Hervey, 22 September
1891. Private letter. Copy. Letter Book No. 4. Hervey subsequently sought
employment as a correspondent with *The Times* on two occasions, in 1893 and in
1894, but was refused. Moberley Bell to Hervey, 6 December 1893. Copy. Letter
Book No. 8, and William Lyddiatt to Hervey, 31 July 1894. Copy. Letter Book
No. 9.

a thoughtless repetition of the plan of political campaign undertaken by the party in power against Colonel North and many
leading and wealthy Chileans associated with him in the development of the resources of Tarapacá.[39]

Amidst the welter of allegation and denial, charge and coun-
ter-charge, the truth is somewhat elusive. On one issue, however, there can be no doubt. The sympathies of the British
community in Chile, including the British squadron, and those
of British business houses were almost entirely on the side of
the revolution. Kennedy's position in Santiago was made quite
difficult by the partisanship of British subjects. Reporting in
June on shipping complaints, he stated that 'Britishers complain and protest more than all other nationalities put together;
they delight to resist and defy and they are encouraged by old
Joel and Captain St Clair.'[40] In an interview with Kennedy in
the same month, the Minister of the Interior, Bañados Espinosa,

stated that about 10% of the British residents of Valparaiso avowed
publicly their sympathies with the opposition. He also complained
[said Kennedy] of the opposition tendencies of *The Chilean Times*
and begged me to convey a warning to that paper.[41]

Admiral Hotham wrote that the British consul at Coquimbo
and the agent of the Pacific Steam Navigation Company there
also sympathized with the revolution, and that the ships of the
company actively aided the Congressionalists.[42] Another witness of the civil war supported this testimony in his account of
how he travelled from Valparaiso to Caldera in April 1891, in
the P.S.N.C. vessel, the *Mendoza*, with over thirty Congressionalists, including Juan Walker Martínez, a leading revolutionist,
on board.[43] It was also in this way, by means of a British
vessel steaming from Valparaiso to the north, that the future,

---

[39] Kennedy to Antony Gibbs and others, Santiago, 30 July 1891. Copy. Encl.
No. 2 in Kennedy to Salisbury, Santiago, 17 August 1891. F.O. 16/265. No. 85.
Diplomatic.
[40] Kennedy to Sanderson, Santiago, 9 June 1891. F.O. 16/265. Private.
[41] Kennedy to Joel, Santiago, 18 June 1891. F.O. 132/33. British Minister to
Consuls, 1891–92. No. 32. Confidential. Copy.
[42] Unaddressed and undated notes of Hotham in F.O. 16/281. Consular, Commercial & Treaty. Various. 1891.
[43] C. C. Morant, *Chile and the River Plate* (London, 1891), pp. 142 ff.

outstanding commander of the Congressionalist army, General Emil Körner, was able to escape from Santiago.[44] And, although on the outbreak of the revolution, the manager of Antony Gibbs at Valparaiso immediately laid down 'the rule of maintaining the strictest neutrality and carefully avoid giving any opinion or doing any action which might be interpreted as giving support to one side more than to the other',[45] there is no doubt on which side the company's sympathies lay. After the revolution was over, Kennedy was quite explicit:

There is no doubt [he wrote] our Naval Officers and the British community of Valparaiso and all along the Coast rendered material assistance to the opposition and committed many breaches of neutrality.[46]

The reasons for these attitudes and actions are not far to seek. In the case of the naval personnel, officers such as St Clair, conscious of the longstanding ties of friendship between the Chilean and British navies, and treated always with courtesy and consideration by Admiral Montt and his colleagues, simply accepted their version of the causes of the revolution as those of trustworthy brother-officers. As Montt himself later informed Kennedy:

Her Majesty's Naval Officers on this station had been his true friends from the beginning to the end of the Revolution and . . . had never faltered in their belief in the success of the cause of the Congress party.[47]

Other British subjects who sympathized with the revolution, many of them longstanding residents of Chile, clearly believed, as did the international press, that the Congressionalist cause was just and that Balmaceda was an aspiring tyrant, and they shared the view expressed by *The Times* in April 1891:

[44] Rojas, *Memorandum*, p. 500. On Körner, see Figueroa, *Diccionario histórico*, iii, 602–3, and Frederick M. Nunn, 'Emil Körner and the Prussianization of the Chilean Army: Origins, Process and Consequences, 1885–1920', *HAHR*, 1 (1970), pp. 300–7.
[45] Antony Gibbs & Sons, Valparaiso to London, 19 January 1891. AAG, MS. 11,470. Vol. 12.
[46] Kennedy to Sanderson, Santiago, 15 September 1891. F.O. 16/266. Private.
[47] Kennedy to Salisbury, Santiago, 2 September 1891. F.O. 16/266. No. 91. Diplomatic. On the back of this despatch Sanderson wrote the wry comment: 'This is charming—as things have turned out. But I think we need not print it.'

It is [the paper said] rather singular that if the President is merely a good man struggling with adversity, he should have against him, by his own showing, all the classes who have secured to Chile a period of tranquil and orderly progress such as no other South American Republic has ever enjoyed ... [48]

And there can be no doubt that a major factor in this attitude was the severely repressive policies adopted by Balmaceda's government, and particularly Godoy, in the areas which they controlled. In the army which was based upon conscription, often of the most brutal kind, discipline was severe, and it is not surprising that desertions were frequent. Godoy's lieutenants, such as Salvador Sanfuentes in Concepción, were little more than thugs who utilized their official positions for personal ends. The revolution gave free play to private passions and the abuses committed under the justification of national necessity brought disrepute on the government itself. Discontent spread throughout the country, as the severe policies of Godoy to stamp out the enemy within not only failed in that purpose, but also, indeed, alienated those sectors of public opinion hitherto uncommitted in the civil war. [49]

How far Balmaceda himself was responsible is a matter of some dispute. [50] Reporting on the flogging and torture of political prisoners by government officials during the war, the diarist of Gibbs added that 'if this is true it must surely be without Balmaceda's knowledge', and he instanced one case suggesting that this might be so:

Pío Fierro [he wrote] the head of the secret police in Valpo [*sic*] who was the leader of the men who entered Mrs. Edward's House on 24th ult° [*sic*] has been removed from his post, after, it is said, a severe reprimand from Balmaceda for his behaviour on that occasion. [51]

---

[48] *The Times*, 28 April 1891.

[49] Encina, *Historia de Chile*, xx, 125–80, is an excellent account of Godoy's dictatorship, to which Velasco, *Memorias, passim*, adds much valuable eyewitness material.

[50] Cf., for example, Encina, loc. cit., where the blame is put squarely on Godoy's shoulders, and Ricardo Donoso, *Francisco A. Encina. Simulador* (2 vols., Santiago, 1969 and 1970), ii, 348–9, where Encina is strongly criticized for this view, and the blame is ascribed to the government as a whole, including Balmaceda.

[51] Gibbs Diary, AAG, MS. 11,470. Vol. 13, p. 110. Entry dated 13 April 1891.

And, after the war, Kennedy himself expressed the view that it was Balmaceda's lieutenants and not the President who were responsible for the bad reputation the government got because of its repression.[52] Nevertheless, the facts remain, and no leader can escape some responsibility for his subordinates since it is he who chooses them. Moreover, it must be remembered that an important factor in the genesis of the revolution was precisely the widespread feeling in Chile that Balmaceda's capacity as a judge of men was weak, a human failing but, in a chief executive, a crucial one.[53] Balmaceda paid dearly for this fault: when, in August 1891, his armies were routed at the bloody battles of Concón and Placilla, weakness of morale, the result of public revulsion, was certainly a major factor.[54]

The widespread sympathy of foreigners in Chile towards the revolution, however, played a minor part in its final outcome, though some were undoubtedly guilty of actual support of the Congressionalists and could be held culpable of unwarranted interference in a domestic struggle.[55] But so far as the nitrate interests, and particularly North, were concerned, the truth is much more elusive, as, no doubt, it is bound to be. The circumstantial evidence, however, is no less strongly against that view than for it. In the first place, no shred of evidence has come to light to support the rumours retailed during the war, such as that reported by Patrick Egan that North himself had provided a contribution of £100,000 to the revolutionary cause. Indeed, in the wartime propaganda of the government and its sympathizers, there is not one single hard fact, though wild charges in strident tones abound as crude appeals to both chauvinistic sentiment and class hatred. The argument that evidence of North's alleged complicity would, by its very nature, be hard to find is no argument at all for accepting the veracity of con-

[52] Memorandum on the Chilean Revolution. Encl. in Kennedy to Sanderson, Burton, 24 September 1892. F.O. 16/280. Diplomatic. Various.

[53] Cf. above, pp. 172–3.

[54] Most writers on the subject agree with this view. It was also the opinion of an eyewitness of the battles, the British Lieutenant Colmore. Report on the Battles of Concón and Placilla, 5 October 1891. Encl. No. 2 in Hotham to Admiralty, *Warspite* at Esquimault, 6 November 1891. Adm. 1/7068/Y. General Letter. No. 287.

[55] Cf., however, Ramírez, *Balmaceda, passim,* where foreign sympathy is regarded as a much more significant factor.

temporary rumour which is itself contradicted by collateral evidence pointing to the opposite conclusion.

Some three years after the war, at a time when the defeated Balmacedists had already returned to full participation in Chilean public life, and were, in fact, the second largest party in the Chilean Congress, the government published an account of the finances of the Congressionalists during the revolution.[56] This set out, in minute detail, their income and expenditure during the war, and it does, indeed, include references to North. These are found in the lists of payments to individuals and companies in Tarapacá for goods and services rendered, where some of North's concerns are listed among the thousands of names set out, including the Agua Santa Company, Balmaceda's former protégé.[57] But the payments were no more than a record of normal commercial transactions between private interests and the authorities in control of the province, precisely in the same way that Balmaceda's government carried on business in the areas it controlled.[58] The account is over four hundred pages long, and it shows a balance of income and expenditure of some $17,000,000, of which, on the income side, more than $10,000,000 came from export taxes, notably on nitrate, the revolutionists' major source of revenue from the time they captured Tarapacá in February 1891. On the expenditure side, and not surprisingly, the largest outlay—some $13,000,000—was for war purposes. Making the crude assumption of an exchange rate of 38 pence to the peso,[59] North's reputed donation of £100,000 to the revolutionary cause would amount to $631,579, about one-thirtieth of the total.

There is, of course, no reference to this sum in the account, however detailed, but the question to be asked is whether it is at all likely that North would, even if he could, have spent so sizeable a sum in this way. North was, of course, a gambler,

[56] *Cuenta Jeneral de las Entradas y Gastos de la Excma. Junta de Gobierno de Chile desde enero a agosto de 1891* (Santiago, 1894).

[57] Ibid., *passim*, but see particularly pp. 219, 221, 224.

[58] See *Diario Oficial de la República de Chile, 1891* (Santiago, 1891), *passim*. It may be interesting to note that during the war Balmaceda's government renewed a contract it had with North's Arauco Company. *Diario Oficial*, p. 655.

[59] This was the rate of exchange in 1890 and also after the revolution, though considerable confusion existed in 1891 itself. Martner, *Estudio de la política comercial chilena*, ii, 475 ff.

though he rarely gambled on unfavourable odds. The story of his 'contribution' was reported by Patrick Egan in March, a mere week after the decisive battle in the northern desert which gave the Congressionalists control of Tarapacá and, therefore, of the export taxes on nitrate shipments. Up to that time, however, the revolutionists lacked funds, arms and a firm base on land, and it was very doubtful that they could overthrow Balmaceda. 'The Fleet are getting very short of money and . . . they are very deficient in rifles and ammunition', wrote an observer on 19 January,[60] and, a week later, the same writer thought that 'the opposition are . . . in a much worse position than they were at the beginning'.[61] This view was shared by the British Minister, whose despatches in February referred more than once to the contrast between the inactivity of the revolted fleet and the energy of the government.[62] And even after the Congressionalists captured Iquique on 16 February, but still had to secure this base and, indeed, take over Tarapacá as a whole, Kennedy thought that the balance of power lay with the government forces.[63] Is it likely, therefore, that in these circumstances North would have made so large a contribution to so doubtful a cause, particularly since such an investment would be highly speculative on another count—his ignorance of what attitude would be adopted towards his interests even if the revolution succeeded?[64]

There is other circumstantial evidence to support this view. As we have seen, North's financial position at the end of 1890 was very far from secure,[65] and it was pointed out to Kennedy only a month before the war ended that 'the bare idea of the embarrassed English Nitrate Companies being the "financial Supporters" of the Revolution affords its own contradiction'.[66] A similar view was expressed by Stephen Williamson, certainly no friend of North, in a letter to *The Times* which was not, in

[60] Gibbs Diary, AAG, MS. 11,470. Vol. 12, p. 740.

[61] Ibid., pp. 766–7, entry for 8 February.

[62] Kennedy to Salisbury, Santiago, 17 and 28 February 1891. F.O. 16/264. Nos. 13 & 21. Diplomatic.

[63] Same to same, 4 March 1891. No. 22. Diplomatic.

[64] On this subject, see below, pp. 209–27.   [65] See above, pp. 189–90.

[66] Antony Gibbs and others to Kennedy, Valparaiso, 27 July 1891. Encl. 1 in Kennedy to Salisbury, Santiago, 17 August 1891. F.O. 16/265. No. 85. Diplomatic.

fact, published, possibly because it consisted of a strong attack on Maurice Hervey's unproved assertions about the complicity of North and other nitrate capitalists in the revolution.[67] And, finally, when Hervey himself was recalled from Chile and ordered to bring back *proof* of his allegations, he could provide nothing to satisfy his employer:

We can only say, with regret [wrote the editor subsequently to Hervey], that you seem to have entirely misconceived the object of your mission. That object was not the glorification of *The Times* by lavish hospitality to one party in a civil conflict . . . but to ascertain by careful enquiry and observation and to describe the condition of the country.

So completely have you failed in this that you did not even call on the British representatives at Santiago and Valparaiso and have returned with sympathies which, however honest they may be, are diametrically opposed to those of every intelligent person we have met, and to those we have ourselves formed after sending [*sic*— reading?] everything you have been able to write in favour of your own views.[68]

That North's sympathies lay with the revolution can hardly be doubted, and he did, in fact, make one appeal to the Foreign Office on behalf of the Congressionalists, when he wrote in May to Lord Salisbury, at the formal request of the Congressional agents in Europe, asking the British government to place an embargo on certain arms from England which were allegedly intended for a Chilean ironclad being built for Balmaceda in France.[69] But that was all, and in the almost complete absence of evidence to the contrary, the only conclusion possible about the wartime rumours of North's contribution to the revolution is that they were rumours, indeed, and nothing more.

Nevertheless, North and other foreign nitrate capitalists were a convenient bogy for Balmaceda's government in 1891, particularly as the government's frustrations increased. The Congressional seizure of the nitrate areas in February–March

[67] Stephen Williamson to the Editor of *The Times*, Liverpool, 24 March 1891. Balfour Williamson Papers, Letter Book No. 3. Copy.

[68] Moberley Bell to Hervey, London, 3 August 1891. Archives of *The Times*, Letter Book No. 4, pp. 13–14. Copy.

[69] Blakemore, 'Chilean Revolutionary Agents in Europe, 1891', p. 432.

1891 provided a steady revenue for the revolution from export taxes on nitrate shipments. Though the Chilean government decreed the closure of the nitrate ports to shipping in April 1891 this was simply a 'paper blockade', since Balmaceda lacked the ships to enforce it, and almost all foreign governments, in accordance with international law and practice, refused to accept closure of ports by mere decree. They also declined to accept other government decrees, one declaring that nitrate shippers were liable to pay double duty if they had paid the Congressionalists at places of shipment, and another refusing to clear foreign ships from Balmacedist ports if they intended to stop at northern harbours on their trade routes.[70] The Chilean government's pertinacity in seeking to apply these decrees was perfectly understandable to the British Minister:

the Chilean government feel [Kennedy reported] that if only they could prevent shipments of nitrate from Tarapacá and transport of provisions to that province, the revolution would be speedily extinguished.[71]

This, however, the government could not do, and throughout the summer of 1891 a general situation of stalemate between the antagonists prevailed, as each anxiously sought abroad the war material it required to launch a decisive attack on the other. In this race, the Congressionalists triumphed, securing the necessary arms to equip a formidable army, recruited from the nitrate workers of Tarapacá and splendidly trained by the better officers who had joined the Congressional cause. Towards the end of August, a Congressional army was transported by the fleet from Tarapacá to the vicinity of Valparaiso, where, in two separate engagements, it crushed the Balmacedist forces, which were weak in arms, feeble in morale and lacking leadership.

Decisively defeated on the field and dejected in spirit, Balmaceda took refuge in the Argentine embassy in Santiago, where, after writing a remarkable prophetic testament on

[70] See the correspondence in F.O. 16/265. Almost half of Kennedy's despatches in the summer of 1891 were devoted to the subject of shipping questions arising from these decrees and the British government's refusal to accept them.

[71] Kennedy to Salisbury, Santiago, 3 June 1891. F.O. 16/265. No. 54. Diplomatic. Cf. von Gutschmidt to Caprivi, Santiago, 26 April 1891. *DVC*, p. 116.

Chile's future political development, he ended his life with a shot from a revolver on 19 September, five years and a day from the date he had assumed the highest office in the republic. It was a dramatic end to the career of the most complex character in Chilean history, a self-inflicted martyrdom which set the seal on a romantic reputation and was to exercise a profound influence on subsequent Chilean history. Yet, in his final political testament, as in his dramatic address to the nation which began the revolution of 1891, Balmaceda made no mention of those economic interests, foreign and national, against which the government had thundered during the civil war. To political ambitions and personal desires alone he ascribed the national disaster of which he was the principal victim.[72]

The Chilean Government and the Nitrate Interest

With the defeat of Balmaceda in the civil war of 1891, says a modern historian, 'the nitrate policy [of the Chilean government] followed lines [which were] diametrically opposed to those enunciated by Balmaceda in 1889'.[73] 'It is certain', says another, 'that the victors felt that they owed something to the nitrate interest, and they put in office a President who cared for his supporters.'[74] This is a view which, in recent years, has come to be widely accepted, and one which continues to exercise considerable influence on contemporary Chilean affairs.[75] It is, indeed, the coping-stone on the edifice built up to explain the Chilean revolution of 1891 in terms of economic nationalism and foreign economic imperialism. But, like the foundations of that argument itself, it is weak in construction and unstable in fact.

There is no doubt that the victory of the Congressionalists was greeted with relief by those foreign interests in Chile which felt in any way threatened by Balmaceda. 'Foreign residents here', wrote Joel from Valparaiso, 'are almost unanimous in

[72] The testament is given in full in Bañados, *Balmaceda*, ii, 644–55.

[73] Ramírez, *Balmaceda*, p. 216. Ramírez reaches this conclusion after citing a good deal of evidence to contradict it.

[74] Hardy, 'British Nitrates', p. 178.

[75] See below, pp. 244–5.

expressing their satisfaction at the result.'[76] Minister Kennedy was even more explicit:

The British Community in Chile [he wrote] make no secret of their satisfaction over the downfall of Balmaceda whose triumph, it is believed, would have involved serious prejudice to British commercial interests.[77]

The British commercial press also expressed its approval: it was 'with great satisfaction' that the *South American Journal* spoke of the realization 'not only of our hopes, but of the expectations we have throughout ventured to express'.[78] Balmaceda's defeat was considered 'matter for congratulation' by *The Statist*,[79] while to *The Times* it augured the beginning of Chile's return to her position of pre-eminence in South America which had been jeopardized by Balmaceda's policies and actions.[80] Nor were these views confined to British subjects. The press of Europe as a whole exulted in Balmaceda's defeat,[81] and the German Minister in Santiago was no less gratified by the outcome of the revolution than was his British colleague.[82]

The nitrate interests in general, and those of North in particular, shared the widespread euphoria. Note was taken of 'Colonel North's friendly relations with the new Government',[83] which was reported to have 'a distinctly favourable' attitude towards foreign nitrate interests.[84] Moreover, a cheerful confidence in the future was the dominant tone at the board meetings of several nitrate companies towards the end of 1891.[85] Only *The Economist*, true to its reputation for realism, injected a note of caution:

[76] Joel to Foreign Office, Valparaiso, 1 September 1891. F.O. 16/269. No. 7. Political.

[77] Kennedy to Salisbury, Santiago, 21 September 1891. F.O. 16/266. No. 97, Diplomatic.

[78] *South American Journal*, 5 September 1891.

[79] *The Statist*, same date.

[80] *The Times*, 31 August, 1 and 2 September 1891.

[81] See A. Fagalde, *La Prensa Estranjera y la Dictadura Chilena* (Santiago, 1891), pp. 54–102.

[82] Von Gutschmidt to Caprivi, Santiago, 29 August 1891. *DVC*, p. 204.

[83] *The South American Journal*, 12 September 1891.

[84] Ibid., 19 September 1891.

[85] Ibid., 5 December 1891.

it will not do [the paper said in September] to be too sanguine that all questions between the nitrate companies themselves and between them and the Chilean Government have been set at rest . . .[86]

For the moment, however, the lone voice of this Cassandra was quite submerged by the chorus of optimistic opinion, confident that the new government in Chile would promptly reverse its predecessor's apparent attitudes and policies.

The Nitrate Railways Company was particularly pleased, and its directors assumed that they now had little to worry about. They showed their confidence soon after the war, when the Chilean government entered into negotiations with foreign powers to establish machinery for the adjudication of claims for compensation for wartime damage suffered by foreigners in Chile.[87] Although the company had a claim for £48,775, its manager at Iquique informed Kennedy that it did not wish to press the matter for the moment,[88] and Kennedy informed London that this claim, with two others, might be 'privately arranged between the Chilean Government and the interested parties'.[89] It seems that the company deliberately held back in its claim in order not to prejudice the excellent relations it was believed to have with the new Chilean administration.

But disillusionment came quickly. Before the year was out, the company's lawyer in London, Mr Budd, was writing a long letter of complaint to the Foreign Office:

It was hoped [he said] that one of the first acts of the new Government at Santiago would have been to reverse the arbitrary decrees of the late Government, but recent telegraphic advices have informed us that the present Government is confirming the Concession of the Agua Santa competing line and is authorising the

---

[86] *The Economist*, 5 September 1891.

[87] The terms of the Claims Convention between Chile and Great Britain is in *British and Foreign State Papers*, LXXXV (1892–93), pp. 22–5. British correspondence on claims comprises 14 volumes of documents, F.O. 16/299–310, 361–2. See also *Tribunal Arbitral Anglo-Chileno. Reclamaciones presentadas al tribunal, 1894–6* (4 vols., Santiago, 1896), and M. A. Martínez, *Informe del ajente de Chile ante el tribunal anglo-chileno* (Santiago, 1896).

[88] Kennedy to Acting Vice-Consul Morrison at Iquique, Santiago, 30 September 1891. F.O. 132/33. Copy.

[89] Kennedy to Salisbury, Viña, 22 December 1891. F.O. 16/266. No. 139. Diplomatic.

Promoters of that line to extend Branches of it to *Oficinas* which have been for many years served by the line of the Nitrate Railways Company.[90]

Budd went on to recapitulate the history of the Nitrate Railways case and to ask the Foreign Office to instruct Kennedy in Santiago to take up the question with the Chilean government.

In fact, however, the hands of the Foreign Office were tied, and it had already taken its decision on future action, or rather non-action, with regard to the Nitrate Railways Company. Shortly before the outbreak of the revolution in 1891, Kennedy had reported that, after consultation with eminent Chilean lawyers, he had concluded that the company's cause was 'hopeless': all were agreed that Balmaceda's appeal to the Council of State when the Supreme Court had questioned his right to annul concessions by administrative decree was perfectly valid, and that the unfavourable decision against the company by the Council could not possibly be annulled. The Court, however, might consider the lawsuit brought by the company against the Agua Santa Railway, and Kennedy had, therefore, advised his superiors that it would be best to await the outcome of this case before proceeding to further diplomatic action.[91] Kennedy also pointed out that Julio Zegers and other Chilean advisers of the company took the same view. Nevertheless, in March 1891 the company in London again appealed to the Foreign Office for diplomatic support.[92] But when the Foreign Office consulted the Law Officers of the Crown, in response to this request,[93] it received a reply which determined its attitude for a very long time to come:

it appears clear [said the Law Officers] that the intervention of the Council of State was justified by the Chilean Constitution, and that further proceedings by the Nitrate Railways Company are now pending before the Tribunals. The final determination as to the propriety of further diplomatic action must now be postponed until those proceedings have come to an end.[94]

[90] Budd to Sanderson, 21 December 1891. F.O. 16/288. Copy also in F.O. 132/30.
[91] Kennedy to Salisbury, Santiago, 2 January 1891. F.O. 16/288. No. 1. Diplomatic.   [92] Budd to Sanderson, 24 March 1891. F.O. 16/288.
[93] Foreign Office to Law Officers, 1 April 1891. F.O. 16/288.
[94] Law Officers to Foreign Office, 14 May 1891. F.O. 16/288.

And that, for the Foreign Office, was that: there would be no renewed diplomatic support for the company until its lawsuit against Agua Santa was concluded, and Budd was so informed.[95] And he received a similar reply to his request for support in December 1891.[96]

Yet Budd was undeterred, and he persisted in bombarding the Foreign Office with appeals, letters and memoranda throughout the following years.[97] Meanwhile, at the end of 1891, one of the Congressionalists' former agents in Europe and now the Chilean Minister to the Court of St James's, Agustín Ross, published a pamphlet in London on the Nitrate Railways question.[98] Although Ross took care to maintain an impartial tone throughout, he held to the view that the decisions taken against the company under Balmaceda were perfectly legal under the Chilean Constitution, and that, in fact, it was really the company's high tariff on nitrate freights which was at the heart of the matter. As it happened, this was precisely the line taken by Balmaceda himself in conversation with the British Minister in Santiago only a few weeks before his final defeat in the civil war. Perturbed by reports in July 1891 that the desperate financial position of Balmaceda's government was leading it to consider seeking a loan in the United States, to be guaranteed by a mortgage on the nitrate works and the Nitrate Railways Company, which would, in effect, be nationalized, Kennedy saw the President personally on 12 August 1891. He received, he reported:

positive verbal assurances that he [Balmaceda] had no intention whatever of applying to Congress for permission to expropriate the Nitrate Railways, nor of interfering with either of the first two concessions possessed by the Company. His Excellency suggested that he would readily promise to give no further concessions for railway

[95] Sanderson to Budd, 5 June 1891. F.O. 16/288.

[96] Sir Thomas Villiers-Lister to Budd, 8 January 1892. F.O.16/288. Villiers-Lister was Assistant Under-Secretary of State for Foreign Affairs.

[97] Already in January 1892, Sanderson was complaining wearily to W. E. Davidson, Legal Adviser to the Foreign Office, that Budd had 'broken out again in great volume'. Notes on reverse of Budd to Sanderson, 25 January 1892. F.O. 16/288.

[98] A. Ross, *Memorandum on the Nitrate Railways of Tarapacá*. It will be recalled that Ross, in 1889, had criticized Balmaceda for his lack of a policy to assist Chilean investment in nitrates. See above, p. 86.

construction in the Nitrate Districts in return for a diminution in the rate of transport charged on the Company's lines.[99]

A long despatch amplified Kennedy's immediate report of this interview, and in it Kennedy stated that Balmaceda had informed him that the proposals concerning nitrate-grounds referred only to those *salitreras* belonging to the state.[100]

The pamphlet published by Ross was a bombshell for the Nitrate Railways Company. Budd complained to Sanderson at the Foreign Office:

We are utterly at a loss to understand what motive can have induced Mr. Ross to print and send about broadcast in the City such a document . . . unless it be his apprehension that his Government might be induced to buy the Nitrate Railways undertaking.[101]

And Budd himself wrote to Ross, though quite affably, expressing the hope that the new government in Chile would rescind the decrees cancelling the company's concession, since the directors of the company had confidence in

the good faith and honour of the Chilean Government which has never been impugned except during the brief period of President Balmaceda's usurpation.[102]

In a later letter, Budd reminded the former agent of the revolutionaries that it was the Nitrate Railways Company which, by conveying nitrate to the coast during the civil war, had really provided the Congressionalists with 'the sinews of war' to defeat Balmaceda, and he concluded, somewhat reproachfully:

We, all of us, who are interested in the . . . Company hoped—nay— I will say felt sure—that one of the first acts of the Constitutional Government in Chile . . . would have been to have redressed these unjust and arbitrary acts of your Predecessors.[103]

Flattery, however, got Budd nowhere, and the company's expectations of the new Chilean government were doomed to

[99] Kennedy to Salisbury, Santiago, 12 August 1891. F.O. 16/288. No. 33. Telegraphic.

[100] Same to same, Santiago, 12 August 1891. F.O. 16/288. No. 84. Diplomatic.

[101] Budd to Sanderson, 25 January 1892. Copy. F.O. 132/30. Encl. No. 2 in Foreign Office to Kennedy, 2 February 1892. No. 14. Diplomatic.

[102] Budd to Ross, 8 January 1891. F.O. 16/288. Copy.

[103] Same to same, 22 January 1891. F.O. 16/288. Copy.

disappointment. It had, indeed, every reason to believe that the new administration, compared with Balmaceda's, would favour its interests: its information from Chile in 1890 had been that the Nitrate Railways case was very valuable to the opposition as a classic instance of Balmaceda's arbitrary conduct, and that the President would eventually be called to account partly on that issue.[104] Moreover, was not the company's chief lawyer in Chile the same Julio Zegers who throughout 1890 had led the opposition against Balmaceda? At the end of 1891, Kennedy had spoken of Zegers as 'one of the leaders of the Liberal party and a politician who will always exercise great influence over the Government of this country'.[105] Events in Chile, however, belied both Kennedy's opinion and the company's hopes. A few weeks later Kennedy wired a very different message to London:

in my opinion [he said] diplomatic action and legal proceedings are alike useless: Government and lawyer of Company accept validity of decree of Council of State. Both subordinate above business [i.e. the Company's case] to political and personal interests.[106]

Though the Chilean Courts decided that the company's case against the Agua Santa Railway might proceed, the latter appealed against this decision, claiming that the affair was *res judicata* and that, meanwhile, the Agua Santa line had been built and was, indeed, carrying traffic.[107] This left the Nitrate Railways Company bogged down in contesting doubtful legal issues while its rival was busily engaged in the work which the company hoped to stop. The total futility of these hopes was soon revealed by the British Minister who, early in 1892, had a number of meetings with the new President, Jorge Montt, with the Ministers of the Interior and of Public Works, and with the Presidents of both Chambers of Congress: all, said Kennedy, took the view that the cancellation of the company's monopoly by Balmaceda and the confirmation of this act by the Council of State was quite legal and valid.

[104] See above, pp. 137-8.
[105] Kennedy to Salisbury, Santiago, 31 December 1891. F.O. 16/288. No. 141. Diplomatic. Confidential.
[106] Kennedy to Foreign Office, Santiago, 7 February 1892. F.O. 16/288. Telegraphic. Confidential, Decyphered.
[107] Budd to Sanderson, 19 February 1892. F.O. 16/288.

I also perceived [he continued] a disposition to speak contemptuously of Señor Zegers as being a lawyer who preferred his personal interests to those of the Company . . .

I have been surprised by the above sentiments because up to the end of the revolutionary period, all the prominent members of the Opposition assured me that the Congress party, if triumphant, would grant especially favoured treatment to the Nitrate Railways Company; and also, because I had counted much on the influence of Señor Zegers with the Congress party, of which he was held to be an important member . . .

No doubt [Kennedy continued] there exists a feeling of jealousy against Señor Zegers, on account of the large sums of money which he is supposed to have received from the above Company; and also because of a conviction which has been expressed to me that in reality he was a great friend of President Balmaceda's, and only turned against him, in consequence of the publication of the Decree of forfeiture [of the Company's privileges] which Señor Zegers looked upon as a blow directed against his sources of income.

In the same despatch, Kennedy reported on conversations he had had with Zegers himself, who tried to persuade the British Minister that if the Courts finally decided against the Agua Santa Company in the case brought against it by the Nitrate Railways Company, the entire situation would be changed. But he failed to convince Kennedy, who asked him what the result would be of further concessions contrary to the interests of the Nitrate Railways Company which might be awarded to yet more companies, and received the reply that Zegers would also initiate legal proceedings against them, as he had done against Agua Santa. Kennedy also pointed out that there were political implications:

I would mention [he added] that the Agua Santa Company is now patronised by two important politicians of the Conservative party, who, during the Revolution were each members of the secret revolutionary committee in Santiago, and who now have greater claims on the Government than Señor Zegers, who gave no active assistance to the Revolutionary struggle.[108]

Kennedy's comments on Zegers were reported, though in a

[108] Kennedy to Salisbury, Viña, 20 February 1892. F.O. 16/288. No. 15. Diplomatic. Confidential. Zegers was in hiding throughout 1891. See Velasco, *Memorias*, pp. 573–4.

different form, to Antony Gibbs and Sons in London by their manager in Santiago. According to him, the Chilean Ministers

spoke contemptuously of Zegers as a 'mess lawyer', carrying on, knowing that he has no case and for his own pecuniary advantage, and no doubt as we pointed out to him, to the advantage of the Nitrate Railways Co. also, who may thus hope to frighten others from attempting to get concessions for new lines.[109]

Others, however, were far from frightened by Zegers's tactics, since they were warmly encouraged by the government itself. In August 1892, even while the case against Agua Santa wound its tortuous way through the Chilean courts, the government invited tenders for building a line in Tarapacá to the port of Junín, an act which showed, in the words of Budd, that it was 'obviously following in this respect the policy of the deposed Dictator'.[110] And in 1893 various other concessions were granted for further lines in the nitrate region, all in breach of the original grant to the Nitrate Railways Company. One of these was to the Agua Santa Company itself, for a branch line from the main line it had already built while the legal wrangle continued.[111] In June 1893 Kennedy reported that there existed

in influential quarters a feeling of intense hostility towards the Nitrate Railways Co., and a sense of undisguised satisfaction that a means had been found for inflicting a serious injury on the above Company, without compromising the Government; namely, by the grant by Congress of a concession to the Agua Santa Company . . .[112]

Two ministers told Kennedy quite bluntly that Congress might grant concessions 'whenever it pleases, in the face of vested interests or previous lawful possession', and, although such concessions contained the phrase 'without prejudice to the rights of third parties', Kennedy thought this a mockery in the case of the Nitrate Railways.[113]

[109] Antony Gibbs & Sons, Valparaiso to London, 26 February 1892. AAG, MS. 11,470. Vol. 13. Letter No. 90. Private.
[110] Budd to Sanderson, 2 September 1892. F.O. 16/288.
[111] Brown, 'Nitrate Railways', p. 476.
[112] Kennedy to the Earl of Rosebery, Santiago, 15 June 1893. F.O. 16/288. No. 38. Diplomatic. Also cited by Brown, loc. cit.
[113] Kennedy to Rosebery, loc. cit.

In separate letters to Edward Manby, a director of the Nitrate Railways Company, Kennedy made a number of other important comments, and placed the railway issue in a much wider context. The hostility to the company, he reported,

is clearly more general and intense than at any time within my recollection, and . . . it is, as I am assured by leading politicians, shared and promoted by British Companies interested in the production or exportation of Nitrate . . .[114]

He had seen the Ministers of the Interior and of Foreign Affairs and had found their language 'unsatisfactory', but 'in other quarters', he added, 'I have heard stronger language used against the Company', in criticism of the series of 'artifices and vexatious lawsuits' by which it had sought to preserve its transport monopoly. He had also been told

that the Railway Company, assisted by Nitrate Companies equally interested in the production and transport of Nitrate, have kept up prices, and by a combination have limited the export: that the Chilian Government is exasperated and determined to liquidate the situation by effecting the reduction of rates of transport, by increasing the output of Nitrate by Chilian Companies, and by upsetting the combination . . .

On all sides [he went on] I am afraid that the above schemes . . . have the approval and support of the majority of British Subjects, including the Agua Santa Company which, I am assured, is a British concern although registered as Chilian . . .[115]

Clearly, then, Balmaceda's successors were quite determined to carry through the policy he had pursued with regard to the Nitrate Railways Company: the effective destruction of its transport monopoly in Tarapacá through the award of concessions for competing lines. The Agua Santa Company was the principal agent for this policy, as it had been with Balmaceda: it had the full support of the Chilean government, and throughout the 1890s was able to delay judgement in the court

---

[114] Kennedy to Manby, 6 June 1893. Encl. No. 3 in Kennedy to Rosebery, loc. cit. Kennedy's recollection, it will be remembered, went back to the critical years of Balmaceda's presidency, when the Nitrate Railways case first became an important public issue.

[115] Kennedy to Manby, 12 June 1892. Copy. Encl. No. 4 in Kennedy to Rosebery, loc. cit.

case brought against it by Nitrate Railways.[116] The Nitrate Railways Company, for its part, persisted in the policy of bringing legal actions against other concessionaires, probably at the insistence of Julio Zegers, and in pressing the Foreign Office to support it through diplomatic representations to the Chilean government. Both courses of action, however, were completely futile so far as the company's formerly exclusive privileges were concerned, and its monopoly was gradually undermined.[117] Indeed, in 1892 the company itself turned to the possibility of stopping further concessions by offering to reduce its freight rates, an expedient regarded by the manager of Antony Gibbs and Sons in Valparaiso as clear proof that the company's directors themselves no longer really believed in their power to prevent Congress granting other concessions.[118] Yet some power they still possessed, as Antony Gibbs discovered in the same year, when the House itself joined in the attack on the Nitrate Railways Company.

Gibbs had never completely abandoned their project to build a railway line from the nitrate-fields of Alianza to the port of Chucumata, a project which had cost them a good deal of time and money when Balmaceda was president. Post-war events encouraged them to revive it.

We have little doubt [wrote Daubeny in mid-1892] that if at the present time we were prepared to build our Chucumata Railway we should have very little difficulty in getting a concession from this Government.[119]

In fact, however, it was the autumn of 1893 before the House began the complicated business of applying to Congress for permission to build the line, and here they ran into opposition from lawyer-politicians who were retained by North, notably the MacIver brothers, Enrique and David.[120] Nevertheless, the first vote on Gibbs' proposal in the Chamber of Deputies was favourable, and Daubeny was optimistic: 'we are trying', he

[116] See Budd to Sanderson, 11 January 1894. With 18 enclosures F.O. 16/298.
[117] See Brown, 'Nitrate Railways', pp. 475–81.
[118] Antony Gibbs & Sons, Valparaiso to London, 18 November 1892. AAG, MS. 11,470. Vol. 14. Letter No. 110. Private.
[119] Same to same, 16 July 1892, in ibid. Letter No. 100. Private.
[120] Same to same, 24 August 1893, in ibid. Letter No. 133. Private. For the connection of North with the MacIvers, see above, p. 183.

wrote, 'to make capital out of the blow that our line will inflict on the unpopular Northite monopoly . . .'[121] At the same time, his superiors in London sought to exploit the delicate situation in which the Foreign Office would find itself if faced with appeals for support from conflicting British interests in Chile.[122] When the bill to extend the privileges of the Agua Santa Company had gone to the Chilean Congress in the summer of 1893, Kennedy had been authorized to make representations on behalf of the Nitrate Railways Company, but only in a 'friendly and unofficial' manner.[123] Gibbs, however, were determined to stop even these quite ineffectual initiatives and they persuaded the Foreign Office to instruct Kennedy to abstain from opposition to Gibbs' petition, although, if successful, it would do no less harm to the Nitrate Railways Company than the petition of the Agua Santa Company.[124]

Yet, despite these initial successes in Santiago and in London, the plans of Gibbs soon ran into heavy weather, for a variety of reasons. A certain Lisandro Vivero put in an opposing petition and Congress had to take cognizance of it: Daubeny assumed that he had been 'set on by the Nitrate Railways Co.' in the same way that other, more prominent, Chileans had been 'got at by the North faction'.[125] Kennedy was said to be 'a notorious partisan of the Nitrate Railways Co.', whatever his official instructions, which clearly did not stop him from talking to people.[126] Gibbs' own lawyer, Eulogio Altamirano, told Daubeny that their original petition had been substantially amended in committee in Congress, and his denial that the Nitrate Railways Company had anything to do with it was far from convincing.[127] And, finally, when a special meeting of the Senate was mooted to discuss the bill, the day before Congress

[121] Antony Gibbs & Sons, Valparaiso to London, 3 November 1893. AAG, MS. 11,470. Vol. 14. Letter No. 139. Private.

[122] Brown, 'Nitrate Railways', pp. 477–8. 'This antagonism between British firms', wrote Sanderson to Rosebery, 'is a very perplexing feature in international disputes'. Notes dated 18 November 1893, in F.O. 16/288.

[123] Brown, loc. cit., p. 477.

[124] Ibid.

[125] Antony Gibbs & Sons, Valparaiso to London, 12 January 1894. AAG, MS. 11,470. Vol. 15. Letter No. 145. Private.

[126] Same to same, 29 December 1893, in ibid. Letter No. 144. Private.

[127] Same to same, 15 December 1893, in ibid. Letter No. 143. Private.

went into recess, the motion was talked out by Senator José Antonio Gandarillas.[128] Gibbs would have to wait somewhat longer to bring their plans to fruition.

In any event, the proposed Chucumata line was a subsidiary issue in the destruction of the monopoly of the Nitrate Railways Company. While the company's lawsuits against concession-aires proceeded tortuously through the Chilean courts, rival railway lines bit deeply into the Company's nitrate traffic.

Attracted by the low railway freights [reported the British consul at Iquique in 1894] a number of *oficinas* have signed contracts with the Agua Santa Company for the transport of their nitrate to Caleta Buena . . .[129]

and in the same year it was stated that, of a total of 20 million quintals of nitrate to be shipped from Tarapacá that year, only 9 million would be carried by the Nitrate Railways Company.[130] Already, under the pressure of competition, the company had been obliged to reduce its freight rates at the end of 1893, and thus finally to give way on the fundamental issue which had sparked off the attack on its monopoly so many years before.[131] It is true that the company's profits remained fairly good in 1893 and 1894.[132] But there were quite specific reasons for this, namely that by that time the very rich nitrate-grounds of Lagunas had come into production: these were served by the branch line from the main nitrate railway which had been constructed under the concession awarded to North by Balmaceda's government.[133] North simply manipulated the heavy Lagunas traffic in the interests of the Nitrate Railways Company: he kept the much shorter line to the port of Patillos closed and obliged the Lagunas *oficinas*—also under his control —to move their cargoes to Iquique, twice as far from the grounds as Patillos.[134] By milking one of his enterprises to benefit another, he managed to keep up appearances for the

[128] Same to same, 25 January 1894, in ibid. Letter No. 146. Private.

[129] Consul Hervey to Kennedy, Iquique, 8 October 1894. F.O. 132/41.

[130] Kennedy to the Earl of Kimberley, Santiago, 12 May 1894. F.O. 132/44. No. 28. Diplomatic. Draft.

[131] Brown, 'Nitrate Railways', p. 477. See also above, pp. 48–9.

[132] Brown, loc. cit., and see also *The Statist*, 9 December 1893 and 2 June 1894.

[133] See above, pp. 136, 147, 154.

[134] *The Railway Times*, 8 January 1898.

Railways Company almost to the day of his death, but the reckoning for the shareholders followed soon after.[135]

No accommodation was ever made between the Chilean government and the Nitrate Railways Company.[136] Moreover, in the immediate post-war years, Balmaceda's successors pursued other policies affecting nitrates which showed that they were no less sensitive than Balmaceda to the country's dependence on an industry over which foreigners exercised so large a degree of control. The government's financial needs were no less than those of its predecessor, but whereas Balmaceda looked for revenue mainly to promote his ambitious and expensive programme of public works, the victors in the civil war had very different priorities. Their primary aim, in fact, was the retirement of the inconvertible paper money of the republic and the return to a metallic standard, seen by leading members of the government as the crucial reform for Chile's economic health.[137] For this purpose, laws were passed in 1892 providing for the incineration of a fixed amount of paper money and for the building-up of a metallic reserve—a scheme which soon ran into serious difficulties, while its supporters came in for heavy criticism.

It is against this background that the history of the nitrate industry after the civil war must be set. In September 1892 *The Economist* published an important article on the relations of the Chilean government and the nitrate combination, pointing out that restrictions on shipments were a blow to Chile's

[135] See below, pp. 246–7.

[136] Ramírez, *Balmaceda*, pp. 224–5, cites an interview between Kennedy and Enrique MacIver, by then Minister of the Interior, in September 1894, in which North's former employee made certain proposals, presumably on behalf of the Chilean government, to the Nitrate Railways Company, which, he said, would be to its advantage. This incident is quoted to show the good relations between the Chilean government and the Company. But, as Brown, loc. cit., p. 479, points out, the terms offered by MacIver were so one-sidedly favourable to the government that the Company had no interest whatsoever in the proposals. What it did do, however, was to revive its claim for compensation for damages suffered during 1891, but even this was dragged out until 1903. The relevant documents are in F.O. 16/298 and 346.

[137] For this question, see in particular Fetter, *Monetary Inflation in Chile, passim,* and Hirschman, *Journeys Towards Progress*, pp. 170–2. But the basic research still needs to be done. This account is limited to the relationship of the question to the nitrate interests.

revenues at a time when the country had embarked on a serious programme of monetary reform: it also quoted a recent speech by the Chilean Minister of Finance who had declared in Congress:

the influence which the acts of the producers of nitrate may have upon the public revenue will be absolutely null if the Government so will it. The maintenance of the revenue derived from nitrate . . . will depend upon the law, and not upon the actions of persons within or without the country.[138]

This was no empty warning: later in the year a bill went to Congress to authorize the sale by government of state nitrate-grounds, a measure which the existing companies opposed, since they already had greater productive capacity than they could utilize, and they wanted neither new competitors nor new burdens.[139] This was a measure which, according to

Kennedy, would

probably disturb many of the important British Commercial interests existing in Tarapacá and elsewhere, but . . . justified on the ground that the future prosperity of Chile cannot be sacrificed for the interest of a few privileged companies.[140]

Verbal attacks on companies supporting the combination increased in volume and intensity. The *Delegado Fiscal de Salitreras y Guaneras* pointed out that many British companies were heavily overcapitalized, and inflated running costs were chiefly responsible for the high price of nitrate produced.[141] And, in his annual report to Congress for 1892, presented the following year, the *Ministro de Hacienda*, while refuting the idea that the nitrate industry should be nationalized, said that native capitalists ought to invest in it.[142] As the months passed, in 1893, so criticism of the combination grew, precisely as the Nitrate Railways Company was attacked for its high tariff and for its fight against Agua Santa to retain its monopoly: indeed,

[138] *The Economist*, 3 September 1892.   [139] Ibid., 19 November 1892.
[140] Kennedy to Rosebery, Santiago, 16 July 1893. F.O. 16/283. No. 12. Commercial.
[141] *The Economist*, 28 January 1893.
[142] *Memoria del Ministro de Hacienda presentada al Congreso Nacional de 1893* (Santiago, 1893), pp. li–lxxxviii.

both issues were seen as part of the same general picture in which Chile's national interests were being jeopardized by the actions of foreigners.[143]

In a long report home, Kennedy discussed Chilean hostility to what had become known as 'the triple syndicate', formed by the Nitrate Railways Company, the nitrate combination, and the Bank of Tarapacá and London. For some months past, the Chilean press had been attacking these interests, and so had others:

the British, and, although to a lesser extent, the German Commercial Community at Valparaiso condemned generally the proceedings of the Nitrate group, especially the action of the Bank and the sale of Nitrate Cargoes direct to London; and Chileans of position asserted that the National Conscience was aroused and that the National dignity required that a check should be placed on the system . . . by which the interest of Chile in the province of Tarapacá had been reduced to the mere collection of the export duty, and the future of the chief source of Chilean State Revenue had been imperilled.[144]

Kennedy enlarged on the reasons for the 'noisy animosity' and 'threatening language': the combination seemed to restrict Chile's income; the nitrate companies had deprived Valparaiso of much business by selling cargoes direct to England instead of through the port, as in the past, and the bank was suspected of causing exchange rates to fluctuate in its own interests.[145] Though tempers cooled with the closure of Congress on 1 September 1893, and also by the grant of concessions to the Nitrate Railways Company's competitors, a Congressional Commission had been set up

to study the expediency of passing laws for regulating the position of the Nitrate industry in its relation to the State, and for determining the taxes to be paid by foreign commercial establishments . . .[146]

And, finally, while many leading newspapers painted a picture of Tarapacá as a British protectorate, some even urged the

---

[143] Cf. above, pp. 217–18.
[144] Kennedy to Rosebery, Santiago, 15 September 1893. F.O. 16/288. No. 63. Diplomatic.   [145] Ibid.   [146] Ibid.

government, as a last resort, to expropriate the foreign nitrate companies,[147] a request which was repeated in the following year.[148]

Although the North group was particularly singled out for attack, other companies were also likely to be condemned, and their representatives in Chile were certainly apprehensive. The manager of Balfour, Williamson and Company at Valparaiso complained bitterly to Kennedy in August 1893 that 'some proceedings of the Nitrate Railways Company and the Bank of Tarapacá' were 'very galling' to the national pride of Chileans and that 'the motives to be ascribed to such proceedings can only be instinctive hostility to the general commercial community on this coast . . .'[149] Kennedy reported that he had received official representations signed by representatives of leading British firms, stating that

the actions of the Bank . . . and of its allies, the English Nitrate Companies, had been, and is, highly prejudicial to a much larger body of Her Majesty's subjects resident in Chile and whose residence and interests there date very much farther back than that of the English Bank and Nitrate Companies.[150]

And, in a long letter to his superiors in London, the manager of Gibbs at Valparaiso was no less explicit:

Remarks have been made [he wrote] both in Congress and in the papers shewing very clearly the intention on the part of the Government to do all they can to hostilize and if possible break up the Nitrate Combination and damage the Bank of Tarapacá, and the feeling is we fear developing into another period of dislike to foreigners generally and perhaps the English particularly as being more closely connected with the Nitrate manufacture and combination.[151]

Daubeny, indeed, went so far as to suggest that Gibbs might

[147] Summary of Nitrate Questions as set forth in the Chilean Press. August 1893. Encl. No. 1 in Kennedy to Rosebery, loc. cit.

[148] By M. J. Vicuña, *Conferencia sobre la industria salitrera dada en el congreso minero de 1894* (Santiago, 1894).

[149] W. R. Henderson to Kennedy, Valparaiso, 4 August 1893. F.O. 132/38.

[150] Kennedy to Rosebery, loc. cit.

[151] Antony Gibbs & Sons, Valparaiso to London, 27 July 1893. AAG, MS. 11,470. Vol. 4. Letter No. 131. Private.

break completely with the combination and resign all their nitrate agencies.

Two events mitigated the growing hostility against the nitrate interests. In the first place, early in 1894 the combination broke down, partly because North refused to bring his new Lagunas interests into it.[152] Secondly, in the summer and autumn of 1894, the Chilean government auctioned a number of state-owned nitrate-fields, and was delighted by the fact that Chilean investors put up more than one-third of the total amount spent on their purchase.[153] The British Minister was also pleased by an auction in which British capital had not been prominent: the investment of substantial Chilean capital would, he thought, not only provide 'a satisfactory guarantee against vexatious state interference', but would also blunt criticism of the so-called British monopoly.[154]

Yet, while it had lasted, Chilean hostility to certain British nitrate interests after the civil war of 1891 was both more general and more bitter than previous manifestations under President Balmaceda. Indeed, before that war, and with the sole exception of his attitude and policy towards the Nitrate Railways Company—an attitude shared by the government which preceded him, no less than by that which came after— Balmaceda confined himself to admonitory speeches on foreign participation in the nitrate industry and took very few practical steps to change the situation. Before 1891, Balmaceda was singularly vague in his pronouncements on the nitrate industry; after the war, the Chilean government was much more explicit, and it suited its actions to its words.[155] The approach of both governments to questions involving British nitrate interests, and notably those of North, was essentially the same, that of seeking to secure to Chile, but for quite different objectives, the revenue due to her from her most important natural resource of the period, though neither government had the

[152] Brown, 'Nitrate Crises', p. 238.

[153] Report on the present financial position of Chile. Enclosed in Kennedy to the Earl of Kimberley, Santiago, 8 November 1894. F.O. 16/289. No. 53. Diplomatic.

[154] Ibid.

[155] Cf., however, Ramírez, *Balmaceda*, pp. 216 ff., taking the diametrically opposite view, with Brown, 'Nitrate Crises', pp. 237–8.

remotest intention of taking the industry completely into Chilean hands. As for North's own relations with both governments, there was no difference whatsoever. He himself may have imagined that he had much to gain as a consequence of the outcome of the revolution of 1891, and he was not alone in this belief. But, as he showed quite clearly in his final years, he at least was a realist in recognizing the facts when Balmaceda's successors proved no more willing than the unfortunate president to give him what he sought. Though he kept the title of 'Nitrate King', he quickly abandoned the throne which he knew was now untenable.

The Final Years of the 'Nitrate King'

North's rise to fame and fortune in the 1880s, culminating in his grand tour of Chile at the end of the decade, had been based on many factors: the growth of nitrate in world trade and his own strong position in the industry; his able conduct of public relations; his ebullient and forceful character; and a gift for business which combined considerable shrewdness with lack of principle. In an age of British entrepreneurship in the exploitation of the world's natural resources, North was a self-made man with a striking personality, though cast more in the mould of Barney Barnato than in that of Cecil Rhodes, and made, perhaps, of baser metal. Yet the title he bore, and was happy to assume, had been conferred by public favour in view of spectacular early successes, and public favour was a fickle thing.

It was in the nature of the nitrate industry to experience periodic booms and slumps which were reflected in wild oscillations of nitrate shares on the London Stock Exchange. While fortunes had been made in a very short time, they could just as soon be lost, and with them the reputations of their makers. The confidence of investors was obviously the key, and in keeping that confidence North was superb. In the uncertain situation of the 1890s, his gifts of personality and persuasion were needed no less than they had been before, and he kept up the image in commerce and society which had taken him to the top. But, at the same time, none knew better than he the unstable character of the nitrate trade, and he took great care to ensure that his own dependence on it was far from absolute.

The acute distress of the nitrate market had forced the formation of the second combination early in 1891.[156] The Chilean civil war then played its part in reducing exports further.[157] Surplus stocks were thus brought down, the price of nitrate naturally rose, and shares in the companies began to pick up, particularly after Balmaceda's defeat.[158] Yet total demand failed to rise fast enough to persuade investors that underlying strength had now returned to the nitrate market, and the value of shares in the nitrate companies fluctuated markedly in 1892.[159] The unexpectedly hostile attitude of the Chilean government towards nitrate interests in general, and those of North in particular, was another factor creating uncertainty, and a lively debate on nitrate filled many columns in the British commercial press.[160] No less important in the general mood of doubt was the government's declared intention, made at the end of 1892, of putting up for auction some state-owned nitrate-fields.[161]

It was this particular development which, more than any other, broke up the combination.[162] Yet it was North, the recognized leader of the combination, who engineered its collapse. By 1893, his own, very rich Lagunas field, the largest in Tarapacá and the latest to be opened, was ready to swing into full production, once the restrictions imposed by the producers' combination were removed. When, in the latter part of 1893, the nitrate market began to show signs of improvement, North, to that point 'the most ardent advocate' of the combination, now declared 'for free trade in nitrate'.[163] This volte-face is not hard to explain. If the Chilean government's decision

[156] See above, pp. 189–90.

[157] See Brown, 'Nitrate Crises', p. 236.

[158] *The Economist*, 22 August and 5 September 1891.

[159] See the useful tables of share values in *The Economist*, 14 May 1892, and *The Statist*, 2 July 1892.

[160] See *The Economist*, *The South American Journal* and *The Statist* for 1892 and 1893.

[161] Brown, loc. cit., p. 238. See also *The Economist*, 19 November 1892, and *The Board of Trade Journal*, xiv (1893), p. 201.

[162] As *The Economist* had prophesied on 28 January 1893.

[163] *The Economist*, 14 October 1893. Letter from M. Nicholson.

to bring more *salitreras* into production once again saturated the world market in nitrates, the Lagunas Syndicate, North's newest venture on the London Stock Exchange, would hardly be launched like a rocket: prudence suggested that the new field, with its up-to-date plant and cost advantage, should cash in at once while the going was good. Since the combination had already been weakened by internal dissension, pressure from the government and adverse comment in the commercial press, it could not survive North's own secession, and in September 1893 the announcement was made of the combination's demise at the end of the following March.[164]

But North was not seeking merely a corner in nitrates. He had another reason for breaking the combination which was no less compelling. By this time it was fairly common knowledge that the former transport monopoly of the Nitrate Railways Company in Tarapacá was virtually dead.[165] Though the company persisted in its legal battles in Chile, the directors must have known that the cause was quite hopeless, and probably maintained it to keep up the drooping spirits of shareholders. But North had a better counter to the serious threat of a drastic fall in railway shares, provided the combination ceased to exist. This lay in opening up Lagunas, giving its large traffic at the customary high tariff to the Nitrate Railways Company, and thus keeping shares buoyant, at least for a time. The chairmanship of both the Lagunas Syndicate and the Nitrate Railways Company, their boards of directors drawn from his intimate circle, and the still potent magic of his business reputation allowed North to get away with these manœuvres.

But this commercial sleight of hand did not go entirely unnoticed by his sharp-sighted critics,[166] nor did the most cogent

---

[164] *The Economist*, 23 September 1893.

[165] In the autumn of 1893, when bills for yet two more competing lines in Tarapacá went to the Chilean Congress, the lower house passed them with unprecedented speed, a fact which one of North's outspoken English critics described as 'striking evidence of the desire of the Chilean nation to get rid of the yoke of the Nitrate Railways monopoly'. Letter from John Harold, *The Economist*, 2 September 1893. Harold, like Nicholson cited in note 163, was a frequent contributor to *The Economist*.

[166] As early as the end of 1892, M. Nicholson drew attention to the fact that Lagunas was a long way from Iquique and Pisagua by the Nitrate Railways

commentator on nitrate affairs turn a blind eye to the Lagunas proceedings. In a long article headed 'The New Nitrate Rig' in June 1894, *The Economist* pulled no punches in attacking North's newest venture, the Lagunas Syndicate. Before the prospectus was even issued, £100 shares in the new company had risen to £450, and the paper was not amused. 'Colonel North', it said, 'is a bold man', for, despite his close association with the dramatic boom in nitrates in the late 1880s and the equally dramatic collapse which had ruined many, 'beguiled by his bluff and confident optimism', he was now seeking further public support 'in the same old vein of jubilant prophecy'. Likely investors should be warned about both North's past and about the current situation in the nitrate industry:

it would be well for them [the paper said] to temper their receptivity by a reference to the vicissitudes of the Primitiva and other companies which were rushed upon the guileless investor under the glamour of his then ascendant influence. . . No sooner do the regulated conditions of the industry seem to give it a chance of emerging from the slough of depression into which it had sunk, than the moment is chosen for floating new companies, opening up new ground, erecting new oficinas, and generally making arrangements for vastly increasing the output. . . Experience has taught us that Colonel North wears very rose-coloured spectacles when he is engaged in bringing out a new company.[167]

The Economist felt that it was its duty to draw attention to 'what has taken place under Colonel North's auspices before': the shares of the Primitiva Company which had been run up on its formation in 1888 from £5 to £39 had, it was true, paid quarterly dividends in 1888 and in 1889, but it had paid none since, and its current share-values were well below par. Now, with Lagunas, the same tactics were evident: overcapitalization and share-rigging as the company was launched in a blaze of confident publicity.

The tactics were, indeed, the same as in the 1880s, and so were the weapons of North and his colleagues to counter adverse criticism. The former Government Engineer and Inspector-General of Nitrate Works in Tarapacá, Robert Harvey, in

route, and there were much closer lines to ports of shipment. Letter in *The Economist*, 17 December 1892.   [167] *The Economist*, 23 June 1894.

writing to *The Economist* on the merits of Lagunas, reminded readers of *his* intimate knowledge of the nitrate regions down to the last capital letter.[168] Other organs, persuaded by such arguments and by North's zestful approach, saw nothing but massive profits for investors in the new company.[169] And the temporary boom in nitrates in 1894 lasted long enough to cajole a gullible public into keeping its confidence in Colonel North, who irradiated bonhomie and optimism, as he pursued the active life in society, sport and politics which his public had come to expect of him.[170] Grand social events at his enormous mansion at Avery Hill, successes on the turf and with his grey-hounds, frequent business-trips abroad—all combined to keep North in the public eye, and were an essential aspect of his business career.[171]

North even sought entry into politics. Counting among his friends and associates many leading lights of the Conservative party,[172] North himself, in 1895, returned to his native Leeds to fight against Herbert Gladstone, the son of the Liberal Prime Minister, in a by-election. Little of politics coloured his campaign, for here was the local boy who had made good, the city's first Honorary Freeman, best known to his fellow-Yorkshiremen for his blunt speech and generous purse. He ran his campaign like a circus, riding on fire-engines with well-known prize-fighters, handing out handkerchiefs bearing his portrait, offering advice to racing enthusiasts, and occasionally showering his audience with gold sovereigns. Only 96 votes kept him out of the House of Commons, though his description of the result as 'a moral victory' was, perhaps, hardly well-advised.[173]

[168] Letter in ibid., 7 July 1894.   [169] *The Statist*, 2 June 1894.
[170] See also above, pp. 38–42.
[171] The local press of the period has many references to North's activities. In addition, North's wife, Jane, kept a simple diary of events at Avery Hill during the last year of his life, and this gives an excellent picture of the very large number of visitors who went there, and of North's extremely busy life. The diary is in the possession of Mr Richard North, and I am much indebted to him for the chance to read it.
[172] In 1889, while on his visit to Chile, North remembered to telegraph Lord Randolph Churchill, 'Be sure contest Birmingham' in the forthcoming election. Winston S. Churchill, *Life of Randolph Churchill* (2 vols., London, 1906), ii, 386.
[173] Data from *The Leeds Mercury*.

How much of North's public behaviour was simply natural zest, and how much careful calculation, is a question which cannot be answered. But in his life as an entrepreneur, there was certainly plenty of guile. Although his business reputation was founded basically on nitrates, his interests were wide.[174] In 1889, he had founded the eponymous company of North's Navigation Collieries in South Wales, with substantial interests in iron foundries as well as in coal-mines: the property was purchased for £350,000 and paid good dividends in the early 1890s.[175] By 1895, he had other interests in factories in Paris and St Etienne in France, in gold-mines in Australia, in tramways in Egypt and in cement works in Brussels.[176] He was, in fact, an international figure in finance, and it was this status which brought him to the notice of King Leopold II of Belgium in a bizarre, but little-known episode of his career.

In the growth of the private empire of Leopold in the Congo, North was recruited by the king as 'a man of straw', a cover for Leopold's own designs in tropical Africa. North founded the Belgian India Rubber Company in 1892, to exploit plantations in the Congo, but, while much of the capital was in his name— and, incidentally, also in that of Ernest Spencer, M.P., another nitrate capitalist—he was merely acting for Leopold and had no real interest in the enterprise.[177] In other dealings with the king, however, North was a more active partner: he was persuaded by Leopold to interest himself in acquiring land and building a hotel on the beach near Ostend, an enterprise which was under discussion for more than a year, partly because it was subsequently discovered that the land was common land and the proposal needed the approval of the Belgian Parliament, and, secondly, because the debate in the Chambers was long drawn out when certain senators discovered that North intended his luxury hotel to have a casino. Nevertheless, the project went through and only North's death, in 1896, prevented the establishment of what the Belgians were already

---

[174] See also above, p. 64.

[175] *The South Wales Daily News*, 6 May 1896. I am indebted for this reference to Professor L. J. Williams of Aberystwyth.   [176] See *Le Figaro*, 23 April 1895.

[177] Roger T. Anstey, *King Leopold's Legacy: The Congo Under Belgian Rule, 1908–1960* (Oxford Univ. Press, for the Institute of Race Relations, 1966), p. 9, note 1. See also A. J. Wauters, *Histoire Politique du Congo Belge* (Brussels, 1911), pp. 121, 124.

calling 'North City'. At about the same time, in 1895, Leopold leased to North his own estate and château at Ardenne, also to create a luxury hotel for tourists, but this project also ended with North's death.[178]

The many other interests which North took up in the 1890s were not merely an enlargement of his nitrate holdings: much more significantly, they were, in part, a replacement for them. The collapse of the second nitrate combination in 1894 had, indeed, ushered in a period of revival for the industry and trade. But the revival was very short-lived. Already in January 1895 supply had overtaken demand, and new discussions were going on about the formation of another combination:

the only means of screwing up prices to a level remunerative to the owners of semi-exhausted and correspondingly dear-producing oficinas.[179]

As the year wore on, the price of nitrate, and therefore share-values, fell with increasing rapidity, and the process of forming a new combination to arrest the downward trend was extremely slow. It might have come into effect, according to one observer, in 1895, 'had not Colonel North, *more suo*, claimed the lion's share for his large new oficinas, themselves the chief culprits in overproduction'.[180] Another contributory factor to the over-stocking of the world market was the entrance into production of the nitrate-fields auctioned by the Chilean government in 1894 and 1895.[181] Exports of nitrate from Tarapacá increased from 24 million quintals in 1894 to 27.2 million in 1895, a year of agricultural depression in Europe, the fertilizer's principal market.[182] By October the situation was very serious:

Nitrate I fear [wrote Stephen Williamson] is to be a heartbreak. My opinion is we have not nearly seen the lowest price. . . We ought to let the article severely alone. Let the Producers now have a taste of

[178] See the short biography of North by J. Stengers in *Biographie Coloniale Belge* (6 vols., Brussels, 1948–), iv (1956), cols. 663–6. I am indebted to Professor Stengers for drawing my attention to the connection between North and Leopold.
[179] Letter from M. Nicholson, *The Economist*, 19 January 1895. Cf. Brown, 'Nitrate Crises', p. 238.
[180] Letter from M. Nicholson, *The Economist*, 24 August 1895.
[181] Semper and Michels, *La industria del salitre*, p. 143.
[182] Brown, 'Nitrate Crises', p. 238.

bad times. They have hitherto squeezed the Merchants and cut them out of the trade. Very well, let them face it. I am told the Lagunas people have some 30,000 tons about due unsold. The result must be disastrous. . . We think the time is approaching when every Coy [*sic*] will lose money in the mere production irrespective of the exhaustion of grounds . . .[183]

Williamson was right: the nitrate industry was already deep into its worst crisis of production in the nineteenth century.

For North also the critical time had arrived. Against the background of shareholders' worries at the state of the nitrate industry, awkward questions began, at last, to be heard. At a meeting of the Lagunas Syndicate in September 1895, in answer to a question as to whether there was any truth in the rumour that the company held lands in Tarapacá to which it was not entitled, North replied that all the property the company owned was held quite legally.[184] A fortnight later it was reported from Chile that judicial proceedings would be instituted against the company for the recovery of 2,000 acres of nitrate-grounds to which it had no legal title.[185] A few weeks later a far more serious situation arose when, at an extraordinary general meeting of North's Primitiva Company, North moved a motion from the chair for the voluntary winding-up of the company and called for contributions of ten shillings a share to settle bankers' advances: searching questions were asked about North's own holdings in the company and he asserted that he had over 5,000 shares; but he did not say, what was soon discovered, that he had disposed of more than that number in recent years.[186] The meeting was adjourned, and when it reconvened a week later the shareholders apathetically accepted the proposals of the directors, but calls were made for a searching enquiry into the company's balance-sheets.[187]

It was, indeed [*The Economist* commented], the Primitiva 'boom' which, for a time made Colonel North the most talked-about man of his generation, the embodiment of British energy, success and

---

[183] Stephen Williamson to Mr Mathison, Liverpool, 10 October 1895. Balfour Williamson Papers. Letter Book No. 3. Copy.
[184] *The Economist*, 14 September 1895.   [185] Ibid., 28 September 1895.
[186] *The South American Journal*, 9 November 1895.
[187] Ibid., 30 November 1895.

opulence; but of late the Colonel's lucky star has not been in the ascendant . . .[188]

And the paper subsequently made its own investigations or share-registers. This revealed that during the previous seven years North had sold over 7,000 shares in Primitiva, quotations having declined from a high point of 38 in 1889 to 4 in 1892; and it was calculated that even at the lowest quotation of 1892 North must have realized some £17,000 by these sales. If, as North had declared, he had actually bought the 5,000 shares he held in 1895 after his return from Chile in 1889, what, asked *The Economist*, had been done with the 8,000 shares he had held at the end of 1888? North must, it concluded, settle these points 'if he wishes to sustain whatever reputation for truthfulness and straightforwardness he may now possess'.[189] North's reply was that he had transferred shares to members of his family, but *The Economist* was far from satisfied, since he did not say how many shares (and at what price) were involved, nor how many shares (and at what price) had been disposed of to the public.[190] To this, however, there was no reply.

Primitiva was North's most spectacular failure, but it was not the only evidence of his declining fortunes. The Tarapacá Waterworks Company announced in 1895 that its dividend for the year would be 7½ per cent, compared with 10 per cent in almost every year since its foundation, and it wrote off nearly

---

[188] *The Economist*, 2 November 1895.

[189] Ibid., 9 November 1895.

[190] Ibid., 30 November 1895. An interesting testimony of North's capacity to beguile the public into taking shares off his hands is given in Sir Henry Lucy, *The Diary of a Journalist* (London, 1920), pp. 71–4. Lucy met North at a dinner a few months before North's death in 1896, and was persuaded to buy 5 £10 shares in North's Buena Ventura Company. Since, however, the Stock Exchange price then ruling was £230 a share, this transaction cost Lucy £1,150 apart from broker's charges, and he only accepted it on North's positive verbal assurance that he would repurchase the shares at the same price whenever Lucy wished to get rid of them. Lucy subsequently grew uneasy, but when he visited North at Avery Hill with a view to getting North's promise in writing 'he was so heartily genial in his welcome, so sanguine of ultimate success of the venture' that Lucy 'felt it would be unworthy of a guest to hint at distrust by asking for a formal pledge of indemnity' so he said nothing. North died not long after, leaving Lucy holding a worthless document saying he possessed 5 £10 shares in what Lucy called 'the phantom nitrate field of the Buena Ventura (somewhere in Chile)'. I am indebted for this reference to Mrs E. MacLeod.

£17,000 at the same time, the cost of a lawsuit in Chile.[191] The
Bank of Tarapacá was passing through a time of troubles, and
'low or missing dividends brought rumbles of discontent from
the shareholders'.[192] And, at the end of 1895, the Chilean
Supreme Court finally dismissed the long-drawn-out suit of the
Nitrate Railways Company against its rival, Agua Santa.[193]
Though this did no more than recognize in law what had long
existed in fact, it was the symbolic end of policies pursued by
the 'Nitrate King' to shore up his crumbling empire.

Yet North persisted to the end. Early in 1896 a new nitrate
combination was formed. This gave him a welcome respite from
his time of troubles, and it was only after his death that the
storm really broke. The warnings of *The Economist* had long
since proved true for most of the shareholders and only North's
astuteness had enabled him to avoid for so long a personal
calamity. While he lived, a certain residual confidence remained, though it was recognized that the palmy days of the
1880s had disappeared for ever. Falling dividends dismayed
stockholders in the companies he had formed during the 1890s,
but those who had enjoyed the spectacularly high dividends of
the previous decade no doubt took a different view. Unfortun-
ately, they were not, in many cases, the same people, and
North himself had carefully unloaded a large quantity of his
own holdings as the storm-clouds gathered. At the end of
March 1888, North had held a total of 15,830 shares in the
Nitrate Railways Company:[194] only after his death was the
news revealed that his stake in the company had been reduced
to 138 ordinary, 246 deferred and 16 preference shares.[195]

North died of a heart attack in the afternoon of 5 May 1896,
a few days after entertaining four hundred guests at a banquet

[191] *The Journal of Gas Lighting*, 7 May 1895.

[192] Joslin, *A Century of Banking*, p. 184. As early as 1892, Gibbs resolved to do no
business with the Bank from that date. Antony Gibbs & Sons, Valparaiso to
London, 20 June 1892. AAG, MS. 11,470. Vol. 19. Letter No. 98. Private. And
early in 1896, the important London and River Plate Bank took a similar decision.
'We have heard', wrote the manager in Buenos Aires, 'that their business on the
W[est] C[oast] is not conducted altogether as it should be, and that they are at
loggerheads with the Government, owing to the gold they have been exporting
from Chile.' London and River Plate Bank, Buenos Aires to London, 10 February
1896. BOLSA Archive, Letter Book No. 92. Confidential. Copy.

[193] *The South American Journal*, 21 December 1895.

[194] *The Financial News*, 10 May 1888.   [195] *The South American Journal*, 9 May 1896.

at Avery Hill.[196] He was taking the chair at a meeting of his
Buena Ventura Company at his City office in Gracechurch
Street and, so it was reported, had just written 'Passed' against
an item on the agenda when the seizure occurred. The news
spread rapidly through the City, and the press on the following
day carried long reports, as well as brief sketches of the career
of the 'Nitrate King'. More detailed consideration of North's
life and work appeared some time later. His funeral at Eltham
was attended by huge crowds, and the vast number of flowers
which were sent testified to the wide range of North's friendships and interests. Eltham itself went into mourning: the shops
were closed, but the telegraph office remained open and, indeed,
was obliged to increase its staff and stay open at night from 6 ·
to 9 May because of the flood of telegrams of condolence
arriving from all parts of the world. Mrs North received letters
from the Prince of Wales and the Khedive of Egypt, while the
King of Belgium sent a special representative to the funeral, at
which the mourners ranged from members of the aristocracy to
representatives of the boxing ring. Over one hundred and fifty
floral tributes decked the bier and it was nine o'clock at night
before the churchyard was finally cleared though the funeral
took place at four in the afternoon.[197]

North's death caused an immediate fall in the prices of shares
in the nitrate companies he had headed, though they soon
returned to their former level when the actual size of his holdings was revealed. Compared with what had been assumed, his
only large stake in nitrates was in the Lagunas Syndicate, in
which he had some 60,000 shares at £5 each: this, as has been
seen, was the most flourishing British nitrate concern in the
mid-1890s. He still had 5,000 £5 shares in the now-defunct
Primitiva Company which he had not been able to unload;
nearly 5,000 £5 shares in the Colorado Nitrate Company, and
over 2,000 £5 shares in the Pacca and Jazpampa Nitrate Company. But his formerly massive investment in the Nitrate

[196] North's last great social event was a dinner for the London Suburban
Railway Officials Association, of which he was President. According to his wife, it
was a great success and 'John Tom was very pleased'. Mrs North's Diary, entry
for 25 April 1896.

[197] Data from the contemporary press, particularly *The Sidcup and District Times*,
8 and 15 May 1896, and *The Leeds Mercury*, 11 May 1896.

Railways Company had been pared down to a very small sum, and his holding in the Bank of Tarapacá amounted to only 336 £10 shares, of which not more than a half had actually been paid. Sizeable transfers had apparently taken place out of nitrates and into other minerals, notably gold and silver concerns in Australia and elsewhere. He held 17,000 £1 shares in his own name in the Londonderry Gold Mines Company, and more than 37,000 £1 shares, jointly with Lord Fingall, in the same enterprise. He also had some 3,000 £1 shares in the Ripanji Quicksilver and Silver Mines.[198]

The value of North's personalty in the United Kingdom entered for probate was £263,866.[199] His lawyer, however, pointed out that the total value of his properties at home and abroad was nearly half a million pounds, excluding real estate and immovable property.[200] It would, of course, have been much more if North had not been quite as well known for spending money as he was at making it. For fifteen years he had been prominent in business circles and in certain sectors of Victorian society. Yet he was never really a prominent social figure, in the real sense of the term, and *The Economist* was correct in its final assessment of him: while recognizing his inherent ability, boldness and dominant personality, it saw him

from first to last [as] just a workman who had made a great fortune, and who loved to proclaim it by extravagant expenditure, by ostentatious display, and by bearing everybody down . . . his great notion of hospitality was to drown his friends in champagne. . . His money was to him a weapon, and he hewed his way through the opposition, social, mercantile or other.[201]

He was, the paper went on, the 'new-made millionaire',

undisguised by acquired refinement, or by cultivation, or by ability for anything but a rough kind of business, and he constantly compelled even men who had profited by his successes to enquire on the whole whether this new aristocracy . . . is beneficial even to the industrial or speculating world . . .[202]

Not all assessments were quite so harsh. *The South American*

---

[198] *The South American Journal*, 9 May 1896.   [199] Ibid., 11 July 1896.
[200] Ibid. The lawyer was Mr Budd.   [201] *The Economist*, 9 May 1896.
[202] Ibid.

Journal was more charitable to North as, indeed, it had been throughout his career:

though not a man of much culture or high educational attainments, he was eminently gifted with the qualities of judgement, prevision and promptitude which lead the way to conspicuous success in business enterprise or speculation.[203]

And, in far-off Chile, the scene of so many of North's former triumphs, the English-language newspaper of Valparaiso took a similar view:

He was [said *The Chilean Times*] in many respects a remarkable man, and was essentially the architect of his own fortunes. . . The Colonel has sometimes been accused of selfishness, but whatever foundation this charge may have in fact, there can be no doubt that his defects were largely outweighed by his many excellent qualities. He was a sterling Englishman and his death will be universally regretted.[204]

Yet the Chilean press itself, which in 1889 had devoted so much space to the 'Nitrate King', barely noticed his death, and the briefest of lines announcing it was really all that appeared.

Six months from the death of John Thomas North, Santiago witnessed a moving and dramatic occasion, when the remains of José Manuel Balmaceda were disinterred from the secret grave where they had been buried at dead of night in 1891. Accompanied by an enormous procession, his body was removed to the family vault, to the accompaniment of stirring orations from many of the leading men of the republic, an act of reconciliation and commemoration which marked the end of the passionate drama of which he was the central figure.[205] It also signified the beginning of a national hagiography which persists to the present day, in which the president and martyr, Balmaceda, stands for truth, nobility and justice, and John Thomas North, the 'Nitrate King', for perfidy, ambition and greed.

[203] *The South American Journal*, 9 May 1896.
[204] *The Chilean Times*, 9 May 1896.
[205] See *Balmaceda, su apoteósis. Corona funebre 29 de noviembre de 1896* (Santiago, 1896), *passim*.

VI

EPILOGUE: BALMACEDA AND NORTH,
THE MEN AND THE MYTHS

In the continuous process of revisionism which has characterized the historiography of the Chilean revolution of 1891,[1] the
career and reputation of Balmaceda have naturally occupied
the central place. Nor is this surprising, given the brilliance of
his political rise, the controversial character of his administration, the dramatic denouement of the civil war and the personal
sacrifice which ended it. It is a human story of initial triumph
and ultimate tragedy which has no parallel in Chilean history
and one which has continued to engage the attention of
historians and statesmen alike.

The process of rehabilitating the reputation of the defeated
president began with Balmaceda himself, when, in one of his
last letters, he charged his faithful lieutenant, Julio Bañados
Espinosa, to justify his administration to posterity.[2] Bañados
did his work well in his massive study of Balmaceda's presidency,[3] and he was assisted in his task by other close associates
of the former president, such as Joaquín Villarino and José
Miguel Valdés Carrera.[4] The immediate post-war circumstances of 1891 and 1892 also contributed to the same end.
The war had been a civil war, and no conflict is more bitter
than one in which members of the same social family take up
arms against each other. Once the Congressionalists had
decisively defeated the Balmacedist forces on the field of battle,
they reacted strongly against the crimes and blunders of Balma-

---

[1] See Blakemore, 'The Chilean Revolution of 1891 and its Historiography', loc.
cit.

[2] Bañados, *Balmaceda*, ii, pp. 643–4, gives the text in full, and also, between
pp. 642 and 643, the letter in facsimile.

[3] The text runs to more than 1,500 pages.

[4] Villarino, *José Manuel Balmaceda. El último de los presidentes constitucionales de
Chile*, and Valdés Carrera, *La condenación del Ministerio Vicuña. El Ministro de
Hacienda y sus Detractores*. Villarino's book was published in Mendoza, that of
Valdés Carrera in Paris.

ceda's adherents during 1891, forcing into exile his former ministers, purging the public administration of all suspected Balmacedists, and instituting searching enquiries and legal processes against them.[5] Yet these proceedings did not go unchallenged, and their opponents (those who defended the accused at the time) were, in effect, defending Balmaceda's reputation.[6] There were those also who glorified Balmaceda and his supporters. Pamphlets commemorated the lives and deaths of young Balmacedists who fell in 1891;[7] a drama in verse 'dedicated to the loyalists of the old Army' dealt with the sack of Balmacedist houses in Santiago after the revolution had triumphed,[8] and a long poem lauded Balmaceda as 'The Genius of the Fatherland'.[9] Prophetically, this panegyric contained the lines: 'You also have conquered with your death, like Christ on the hill of Calvary'. The parallel may have seemed blasphemous, but some twenty years later, it was reported from the nitrate desert of Tarapacá that in many workers' camps, 'the first thing one found when entering a . . . house was a picture of Balmaceda with a candle in front of it': a commission of investigation into social conditions in the region stated that:

One thing that is noticeable is the truly 'cult' feeling which the workers have for President Balmaceda. In the north, Balmaceda has

[5] See *Minuta de Acusación al Ministerio Vicuña-Godoy, presentado por la Cámara de Diputados ante el Senado, en sesión de 5 de agosto de 1892* (Santiago, 1892), and *Acusación a los Ex-Ministros del Despacho. Pruebas Rendidas durante el Juicio ante el Senado* (Santiago, 1893), a book of some 400 pages, setting out in detail all the alleged illegal acts of Balmaceda's government during 1891, and the names of those who perpetrated them.

[6] See particularly Nemo (pseud. Rafael Balmaceda), *Chile. Una Página de Historia. La Acusación al Ministerio Vicuña y la Tercera Amnistía Parcial* (Buenos Aires, 1893) and the same author's much larger work, *Chile. Páginas de Historia. La Revolución y la Condenación del Ministerio Vicuña* (Buenos Aires, 1893). See also Juan E. Mackenna, *La Revolución en Chile. Carta Política*, published originally in New York, but also in Valparaiso as early as 1893.

[7] E.g. Juan Arellano i Yecorát, *El Martirio de un Leal o sea la Vida y Muerte de Luís Alberto Garín* (Santiago, 1893), and Victor J. Arellano, *El Tribunal de Sangre. Rodolfo León Lavin, Su Vida y Su Muerte* (Valparaiso, 1892). For these works, and for those cited in notes 8 and 9, I am indebted to Señorita Jacqueline Garreaud.

[8] Juan Rafael Allende, *Sin Desenlace. Drama en Cuatro Actos i en Verso* (Santiago, 1892).

[9] A. P. Echeverría, *El Jénio de la Patria* (Santiago, 1892).

a cult of affection, sympathy and respect such as no one else receives; he is a venerated saint and an illustrious person.[10]

Balmaceda's political rehabilitation in Santiago itself came fairly soon after the civil war. Although under the persecution instituted by the Congressionalists in 1891 to 1893, his former ministers were condemned *in absentia* to fifteen years' exile and the forfeiture of all civil rights,[11] the sentences were never applied. In fact, in August 1893, while the 'trial' of the ex-ministers was still proceeding, an amnesty had been passed by Congress which covered all Balmacedists except the ministers,[12] and the Government's lenient policy enabled the followers of the dead president to win 26 seats in the chamber of Deputies and become the second largest party there.[13] The natural corollary to this surprising political event was the passing of a bill for a complete amnesty in August 1894.[14] By the end of 1894, therefore, the vanquished side in the civil war had re-entered Chilean politics, most of the exiles had returned to Chile and, at the close of Jorge Montt's term of office in 1896, it could be claimed, in one sense at least, that 'all possibility of further complications arising from the events of 1891 has now disappeared for ever'.[15]

Reconciliation of formerly bitter antagonists harmonized with the Chilean political tradition.[16] It testified to the underlying social unity of the governing class, and it also underlined the fact that the revolution of 1891 had been a struggle for power in which 'no great social reform [was] involved. Neither Congress . . . nor the President really spoke for the lower classes. Both represented the aristocracy.'[17] The reincorporation of the Balmacedists into the national life also helps to explain why the historiography of the revolution until fairly

[10] Cited in Jordan M. Young, 'Chilean Parliamentary Government, 1891–1924', unpublished M.A. dissertation of the Univ. of California, Berkeley, 1947, p. 62.

[11] Kennedy to Kimberley, Santiago, 6 June 1894. F.O. 16/289. No. 32. Diplomatic.

[12] Anguita, *Leyes promulgadas en Chile*, iii, 272.

[13] León Echaíz, *Evolución histórica de los partidos políticos chilenos*, p. 79.

[14] Anguita, loc. cit., p. 307.

[15] *Memoria del Ministro del Interior presentada al Congreso de 1896* (Santiago, 1896), p. 5.

[16] Cf. above, pp. 4–5, n. 16.   [17] McBride, *Chile: Land and Society*, p. 205.

recently was characterized by 'calm of mind, all passion spent', as historians agreed that the most serious conflict in modern Chilean history was an honourable battle of principles on both sides.[18] Balmaceda could be presented as a great statesman, a patriot and a visionary and Congress as no less high-minded, since both were caught in an ineluctable conflict. Nevertheless, the interpretation of Balmaceda as the most progressive president in Chilean history had already emerged: when, in July 1927, General Carlos Ibáñez del Campo, the only Chilean executive to become a dictator, assumed the presidency of the republic, he was invested by Balmaceda's son, Enrique, with the very sash his father wore at his own inauguration and which he had entrusted to his son, to confer on the future executive of Chile 'worthy of wearing it as the continuer of his program and regenerator of the grand design he saw for the future . . .'[19]

By the 1920s, however, there were other reasons for the rehabilitation of Balmaceda's reputation besides the dramatic story of his life and death. No less important in the making of the legend was the course of Chilean history after 1891. The revolution came to be seen as a critical watershed in Chilean history, since it marked the end of the strong presidential system of the nineteenth century and ushered in the so-called Parliamentary period, from 1891 to 1920.[20] The dominant constitutional and political feature of these years was the impotence of the executive in the face of party faction at a time when population was growing, urbanization was increasing and social problems were beginning to loom large on the national scene. Changes in Chile's economic and social structure were not reflected in her political framework. The national mood of exuberant confidence in Chile's destiny which reached its peak after the War of the Pacific and which Balmaceda himself believed he personified gave way in the early years of this century to feelings of pessimistic self-criticism in which a sense of

[18] See Blakemore, loc. cit., pp. 397–8.

[19] Frederick M. Nunn, *Chilean Politics, 1920–1931. The Honourable Mission of the Armed Forces* (Univ. of New Mexico Press, 1970), pp. 130–1.

[20] The Parliamentary period has been painted in almost universally unfavourable colours by historians, and my brief summary here conforms to that view. The fact remains, however, that very little systematic research has been done on it, despite its assumed importance.

missed direction and growing apprehension for the future predominated.[21] As the oligarchic political system of Chile failed
both to reflect a society in transition and also to cater to its
needs, so there emerged in Chile 'the social question', the
consciousness of 'two nations', an increasingly divided society,
saddled, apparently, with an economic structure which in-
hibited development,[22] haunted by fears of social conflict,[23]
and burdened with a political system in which petty squabbles
of personalities and parties took precedence over attention to
national needs.

Highly simplified though this picture is, it is one which is
widely accepted, and many historians, particularly in the last
twenty years, have succumbed to the natural temptation to ask
moral questions about Chile's past: namely, what went wrong
and who was responsible?[24] Among the many attempts to
answer such questions, the most clearly-identifiable and
influential school of thought is marxist, the work of historians
whose interpretations differ markedly in detail but are in
essence the same: it was the dominant internal oligarchy
in Chile—landowners, bankers and commercial figures—in
alliance with foreign capitalists in control of a large proportion
of Chile's export economy who not only perpetuated in their
own selfish interests a particular economic, social and political
system, but who also destroyed the few, far-sighted Chileans
who wished to change it, pre-eminent among whom was Balmaceda.[25] This brief summary cannot do justice to these
writers, but their importance should be recognized. Their
interpretation of Chile's past has influenced many economists
concerned with Chile's, and Latin America's, current prob-

[21] There is a large literature on these themes, but see particularly Fredrick B.
Pike, *Chile and the United States, 1880–1962: the emergence of Chile's Social Crisis and
the Challenge to United States Diplomacy* (Notre Dame, 1963).

[22] The classic expression of contemporary preoccupation with economic back-
wardness is F. A. Encina, *Nuestra Inferioridad Económica* (Santiago, 1911).

[23] An important literary characteristic of the period is the novel of social
protest, exemplified by the works of Baldomero Lillo. See also Pike, loc. cit.,
pp. 344–5.   [24] See Blakemore, loc. cit., pp. 400–1.

[25] Typical works in this vein are Ramírez, *Balmaceda*, the same author's *Historia
del Imperialismo en Chile* (Santiago, 1960), and Julio César Jobet, *Ensayo crítico del
desarrollo económico-social de Chile* (Santiago, 1951). On the intellectual influence of
marxist interpretations in general, and of these two authors in particular, see Pike,
loc. cit., p. 265.

lems,[26] and their views have been adopted, without, it must be said, any attempt at critical evaluation, by other influential social scientists seeking to provide easily-understood explanations for the complicated reasons for underdevelopment in Latin America.[27]

In this process of using Chile's past not only to explain the present but also to shape the future, Balmaceda occupies a crucial place, and his personal tragedy assumes the dimensions of a national catastrophe. To marxists, he appears as a president with clear ideas about state intervention in the economy and as an economic nationalist who was determined to recover the national patrimony which had been alienated under the ruling philosophy of *laissez-faire*: had he succeeded, it is suggested, he might well have changed the course of Chilean history, setting the country on the path of democratic politics, social justice, and economic growth based on national ownership of basic resources.[28] It is an image which has proved useful in recent Chilean history: in the presidential election of 1970 and subsequently, Balmaceda was used as an exemplar for the left-wing coalition of parties under Dr Salvador Allende whose programme included massive state intervention in the economy and the expropriation of foreign assets.[29] This use of the past was, in its turn, refuted by the opposition to the marxist government as a perversion of the truth about Balmaceda himself and about his administration.[30]

[26] E.g., Aníbal Pinto, *Chile, un caso de desarrollo frustrado* (Santiago, 1962). Hirschman, *Journeys Towards Progress*, pp. 212–16, points to the significant role of Chilean economists and of Chilean experience in the influential 'structuralist' school of thought on Latin American economic development, espoused by the Economic Commission for Latin America, based in Santiago.

[27] See particularly André Gunder Frank's 100-page essay on 'Capitalist Development of Underdevelopment in Chile' in his *Capitalism and Underdevelopment in Latin America* (rev. and enlarged ed., Monthly Review Press, 1969). Frank's indebtedness to Ramírez, whom he quotes extensively, is no less striking than the very limited range of his sources as a whole.

[28] This is not an exaggerated summary of this view. See H. Ramírez Necochea's essay on Balmaceda, the text of a lecture given at the University of Chile in 1959 and published together with a lecture by Alberto Baltra Cortés entitled *Pedro Aguirre Cerda* (Santiago, 1960). I am indebted to Professor John Lynch for this reference.

[29] See, e.g., *El Siglo*, 22 August 1970; *Punto Final*, 17 August 1971, and *El Clarín*, 20 August 1972.

[30] See, e.g., *El Mercurio*, 11 January and 14 May 1972. Interest in Balmaceda

While Balmaceda's historical reputation was enhanced with the passage of time, that of John Thomas North virtually disappeared with his death. The removal of his dominant personality from the boards of companies he had founded exposed his friends to the shareholders' wrath: within two months of his death the entire board of the Lagunas Nitrate Company had been replaced and the extent to which North had manipulated affairs discovered.[31] At about the same time, a shareholder in the Nitrate Railways Company, Mr Herbert Allen, who was also the editor of the transport journal, *The Railway Times*, began a campaign to arouse shareholders to press for an investigation into that Company's affairs, and finally, in the spring of 1897, he succeeded: an investigating committee was established 'to inquire into the past administration of the company and its present position and prospects'.[32] The searching enquiry lasted several months, and the committee's report appeared on 15 July 1897. It was a damning indictment of North's business methods, and of those still alive who had worked with him for it showed quite clearly how the Nitrate Railways Company had been stealthily shored up by North's other interests in Chile. For the remainder of 1897 and well into 1898 a bitter battle raged between the board of directors, led by Robert Harvey, and a group of shareholders led by Herbert Allen, but the board finally won and kept itself in office.[33] Allen, however, was not quite finished, and on 1 January 1898 he published an extensive account of the entire business, with verbatim reports of the committee's sessions.[34]

This issue of *The Railway Times* found its way into the Chilean press, and one piece of news in particular excited considerable

has grown enormously in Chile since 1970. Supporters of the government promoted a series of television programmes about him in 1971, and a year later it was announced that a film was to be made, with the services of a British actor as John Thomas North. *El Mercurio*, 27 September 1972. For its part, the Club José Manuel Balmaceda, which did not support the government, organized a series of lectures in 1971 which were subsequently published as *Visión y Verdad sobre Balmaceda* (Santiago, 1972).

[31] *The Statist*, 11 July 1896.

[32] *The Railway Times*, 17 July 1897.

[33] Ibid., July–November 1897, *passim*. Apparently the members of the investigating committee were persuaded by the directors to join the board themselves, depriving Allen and his supporters of the necessary votes they required to unseat it.

[34] *The Railway Times*, 1 January 1898.

comment. The committee had discovered that between 1887 and 1895, over £96,000 had been paid to North: no vouchers could be found to relate to this money which appeared under the heading of legal expenses, losses and compensations in Chile.[35] In addition, during his testimony, Harvey made no bones about suggesting that this money had been employed to pay the company's lawyers in Chile and also as funds to them for what they might regard as useful expenditures in the company's interests.[36]

Naturally, this news created a furore in Chile, and not least because it was easy to identify the Chileans who had been involved, although they had been referred to in the investigation by capital letters only. North's leading lawyer, Julio Zegers, felt obliged to write several long letters to a leading paper, giving his side of the story,[37] and he also petitioned the Comisión Conservadora for a full enquiry, Congress being then in recess: the Comisión, however, declined to act, on the grounds that it did not have, and could not hope to get, such information as it felt it would require.[38]

The Nitrate Railways' corruption case, as it came to be called, was the last straw for many who had believed in North. *The Chilean Times*, which had paid a warm tribute to North when he died, now changed its tune, and charged him with an 'inordinate desire for prompt profits' and 'stubborn insistence in his bad policy'.[39] The verdict of historians has been no less unfavourable, and while many regard North as the colourful personality he undoubtedly was, of his business practices there is common condemnation. In England, as in Chile, he left no memorial.[40]

Yet, in the rehabilitation of Balmaceda's reputation, North played an important part. To the marxists, he is the incarnation of foreign imperialism who played a considerable role in the revolution of 1891, and the baseness of his motives, selfish as they were, provides a useful contrast to the altruistic ideals of

[35] Ibid., 17 July 1897, and *The Economist*, same date.
[36] *The Railway Times*, 1 January 1898.
[37] Letters in *El Ferrocarril*, 10, 16, 18, 25 February 1898.
[38] *The Chilean Times*, 11 March 1898.
[39] Ibid., 23 February 1898.
[40] North does not figure in *The Dictionary of National Biography*.

President Balmaceda. The comparison, however, is irrelevant
to the evaluation of both Balmaceda himself and the revolution
which overthrew him. The main theme of this book is the
relationship between British nitrate interests and Chilean
politics in the period of Balmaceda and this is an important
segment of the total argument for regarding Balmaceda both as
an economic nationalist and as a president with clearly-
defined ideas about the organization of the Chilean economy
and the state's role in that process. The evidence shows that
Balmaceda's attitude towards foreign nitrate interests contained very little either of economic nationalism or of state
intervention and that, indeed, the specific interests he sought
to control, namely those of North, could best be attacked
through the agency of other foreign interests.[41] With those
interests he was prepared to enter into arrangements, even to
the grant of concessions which, constitutionally, he had no
exclusive power to award, provided he received in return their
co-operation in frustrating a possible monopoly of nitrate production in Tarapacá in the hands of North.[42] At that time, the
monopoly was far from being established, not least because it
was opposed by other British interests in the province, no less
averse from North's designs than Balmaceda was himself. And
his successors pursued precisely the same policy. Secondly,
even with regard to North's own interests, Balmaceda had no
antagonistic policy except the prevention of monopoly control.
Provided he could assure to Chile high income from export
taxes on nitrate shipments, income to finance his programme
of public works, he was prepared to allow North to extend his
interests and, on occasion, even encouraged him to do so.
During the Nitrate Railways' corruption case, one of the
directors, Mr Edward Manby, made the following statement
relating to North's meetings with Balmaceda in 1889:

Amongst other things connected with our railways and lawsuits,
President Balmaceda mentioned this claim of the Chilean Government upon the Patillos Railway, and he said it amounted to
£150,000 and he would be glad to enter into some arrangement
with the Nitrate Railways Company about it . . .

[41] Brown, 'Nitrate Railways', *passim*, came to the same conclusion on much
less evidence.   [42] See above, pp. 145–51.

and when North and his colleagues said that the amount involved was £90,000

still President Balmaceda insisted that something ought to be done, that it was our interest to acquire the railway, and Colonel North, to pacify him, but I believe, without any intention of moving any further in the matter, said he would look into the matter in London.[43]

Balmaceda's government, in fact, did nothing whatever about the Patillos line: North was able to acquire it two years later, and he acquired it to keep it closed.[44]

The argument related to the corruption of Chilean public men by North's gold, which has been linked to the fact that almost all the Chileans involved opposed Balmaceda in 1891,[45] simply cannot be sustained.[46] When Julio Zegers wrote to *El Ferrocarril* in 1898, he set out in minute detail all his financial transactions with the Nitrate Railways Company.[47] This satisfactorily accounted for the sum of over £90,000 which North had spent, fruitlessly, in defence of the company's privileges, so much so that *The Chilean Times* declared:

In fine, no impartial person, after perusing the communications of Mr. Zegers, can fail to be convinced of the fact that his comportment, as Standing Counsel of the Nitrate Railways Company, has been worthy of the best traditions of the Chilian bar.[48]

If the role of nitrates in the Chilean revolution of 1891 was, indeed, very different from that which has been ascribed to it, it is also possible that other features of the Balmaceda legend would yield different interpretations if subjected to detailed scrutiny. Little research has been done, for example, on Balmaceda's taxation policies, though superficial investigation poses interesting questions. In 1889, Balmaceda himself proposed the abolition both of the income tax, instituted in 1879,

[43] *The Railway Times*, 8 January 1898.   [44] Cf. above, pp. 52–54.
[45] Ramírez, *Balmaceda*, pp. 71–86.   [46] Cf. Blakemore, loc. cit., pp. 414–17.
[47] *El Ferrocarril*, 18 February 1898. Ramírez, loc. cit., pp. 75–6, notes this letter briefly but says hardly anything about its contents. Zegers showed conclusively that a large proportion of the total sum involved was spent after 1891, when the battle against the Nitrate Railways Company was really intense. Whether this money corrupted Chilean politicians or not, it can hardly have affected their conduct towards a president who was already dead.
[48] *The Chilean Times*, 26 February 1898.

and of the inheritance tax, introduced in 1878, preferring to rely for government revenue on customs duties and on a state monopoly of tobacco. One of the chief opponents of this proposal was Julio Zegers who argued that the taxes Balmaceda proposed to abolish were the only satisfactory ways of taxing the rich.[49] Since it is a major premiss of the economic interpretation of the revolution of 1891 that Balmaceda threatened the economic interests of the Chilean oligarchy, this issue clearly has some importance. Another important question which remains unanswered concerns the degree to which Balmaceda's policy of public works affected the political balance of forces in Chile. Certain pointers to this question have been suggested in this book,[50] but more detailed investigation of the Chilean administration in the period is required.[51]

How far such investigations would change the historical reputation of President Balmaceda is a matter of conjecture. But they would be unlikely to detract from his stature as a distinguished Chilean president and patriot who, nevertheless, like most great men, also had great faults. A belief in perfect leaders may serve the purpose of political propaganda, but it bears little relation to historical truth.

[49] I am indebted for this information to Professor William Sater.
[50] See above, pp. 124–5, 173–4.
[51] Other possible lines of enquiry are suggested in Blakemore, loc. cit., p. 420.

BIBLIOGRAPHICAL INDEX

References are to the first citation, where the name of the author, full title, and place of publication will be found. The index excludes archives, newspapers, and such sources as the Chilean Congressional debates.

Acusación a los ex-ministros, 241

Aldunate Solar, C., *Leyes, decretos y documentos*, 15

Allende, J. R., *Sin desenlace*, 241

Amengual, N., *Episodios de la revolución*, 192

Amunátegui Solar, D., 'El orígen del comercio inglés', 10–11

Anguita, R., *Leyes promulgadas en Chile*, 19

Anstey, R. T., *King Leopold's Legacy*, 232

Aracena, F. M., *Apuntes de viaje*, 8

Arellano, V. J., *El tribunal de sangre*, 241

Arellano y Yecorát, J., *El martírio de un leal*, 241

Arteaga Alemparte, J. and D. A., *Los constituyentes de 1870*, 76

Aston, G. B., *Letters on Amphibious Wars*, 193

Atkins, J. B., *The Life of Sir William Howard Russell*, 94

Balmaceda, R., *Chile, una página de historia*, 241; *Chile, páginas de historia*, 241

Balmaceda, su apoteósis, 239

Baltra Cortés, A., *Pedro Aguirre Cerda*, 245

Bañados Espinosa, J., *Balmaceda*, 69; *Letras y política*, 160; *Gobierno parlamentario*, 160

Barros Arana, D., *Historia jeneral de Chile*, 12

Bascuñan Montes, A., *Recopilación de tratados*, 19

Bellesort, A., *La jeune Amérique*, 141

Bermúdez, O., *Historia del salitre*, 15; 'El salitre de Tarapacá', 19

Billinghurst, G., *Estudio sobre la jeografía*, 24; *Los capitales salitreros*, 15

Biographie coloniale Belge, 233

Blakemore, H., 'The Chilean Revolution', 28; 'The Chilean Revolution . . . Historiography', 69; 'Chilean Revolutionary Agents', 193; *and* Smith, C. T. (eds.), *Latin America*, 2

Blanlot Holley, A., *Historia de la paz*, 15

Bowman, I., *Desert Trails of Atacama*, 13

Bravo Kendrick, A., *La revolución de 1891*, 193

Brown, J. R., 'Nitrate Crises', 31; 'The Chilean Nitrate Railways', 45

Bulnes, G., *Guerra del Pacífico*, 15

Burdetts Official Intelligence, 32

Burr, R. N., *By Reason or Force*, 71; *The Still-Born Panama Congress*, 71

Cáceres, A. A., *La guerra entre el Perú y Chile*, 15

Caivano, T., *Historia de la guerra de América*, 15

Castle, W. F. M., *Sketch of the City of Iquique*, 23

Centner, C. W., 'Great Britain and Chilean Mining', 13; 'Relaciones comerciales', 10

Churchill, W. S., *Life of Randolph Churchill*, 231

GENERAL INDEX